Theater of Solitude

The University Press of New England

Sponsoring Institutions
Brandeis University
Clark University
Dartmouth College
University of New Hampshire
University of Rhode Island
University of Vermont

Theater of Solitude

The Drama of Alfred de Musset

by David Sices

p. 103

la grêle

Published for Dartmouth College by
The University Press of New England
Hanover, New Hampshire 1974

To my mother,

Henrietta Finger Sices,

this fruit of my long absence.

Acknowledgments

My thanks go first of all to the American Council of Learned Societies, whose generous fellowship made possible the year's leave in France during which this work was written. Also to Dartmouth College for the sabbatical term in which much of my work was carried out; to my friends, mentors and colleagues— Henri M. Peyre, Victor H. Brombert, Eugene H. Falk and Lawrence E. Harvey—for their encouragement and support in the accomplishment of this study; to Peter W. Lock and G. W. Ireland, for their helpful comments and suggestions; to Madame Marguerite-Marie Chalufour, whose aid was instrumental at several points in carrying through my project; and above all, to my wife, Jacqueline, without whose patience, encouragement, and love the entire venture would have been impossible.

The chapters on *Fantasio* and *On ne badine pas avec l'amour* appeared first, in somewhat different form, in *The Romanic Review* and *The French Review.* I am grateful to these journals for permission to reproduce the texts here.

All quotations from Musset's dramatic works and all citations of commentators and critics which were originally in French or German have been translated by me for the present edition.

Hanover, New Hampshire   D. S.
June 1973

Contents

Chapter 1 Introduction

"Quelles solitudes que tous ces corps humains!"
(Fantasio, I, 2)

 The most imaginative, "contemporary," and, by general consensus, significant playwright of the nineteenth century in France is, paradoxically, one whose work is virtually unknown on the American stage. Alfred de Musset's literary reputation in this country is based principally upon a somewhat faded collection of lyrics which were once in vogue with young ladies and French teachers—the celebrated "Nuits"—and a lachrymose autobiographical novel aptly entitled *Confession*. Both of these appear to justify one American critic's typical lumping of him with Vigny, Sainte-Beuve, and "other sad young men of the nineteenth century."[1] But the stereotype, if it may be applied more or less exactly to Musset's distressingly humorless Romantic compatriots, seems inapt to a man noted by contemporaries for his flashing wit and verve. It is all the more unsuitable if we think that he is the author of five or six of the most delightful comedies ever to grace the French stage, not to mention what has come to be considered the finest example of French Romantic historical drama. A poet who has accomplished a feat of this magnitude by the age of twenty-five, after making a brilliant début at nineteen with a volume of hyper-Romantic (and in good part ironic) narrative verse, merits consideration as more than a "sad young man." Concealed behind the stereotype is a complex and inventive literary personality, whose dramatic works harbor a rich vein of material largely unexplored outside of France. Yet

1. Maurice Shroder, *Icarus: The Image of the Artist in French Romanticism* (Cambridge, Mass., 1961), p. 152.

they can speak to us now more fully, more insistently, than they did to Musset's contemporaries, and their dramatic technique has begun to be fully exploited only through the expanding stage resources of the past twenty or thirty years.

The comedies—*Les Caprices de Marianne, Fantasio, On ne badine pas avec l'amour, Le Chandelier, Il ne faut jurer de rien,* to mention the most important—and the historical drama *Lorenzaccio,* have become standard French classical repertory at the Comédie-Française and the Odéon. Moreover, they have inspired independent directors like Jacques Copeau, Gaston Baty, René Clair, and Otomar Krejca to mount them in imaginative experimental stagings. *Marianne, On ne badine pas avec l'amour,* and *Lorenzaccio* provided Gérard Philipe with three of his finest roles, and Jean Vilar with some of his most exciting productions, at the Théâtre National Populaire. Yet Musset's stage works are little known by theater people outside of France. In Germany, where the poet's direct influence on so vital a dramatist as Georg Büchner might be expected to promote his reputation, little attention has been paid to his plays.[2] As for the English-speaking world, only specialists in French literature—and by no means all of them—seem to be aware of Musset's importance in the theater, and of the original, delightful quality of his works.

Why this should be so is difficult to pin down. Many of Musset's compatriots have found a place on the American stage: Molière, Beaumarchais, Dumas fils, Feydeau, Rostand, Giraudoux, Anouilh, Sartre, Ionesco, Genet. Only one or two of these have made a contribution to their national theater equal to Musset's, or represent dramatic talent of comparable stature. Victor Hugo and Alexandre Dumas père, who reigned together over the Paris theater of the 1830's in the brief but intense moment of Romantic glory, achieved considerable success in its belated extension to the American stage, whereas Musset seems hardly to

2. Cf. Werner Bahner, *Alfred de Mussets Werk. Ein Verneinung der bürgerlichen Lebensform seiner Zeit* (Halle, 1960), p. 9; Maurice Gravier, "Georg Büchner et Alfred de Musset," *Orbis litterarum,* 9 (1954), 29–44; Henri Plard, "A Propos de 'Leonce et Lena,' Musset et Büchner," *Etudes Germaniques,* 9 (1954), 26–36.

have been noticed.[3] Of course, several of Musset's most illustrious countrymen are victims of similar neglect. Corneille, Racine, and Marivaux have never succeeded in transplanting their peculiar appeal to the English-speaking theater. At first glance there would seem to be no basis of comparison between the first two and Musset. Their inexorably regular alexandrine verse in relentless heroic couplets appears untranslatable into English idiom without generating an excruciating monotony; and the *diktat* of neoclassical doctrine does not hold sway beyond the sphere of the cultural brainwashing which inculcates it into French *lycéens*. Musset, like the other Romantics with whom he is lumped, was trying to break the neoclassical order, to introduce a more Shakespearean drama into the French theater. Nonetheless, the problem with Musset, as with the neoclassics, seems in great part one of translation, to judge by the evidence of published texts.[4] Not for lack of prosodic equivalents, since his best work is written in prose; but, like Marivaux's subtle and elegant language, Musset's has a peculiarly Gallic balance which seems to resist efforts to English it. In the hands of journeyman translators, the passion of *On ne badine pas avec l'amour* becomes bombast; the sallies of *Fantasio* evaporate, or degenerate into heavy-handed puns; and the political tirades of *Lorenzaccio* are transformed into awkward, tiresome moralizing—none of which is true of the original. Yet is should be possible for a sensitive writer to find an English

3. Except for French-language productions in New Orleans. See Charles M. Lombard, "French Romanticism on the American Stage," *Revue de Littérature Comparée*, 43 (1969), 161–72.

4. The list includes translations by Raoul Pelissier, E. B. Thompson and M. H. Dey of the Comedies in *The Complete Works of Alfred de Musset* (New York, 1905); *A Caprice*, translated by Anne Grace Wirt (Boston, 1922); the versions of *Fantasio* and *Lorenzaccio* in Eric R. Bentley's *The Modern Theater* (Garden City, N. Y., 1955–60), translated by Jacques Barzun and Renaud C. Bruce; *Il faut qu'une porte soit ouverte ou fermée* in Bentley's *From the Modern Repertoire*, series three (Bloomington, 1956), translated by Barzun; George Graveley's translations of *Un Caprice, Il faut qu'une porte soit ouverte ou fermée* and *On ne saurait penser à tout* in *A Comedy and Two Proverbs* (London, New York, 1957); and *Seven Plays*, translation and introduction by Peter Meyer (New York, 1962).

equivalent of this alert prose, which Théophile Gautier wittily labeled "pure French dialect."

If Musset's theater has been so long in finding receptive audiences in the non-French world, that is also explainable in part by its difficult history in France itself. The poet's isolation from the theater of his time was consecrated by a tragicomic stage debut, the ignominious fiasco of his one-act play, *La Nuit Vénitienne* in 1830. That work, whatever its intrinsic merits (it is somewhat less than halfway between Musset's earlier pastiche Romanticism and his mature style), today seems too slight to justify the hostile reception accorded it. Even without the legendary encounter between the heroine's white dress and a freshly painted green trellis, the "Cabale" seems to have been ready to inflict humiliation on this young upstart whose wit had offended Romantics and classics alike.[5] Out of this defeat, it is true, emerged the "armchair theater" which permitted the young author to explore a drama freed from the practical imperatives of the contemporary stage. But it was also the start of a long series of delays and misunderstandings which were to keep most of Musset's best plays from reaching the stage until after his death—in the case of *Lorenzaccio*, some fifty years afterward. And then they were so adapted and restructured, either by the author himself or by tinkerers, as to lose a great deal of their freshness and originality. It was not until well into this century that all of Musset's plays finally had been produced in their authentic text and according to the original stage directions. As for *Lorenzaccio*, the first productions respectful of the poet's dramatic intentions took place only in 1945 and 1952, at the Théâtre Montparnasse and the Théâtre National Populaire.

When Musset experienced such difficulty at home, it is not so surprising that he was unable to establish himself on foreign stages. Despite the belated success which Paris first granted several of his minor plays in 1847–48—more than a decade after the publication of his major stage works—Musset's theatrical career can be categorized as a resounding failure, one which goes beyond the limits of his personal life and fortunes and extends

5. See Henry Lyonnet, *Les "Premières" d'Alfred de Musset* (Paris, 1927), p. 7.

over the French stage itself. For Musset could have revitalized a theatrical tradition that was in a sad state of decay and remained so for most of his century. In the words of Jean Vilar, "It is significant, I think, that Musset's theater, which might after 1830 have provoked a wholesome dispute, was of use to no one under Louis-Philippe's know-nothing monarchy and under the Empire, not even to Musset himself."[6] Not to Musset himself, for when it came time to stage his works during the last decade of his life, he rejected the innovations he had made in his earlier plays, either adapting and regularizing them (as was the case with *Marianne* in 1851) or creating trivial new ones which no longer followed his original system. It was not until the latter years of the century, with the Symbolists, Maeterlinck, and Claudel, that drama so imaginative and adventurous, so close to the real sources of the theater, was to replace the bourgeois comedies and melodramas, the post-Romantic spectacles, the realist thesis-plays that inhibited theatrical renewal. Even then the new productions of Musset's plays remained timid compared with the freedom and fantasy inherent in their original texts. For many years it seemed as if an anonymous reviewer of *La Nuit Vénitienne* might in fact be right: "I believe . . . I heard the name of Monsieur Alfred de Musset pronounced [at the curtain]. That is a name which will never emerge from its obscurity."[7] Despite the insistent pleas of such contemporary admirers as Gautier, we are confronted in Musset's work with the paradox of a writer who is without doubt the greatest French dramatist of his century, yet who had little influence on its theatrical practice and traditions.

To understand this failure and, at the same time, the tremendous distinction of Musset's dramatic creation, it is useful to view it in the context of the theater of his time. If the author withdrew from the stage and devoted himself to a literary drama, divorced from the cares—and the triumphs—of production, it was evidently because that stage and his concept of theater had little in common. Musset was thus free to create without concern for theatrical "possibility." The experience had both advantages and drawbacks. To quote another theatrical innovator, Jacques Co-

6. *De la Tradition théâtrale* (Paris, 1955), p. 15.
7. *Courrier des Théâtres* (December 3, 1830), cited by Lyonnet, p. 8.

peau: "The greatest dramatic authors are those who have lived on the stage, provided they were its masters. But when the stage is in the hands of poor craftsmen, it is better for the poet to stand aside, to create his world apart, provided he has an intuition of the laws which govern a play.—Musset had it."[8] Musset did not have the opportunity, like Shakespeare or Molière, to experiment with staging, to play his roles himself and to experience their effect, to evolve through the dialectic of creation and production a constantly refined definition of theatrical art—and thereby to modify the givens of stage practice in his time. In any case, his aristocratic temperament and his impatience with the necessities of practical life would never have permitted him such a career (unlike his contemporary Dumas). What he did, he did in isolation, and he never had the pleasure of seeing his best works realized in suitable productions.

When we examine the milieu in which Musset's dramas were written, it is difficult not to be struck by two conflicting facts: the intense theatrical activity of Paris in the second quarter of the nineteenth century, and the pitifully small number of contemporary plays that have survived the passage of time. No doubt the latter is true of most periods of theater history: we tend to ignore the immense quantity of trivia and hackwork produced by the contemporaries of Shakespeare, Lope de Vega, Molière, or Tchekhov, and think of their ages as fertile in works of genius thanks to their presence. Perhaps Musset's period is disappointing because there were so many treatises and manifestos promising a "new" theater and such violent polemics in the journals of the time. When we follow the debate, and read of the Romantics' noisy battle to capture the Comédie-Française, it is hard not to wonder that so much sound and fury produced so remarkably little in the way of enduring results. A good deal of theoretical literature, of course: Stendhal's *Racine and Shakespeare*, Hugo's Preface to *Cromwell*, Vigny's "Dernière nuit de travail" and his "Lettre à Lord * * * ." But the dramatic works corresponding to these statements seldom come close to living up to their promises. The ferment in which the French theater was involved during

8. *Comédies et Proverbes*, with an introduction by Jacques Copeau (Paris, 1931), p. x.

this period should have given birth to an unusually rich repertory of stage works. In the words of an English critic, "Much of the romantic theoretical writing tended to become divorced from the theater . . . It might almost be said that, for the only development of romantic theory which is intimately related to practical theater affairs, we must turn to the controversy which was excited in Paris by the production of Victor Hugo's *Cromwell* in 1827. It was at this time that the romantic concept of the dramatic 'grotesque' was evolved. In England and in Italy the public theaters pursued their own melodramatic course, the poets turned out their dull bookish verse-plays, and criticism more and more remained 'literary'."[9]

But somewhat as Romantic poetic theory, despite the enormous profusion of lyrical works in France at the movement's height, only finally achieved its real summits with Baudelaire and Rimbaud, so the theater, which was even more central to the movement's ambitions, does not appear to have then reached the promised level of achievement. It is not until our century that the liberation called for by the Romantic publicists can be said to have taken effect. Examined objectively from the vantage point of history, the Romantic theater seems strangely hollow despite the great names it invoked for its inspiration: Sophocles, Shakespeare, Schiller. "The life of Romantic drama? It is not to be found in its paradoxical themes, with their deliberate 'immorality,' nor in its historical tableaux which too willingly evoke mere tintype images, nor in its oversimplified psychology, nor in its artificial structure, cluttered with misunderstandings, mistaken identities, fatal quiproquos and final recognitions . . . It is no more to be found in its settings' claim to local color . . . The life of romantic drama is contained in the inner tremor, the bursts of lyricism, the generous inspiration which animate it. Once that inspiration falls, there remains nothing but puppets in pasteboard buildings."[10] A good deal of that "inspiration" seems to

9. Allardyce Nicoll, *The Theater and Dramatic Theory* (London, 1962), p. 208. Hugo's play, the celebrated preface of which appeared in 1827, was not produced and is generally considered to be unproducible.
10. Gaston Baty and René Chavance, *La Vie de l'art théâtral des origines à nos jours* (Paris, 1932), pp. 238–39. Cf. also Charles Affron,

have been in the atmosphere surrounding production, rather than in the plays themselves. Contemporary accounts evoke a frenetic emotional climate generated by the great triumphs of the Romantic theater: Dumas' *Henri III et sa cour* and *Antony*, Hugo's *Hernani*, Vigny's *Chatterton*. Reading the plays today, it is difficult not to be surprised at the vehemence of both their partisans and their opponents. Dumas' vulgar grandiloquence and "immorality" and Hugo's prosodic virtuosity and air of dark mystery thinly mask a remarkable degree of theatrical conservatism. The atmosphere of their premieres can be judged from reports like Gautier's in *Les Jeunes-France*, which have become part of literary legend. The actors themselves, even at the august Comédie-Française, entered into the hysteria fomented by the young Romantics in the balconies. Inspired by recent Paris productions of Shakespeare by Kemble, they attempted to regenerate classical tradition by massive injections of primordial quaking and bellowing. "Alongside Firmin (Hernani) who, according to Madame Dorval's quip, gave 'the impression of a man being tickled standing up,' adopting 'a febrile nervousness which was his substitute for warmth' and which made people take him for an epileptic, Mademoiselle Mars went so far in the last act as to 'imitate the frightful convulsions of a lengthy death-agony' in the English manner so decried by the 'tribe of the beardless' (the classics)."[11] Dispassionate reading of these works leaves many modern readers with the feeling that standards of judgment had been impaired by the prevalent "enthusiasm" which Mme. de Staël had brought into fashion.[12]

A Stage for Poets: Studies in the Theater of Hugo and Musset (Princeton, 1971), p. 10 and passim, for a discussion of Hugo's verse drama as "opera."

11. Quotations from *Les Jeunes-France* cited by Marie-Antoinette Allevy, *La Mise en scène en France dans la première moitié du dix-neuvième siècle* (Paris, 1938), p. 95.

12. Eugene Ionesco's reaction to the Romantics' splashiest theatrical triumph, while exaggerated, represents one significant modern evaluation of its theatrical viability: "As for Hugo, he is ridiculous... When I attended a performance of *Hernani* they had to eject me from the theater because I was laughing too hard..." Quoted in *Le Figaro* (May 28,

Even *Chatterton*, which reflects its author's intellectual sober-
ness and his disdain for vulgar publicity, seems to have benefited
from a powerful current of emotion from its first audiences, as
well as a sensational performance by Vigny's leading lady (and
mistress) Marie Dorval. In typical Romantic theater fashion, she
triggered the premiere's success by her unrehearsed (but long-
meditated) fall down a flight of stairs, at the climactic moment
when Kitty Bell learns of the hero's suicide by poison. It is ironic
that the "philosopher" Vigny's painfully serious social treatise
should have been acclaimed in large part on the basis of this
stunt. The frenzy of enthusiasm which Madame Dorval aroused
is a measure of the peculiar blend of cynicism and naïveté which
reigned in the Paris theater of 1835. The theatrical demands and
aspirations of a Musset were of a different nature.

The odd combination of enthusiasm and charlatanry which
characterizes the Romantic drama as a whole is reflected on all
levels and in all facets of its construction. For classical tragedy's
subtle, overrefined prosody it substituted the superficial brilliance
of *Hernani*'s or *Ruy Blas*'s alexandrines (though they were still
alexandrines), or the brutal vulgarity of Dumas' prose. On the
level of social commentary, its heroes were accursed Byronic out-
casts (Hernani); bastards and other nonquintessential pariahs
(Antony); disguised valets who became prime ministers of Spain
(Ruy Blas), poets hounded by a pitiless society, their genius condemned as a sickness (Chatterton); regal libertines and hunch-
backed jesters (in *Le Roi s'amuse*): exceptional types meant to
cast a gauntlet in the face of the bourgeois public, which ap-
plauded these dramas as it might applaud adventure stories or
fairy tales. The taste for antithesis and paradox personified by
Victor Hugo was especially remarkable in the reigning psychology: beside the dark-souled, haunted heroes stood lily-white heroines like Kitty Bell, or the Queen of Spain (in *Ruy Blas*), loyal
to their persecuted lovers despite the villains' machinations, pre-
served in innocence by ignorance even when poised on the brink
of adultery. The "realistic" experiments in local color, historical

---

1970), p. 30. (Could *Hernani* be one of the sources of the theater of
the absurd?)

verity, and the mixture of genres often seem to be merely spice for familiar dramatic recipes.

Nowhere was the prevailing bad taste more evident than in the staging. This was the age of panoramas and dioramas (cf. the joyous play on the suffix "rama" in Balzac's *Père Goriot*), the mammouth pseudo-historical "mimodramas" of the Cirque-Olympique (half theater, half circus), the spectacular machinery which had begun to take top billing in Paris toward the end of the eighteenth century and reached its climax in the 1830's.[13] The storms, fires, floods, and other forms of violent transformation which had constituted a major attraction of Paris' boulevard theaters finally got a foothold on the austere stage of the Comédie-Française at the same time as the Romantics, when Baron Taylor's administration hired the celebrated Ciceri to do the sets for Dumas' *Henri III et sa cour*, Vigny's translation of *Othello*, and Hugo's *Hernani*. The exaggerated taste for mechanical spectaculars which found its true home in the Opéra has remained a constant of the Paris stage for better or worse until the present, in the splashy shows familiar to tourists. So, at the other end of the spectrum, have the machine-made comedies of Scribe, whose unimaginative *mise en scène*, formulistic plot-construction, and facile, cynical "realism" are still very much alive in the boulevard theater.

Musset's noisy rejection by the public which acclaimed all this gimcrack merchandise would be worthy of the term "symbolic" if *La Nuit Vénitienne* were not such an imperfect play. In the circumstances we may see it only as a stroke of good fortune. It is difficult to imagine what the poet's evolution as playwright might have been if his first venture in the theater had been a success. It seems evident, however, that Musset's wonderful plays written for the reading public would have been a very different affair if he had intended them for immediate production. This is not merely matter for conjecture: we have only to look at his revisions of plays for production after 1847 and the plays written for the stage during that period to see the effect of the practical theater on his literary creation. (These revisions, and some of the

13. See Nicole Decugis and Suzanne Reymond, *Le Decor de théâtre en France du Moyen Age à 1925* (Paris, 1953), p. 141; Allevy, passim.

later plays, will be examined in subsequent chapters.) The important thing is that Musset, hurt and angered by the public humiliation his talent had received, devoted himself during a particularly fruitful period of his literary life to the creation of a free, "ideal" theater, responsible only to the dictates of his imagination and his intelligence.

Musset's dramatic message was expressed with startling rapidity and density; not in one of the innumerable prefaces on which the Romantics lavished their creative energies, but in four masterful, varied, and elegant plays which, written in the space of less than two years (1833–34) by a very young author, have become pillars of the French classical repertory. In the next chapter, I will deal briefly with the period of Musset's apprenticeship in the drama, during which some of the foundations for his great works were being laid.[14] In four subsequent chapters of this study —on *Marianne, Fantasio, Lorenzaccio,* and *On ne badine pas avec l'amour*—I will analyze some of the structural, thematic, and linguistic elements that contribute to the artistic integrity of these works. In two succeeding chapters I examine more briefly two plays dating from the years immediately following this precocious flowering: *Le Chandelier* (1835) and *Il ne faut jurer de rien* (1836). My analyses seek to illuminate both the considerable strengths of these latter comedies and the symptoms of Musset's premature decline which pervade them. Although the emotional climate in which all these plays were created was an intensely pathetic and fascinating one, my observations are restricted for the most part to internal and aesthetic questions: a large body of Musset biography already deals in sufficient detail with the "drame de Venise" and the poet's Muses. Rather, I hope to show from the evidence of the plays themselves—their moral basis as well as their dramatic technique—how the particular set of values and aesthetic aims which was fused into the remarkable artistic whole of Musset's greatest dramas deteriorated in the works of subsequent years and, after his astonishingly rapid accession to artistic maturity, succumbed to his premature decline

14. For a detailed study of this formative period, cf. Herbert S. Gochberg, *Stage of Dreams* (Geneva, 1967).

and senility. In a final chapter I examine one of the author's last plays—*Carmosine* (1850)—in which, although Musset experienced a brief resurgence of his creative energy, we sense a spiritual lethargy, an abdication of revolt, which makes this bourgeois fairy tale doubly pathetic.[15]

15. Among the most familiar plays of Musset are his one-act "proverbs" *Un Caprice* (1837) and *Il faut qu'une porte soit ouverte ou fermée* (1845), which are frequently performed at the Comédie-Française as curtain-raisers. If I have chosen, somewhat arbitrarily, to eliminate them from consideration in this work, it is because they seem to me to belong to another genre than the plays I study, equally subtle and perfected, no doubt, but more limited in its imaginative and moral scope by the salon origins from which it sprang. Another proverb, *On ne saurait penser à tout* (1849), owes so considerable a debt to *Le Distrait* of Carmontelle that it would not bear study as an authentic Musset work, even if it were a better play.

Chapter 2 The Formative Years

The principal phases in Musset's literary career have been admirably retraced by the late Pierre Gastinel in his monumental *Le Romantisme d'Alfred de Musset*. Moreover, much of the author's creative life, as it is linked with his well-publicized sentimental adventures, has become part of literary legend. It is sufficient, then, to examine only the beginnings of Musset's dramatic career, as a prelude to studying the works of his mature years. His later career, where it is relevant, will be dealt with in the chapters on individual plays.

According to his brother Paul, Musset's theatrical gifts can be traced back as far as his maternal grandfather, Claude-Antoine Guyot-Desherbiers, who recited the dramatic proverbs of Carmontelle by heart, and to the poet's tendency as a child to dramatize his feelings within the admiring family circle.[1] The first manifestation of his talent which concerns us, however, came with the publication of his *Contes d'Espagne et d'Italie* in December 1829, when the poet was barely nineteen years old. The volume, in which most of the stylish Romantic themes and attitudes were liberally seasoned with Musset's precocious irony, had a great success, adding a note of literary solidity to the brilliant social reputation he had already earned in Paris salons. Although their precarious balance between seriousness and pastiche did little to reassure the disciples of Hugo's Cénacle as to Musset's

1. *Biographie d'Alfred de Musset*, in *Oeuvres complètes*, text established and presented by Philippe Van Tieghem, "l'Intégrale," (Paris, 1963), pp. 16 ff.

loyalty to the Romantic sect (the closing poem in particular, "Mardoche," contains some outrageous snipes), the *Contes* established the young poet as one of the rising stars of Romanticism. Despite their title, probably inspired by La Fontaine's rhymed tales, they are a collection of narrative and lyric verse.[2] Yet one of its first critics, writing in *Le Figaro*, remarked on the dramatic quality of the volume's chief works—*Don Paez, Les Marrons du feu, Portia* and *Mardoche*—and encouraged the young author to turn his gifts toward the theater. *Les Marrons du feu* in particular is written as a one-act play in nine scenes, with action and setting indicated by stage directions. Like its companions, it is a horrendous, tongue-in-cheek hodge-podge of Romantic clichés, replete with illicit passion, revenge, casual murders, a lecherous priest, a blasé Byronic hero, and a jealous actress.

Others as well were impressed with Musset's dramatic promise, for the following year saw the creation of two works commissioned for performance by theater directors. One, *La Quittance du Diable* ("The Devil's Due"), was adapted for the Théâtre des Nouveautés, a vaudeville house, from an episode of Sir Walter Scott's *Redgauntlet* (Musset, who used a recent French translation of the novel, names his villain, with typical Gallic confusion, "le Sir de Redgnauntley"). Why it did not actually reach the stage is matter for conjecture: both the contemporary political situation and a lack of singable lyrics have been alleged. Certainly the work's slapdash plot and solemn Gothicism were no worse than many similar pieces of hokum being produced. In any case, *La Quittance du Diable* cannot be considered a landmark in Musset's literary progress. It is typical period spectacle, undistinguishable from the mass of bad melodrama prevalent in its time. Balzac, Hugo, and Nerval went through this phase too.

The second play, *La Nuit Vénitienne* (subtitled "Lauretta's Wedding"), was commissioned for performance by F. A. Harel, director of the Odéon, with the catastrophic results already noted.

2. Musset often had difficulty adhering to a title: two years later his dramatic collection, *Un Spectacle dans un fauteuil*, was to close with a narrative poem, *Namouna*, subtitled "Oriental tale." It must be noted, however, that the poem was composed at the last minute to fill out the slim volume.

Though it is a considerably more characteristic piece which fore-shadows Musset's later use of puppet-characters, his ambiguous, ironic heroes, and elegant prose dialogue, its status as the author's first produced play is more significant as an event than as part of his creative development. Had it not encountered the humiliating failure fostered by the stage accidents, Musset might have been encouraged to pursue his search for success following the prevailing theatrical formulas. The world might well have had several more one-act Romantic pastiches and Gothic vaudevilles; but probably not *Marianne, Fantasio, On ne badine pas avec l'amour,* and *Lorenzaccio.* Romantics and classics alike seem to have been outraged by this slight work. Its lack of action and its excessive length-to-content ratio make it likely that the work would soon have been forgotten had it not contributed so riotously to Musset's subsequent career. We cannot take much to heart the hero's ultimatum to Lauretta on the eve of her marriage: kill your princely fiancé and elope with me before the clock strikes eleven, or my suicide will be on your conscience. Neither can Razetta, for the perfidy of his hesitant mistress, won over by the Prince's mature realism, decides him finally to drown his sorrow only in wine, women, and song. Of all the characters, the charming, sardonic Prince alone is worthy of Musset's later heroes; and he is more prophetic of the poet's decline than of his prime. The rest are cardboard figures or sketches of what was to come.

The year 1831 seems to have been one of unfinished projects and studies for later plays. But December 1832 saw publication of the first volume of *Un Spectacle dans un fauteuil.* Its title appears to link this book with Musset's stage fiasco: having renounced the boards, the author offers his new kind of dramatic works to a homebound reading public. But this first installment cannot be said to represent the real fruition of Musset's theatrical gift. Apart from a narrative poem, "Namouna," it contains but two verse plays, *La Coupe et les Lèvres* ("The Cup and the Lip"—Musset's predilection for proverbial titles was already developed) and *A Quoi rêvent les jeunes filles* ("What Young Ladies Dream Of"). The former is preceded, it is true, by a fairly lengthy "Dédicace" to his friend Alfred Tattet, in which Musset expresses his insouciance, his eclecticism, and his break with Romanticism (as well as other -isms); and he signifies his penchant for fantasy and dream in the style of Racine and Shakespeare, rather than Calderon's or Mérimée's realism.[3] The dramatic content of the volume is quite slim, though; and neither of the plays really hints at the series of masterpieces which Musset was to write during the two following years.

La Coupe et les Lèvres is more ambitious than any of Musset's previous dramas. Its hero is one of those restless, damned souls that Byron planted in the imagination of his Romantic imitators. Haunted by the evil spirit of his insatiable desire, the hunter Charles Frank bids farewell to his native Tyrol after setting fire to his house. Down on the plain, he rejects a warning voice and chooses the route of ambition. It leads him to murder a passing knight and to take his mistress, Monna Belcolore. He wins an immense fortune at the gambling table. But boredom with his life of ease and Belcolore's facile seductions spurs him to join the Emperor's army, where his reckless courage soon raises him to a post of command. Even this glory pales: the sight of a pure young girl he knew in the mountains reminds him of the vanity of his present life. Frank stages a mock funeral for himself, and attends it disguised as a monk. Cynically, he turns a comrade's eulogy into a mass demonstration of hatred for the "departed," before revealing himself to the abashed throng of fickle mourners. Donning his disguise again, he seduces the disconsolate Belcolore on his own coffin, then chases her away in derision. In a long monologue he expresses his disdain for men and gods. A faded bouquet reminds him of Deidamia, the girl he loved. In the final act, Frank, regenerated, is about to marry her when Belcolore appears and stabs the young girl to death.

La Coupe et les Lèvres, although it represents progress over the inanities of *La Quittance du Diable* and the inconsequence of *La Nuit Vénitienne*, is still far from the mastery which Musset was to attain. Its unbroken, juvenile seriousness, its pedantic allegory of vice and virtue, its Romantic mixture of *Macbeth*, Schiller, Byron, and Goethe, its static dramatic structure, with

3. The relaxed association of Racine and Shakespeare is, of course, a further gesture of independence from the Cénacle.

a striking abuse of long monologues, disembodied voices and choruses—not to mention the monotony of its alexandrines—give no hint of the brilliant prose comedies to come. Little besides its themes of ennui and the irreversible fatality of vice links it with *Les Caprices de Marianne, Fantasio,* and *Lorenzaccio.* This thematic affinity is not enough to lift the play out of the common run of Romantic symbolic drama, a devil-ridden, outlaw-populated "literature of protest" which seems quaint today.

A Quoi rêvent les jeunes filles bears almost no resemblance to its companion piece, aside from its alexandrine verse. It thus at least gives a measure of Musset's precocious versatility. The play's freshness and the charming humor of its hymn to young love and mature nostalgia make it the most perfect of Musset's verse dramas, if not one of his more consequential works. Duke Laertes, in order to give his daughters Ninon and Ninette the impression that their carefully arranged marriages are romantic love-matches, stages false abductions and disguised serenades, encouraging young Silvio to play the part of Don Juan. Silvio finally chooses and wins Ninon, the grotesque Count Irus abandons his suit in fright after a comic duel with Silvio, and Ninette resigns herself to waiting for a suitable match. The action of the play is confused enough to lead one critic to view it all as Ninon's dream.[4] The graceful symmetry and echo of the speeches of the two sisters, the puppet-figures (Irus, and the mechanically contradictory servants Spadille and Quinola), the dialectic of innocence and experience, sentiment and ruse, give this play a closer relationship in both form and content to what follows than we find in *La Coupe et les Lèvres,* despite a considerable difference in moral and artistic level. *A Quoi rêvent les jeunes filles* is recognizable as pure Musset, marked by the imprint of his artistic personality. Its easy, conversational, yet far from pedestrian verse, reminiscent of Musset's best ironic lyrics, bears the same stamp as that elegant poetic prose in which his later comedies were written. The freedom of its construction, with multiple scene changes during the course of its two acts, together with the rapidity of

4. Steen Jansen, "Alfred de Musset dramaturge. *A Quoi rêvent les jeunes filles* et la technique dramatique d'*Un Spectacle dans un fauteuil,*" *Orbis Litterarum,* 21 (1966), 222–54.

its action make this play the first measure of Musset's dramatic originality.

Nevertheless, *André del Sarto*, written in the initial quarter of 1833 and published in the *Revue des Deux Mondes* on April 1, is the first true herald of Musset's major theater. Despite its structural flaws and vestiges of Romantic grandiloquence, it marks the advent of the author's mature prose style. By its content—psychological and thematic—it belongs to the great series of theatrical works which the period from 1833 to 1834 produced, in a sudden, intense flowering of Musset's dramatic talent. It is not a perfect work: it is too long and diffuse, and verbosity and melodrama often take the place of Musset's usual justness of speech and action. That is probably why, although the play was among the first of Musset's mature works to be staged, it has never enjoyed the popularity which the others of its series attained. Yet it remained close to its author's heart, no doubt because of the personal significance of its two main themes—the artist as failure, and the difficult relationship between art and love—to which Musset was to return later, notably in the short story "Le Fils du Titien." Despite its flaws, the play has kept its hold on the stage, thanks to the passion and generosity of its sentiments, the rare dignity, and the stature which the young Musset succeeded in giving to the traditionally comic role of the cuckold.

The painter Andrea del Sarto, in order to cater to his young wife Lucretia del Fede's whims, has sacrificed talent, integrity, even a large sum of money entrusted to him by François Ier of France to purchase works of art for his collection. As the play opens, Andrea's friend and disciple, Cordiani, emerges from Lucretia's window after their first night of love. Surprised by the doorkeeper, Gremio, Cordiani wounds him in his flight. When Andrea, thinking only to protect Lucretia's reputation, sets a trap that night for the unknown "prowler," Cordiani again wounds Gremio, this time mortally, then, unexpectedly meeting Andrea in his wife's bedroom, pretends to be chasing the culprit. Andrea, finding blood on his hand after shaking Cordiani's, realizes the duplicity of his wife and his best friend. Overwhelmed by disillusionment and the disintegration of his artistic hopes, he receives news that François' ambassador has arrived to settle accounts. When Cordiani is discovered hiding in Lucretia's room, Andrea sends his wife off to her mother, then gravely wounds the unresisting Cordiani in a duel. Forced to confess his embezzlement to the king's ambassador, Andrea grows delirious with grief and shame. The news that Cordiani, recovered from his wound, has fled the city with Lucretia completes Andrea's despair. He sends a servant off to them with the message, "Why are you fleeing in such haste? Andrea del Sarto's widow can wed Cordiani"; then he takes poison and dies. Cordiani and Lucretia, in flight, receive Andrea's message as the curtain falls.

André del Sarto was the first of Musset's 1833–34 plays to be performed: at the Comédie-Française, fifteen years after its publication.[5] It was thus also the first of his works from this period to be subjected to the extensive revisions which the author considered necessary to adapt them to the practical requirements of the stage. I shall examine the nature of these adaptations particularly in the chapter on *Les Caprices de Marianne*. In the present case, the effect of Musset's revisions is less symptomatic of the author's decline than in the latter play: *André del Sarto* was badly constructed and too long. Musset reduced it to two acts in 1850, for production at the Odéon, by eliminating the scene with François' ambassador and one in front of Lucretia's house, cutting a certain number of speeches and having the play end with Andrea's death. This resulted in a tighter, more cohesive structure. Another of its effects (indeed, one of the primary aims sought by Musset) was to permit the play to be produced in a single set

5. In a letter to his mother written in 1848, Musset says that the play is seventeen years old, therefore written in 1831: cf. *Comédies et Proverbes*, ed. Gastinel (Paris, 1952), I, 246. According to his brother Paul, its plan dated from 1830, when Harel asked Alfred for another play to be produced at the Odéon, after the *Nuit Vénitienne* fiasco. But Paul insisted that nothing came of this offer, and that the play itself dates only from 1833. According to a widespread but somewhat doubtful account originated by Paul, the initial idea for *André del Sarto* came from reading the biographical notice accompanying engravings in the *Musée Filhol*. This play was the author's first creative work in a long, distinguished series published by the *Revue des Deux Mondes*. See *Théâtre complet*, text established and annotated by Maurice Allem, "Bibliothèque de la Pléiade" (Paris, 1958), pp. 1186–87.

representing the courtyard of Andrea's house. Thus the process of retrenchment, the rejection of that free dramatic system which Musset himself created in 1833, has its origins in this, the first of his works from that period to be staged. Like the others, it was to be subjected to considerable bowdlerization and revamping to satisfy government censorship, scandalized by its indulgence toward adultery, and by Cordiani's unpunished crime (all of which was resolved by having him die of his wounds!). Musset is said to have regretted the extremes to which he was forced by his producer's fear of scandal; nonetheless he was to initiate with *André del Sarto* the series of compromises and abjurations which casts such a pitiable light on his maturity, after the daring and brilliance of his youthful years.

André del Sarto shares with the later, more ambitious *Lorenzaccio* the distinction of being Musset's only completed historical drama.[6] Like *Lorenzaccio*, it represents the problem of artistic and moral decadence in the context of Renaissance Florence in the 1530's. In both cases the parallel with Musset's own time suggested by the '30's date is not fortuitous: as the opening of the *Confession d'un enfant du siècle* made explicit in 1836, the author saw his generation as caught in a cycle of impotence and spiritual disorder following the heroic days of an earlier generation, those of the Napoleonic campaigns. But in *André del Sarto*, unlike *Lorenzaccio*, the political and social decadence of Florence is subordinated to the protagonist's central problems: the reconciliation of art and love, the realization of a diminished talent which has succumbed to moral abuse and compromise. Andrea regrets the time of artistic heroes—the age of Raphael (of Michelangelo, as Musset anachronistically wrote in his original text)—of which he is the last surviving representative. Now the world of art is dominated by mannerists and facile innovators: Pontormo and his crowd. Andrea's own weakness, the dishonest acts into which he has fallen, are symptomatic of this degeneration. His suicide represents the inevitable death of what was strong, believing, and impassioned.

6. His unpublished works include plans and fragments of two historical plays, *Le Comte d'Essex*, an early project, and *La Servante du Roi*, a verse tragedy he undertook to write for the actress Rachel in 1839.

The theme of time's dissolution of men's dreams is thus intro-duced here in premonitory fashion. Musset's great plays were to deal with this problem, which obsessed the major Romantic poets. But unlike its successors, *André del Sarto* views the theme from the vantage point of maturity. The young poet identifies his anxiety with that of the middle-aged artist who, conscious of his own failure and surrender, sees a cynical new generation vying to take his place. The surprise of this emotional identification by a twenty-year-old with an elder generation, and with that stan-dard butt of mockery, the deceived husband, is all the greater when we realize that in *Marianne, Fantasio,* and *On ne badine pas avec l'amour,* idealism and passion are the properties of youth alone. There Musset substitutes for the traditional virtues of ma-turity a sclerosis or fossilizing which ineluctably accompanies the passage of time in human experience. In these three subsequent comedies, the generation gap is strikingly represented by a differ-ence in characterization between young protagonists and older roles (they cannot be called antagonists) : the latter are presented as *fantoches,* puppet-figures whose grotesque manias and tics take the place of fluid, three-dimensional characterization.[7] Curi-ously, Musset rediscovered a degree of empathy with these older characters in *Lorenzaccio,* another trait of resemblance linking his two historical plays: Philip Strozzi, the aging humanist and republican, is endowed with a pathetic grandeur reminiscent of Andrea's; but the primary focus is on the young hero Lorenzo de Medici, who has sacrificed his youth to a cause and finds himself and his dream undone by the passage of time. In *André del Sarto,* youth is represented rather by Andrea's faithless students, who abandon him and his teachings; and by Lucretia del Fede, who betrays her adoring husband to follow his best friend and leaves Andrea with no recourse but suicide. Youth's unconsciousness under the spell of passion, the unwitting but inevitable pain in-flicted by young men and women driven by love, pride, and jeal-ousy, is taken up later in *On ne badine pas avec l'amour;* but

7. It is interesting to note that a production of *On ne badine pas avec l'amour* by the Tréteau de Paris which toured America in 1968 used projected cartoons to represent the grotesques—a valid modern expres-sion of their two-dimensionality, their "otherness."

sympathetically, from the viewpoint of the suffering young protagonists themselves rather than the astonished, uncomprehending elders who surround them. *André del Sarto* thus represents an initial statement of the predominant themes and of the dramatic technique which Musset was to develop in his later works; but they are treated in a way which distinguishes this earlier work from its companions, and makes it a prophet of things to come rather than the bearer of Musset's integral message.

A month and a half after *André del Sarto* (May 15, 1833), the *Revue des Deux Mondes* was publishing the first of his great cycle of dramatic works: *Les Caprices de Marianne*. In less than six weeks' time, according to his brother Paul, Musset had succeeded in perfecting and applying the new theatrical doctrine which was to distinguish his best work henceforth.[8]

8. *Biographie d'Alfred de Musset*, in *Oeuvres complètes*, "l'Intégrale," p. 28.

Les Caprices de Marianne, Act II, Scene 1.
Théâtre National Populaire:
Geneviève Page (Marianne), Gérard Philipe (Octave).
Courtesy of Agence de Presse Bernand, Paris.

Chapter 3 Les Caprices de Marianne:

The Solitude of Lovers

 If we could be carried by a time capsule to the Comédie-Française on the evening of June 14, 1851, for the premiere of *Les Caprices de Marianne*, we would witness not only a great theatrical success but a singularly moving occasion. It was the first of the quartet of Musset's great plays to be performed, and the only one to reach the stage during his lifetime. The national theater had assigned some distinguished players to the production: the comics Provost and Got as Claudio and Tibia, the *jeune premier* Brindeau (Octave), the sparkling Madeleine Brohan as Marianne, and as Coelio, Delaunay, whose name remained identified with Musset's dramas for years afterward. The importance of the occasion may be measured by the critical force which turned out: nineteen reviews were devoted to this premiere.[1] Théophile Gautier, (whose drama column in *La Presse* had been demanding Musset's instatement at the Théâtre-Français for years), felt somewhat vindicated at last.[2] Only a few defenders of public morality, disturbed by the play's attitude toward marriage, denounced its charm on behalf of the young ladies who might venture into the Comédie some ill-fated matinée. But most of the critics shared the enthusiasm of Augustin Lireux, of the *Constitutionnel*: "The work's originality [is precisely what] charms us: in one hour, it moves us more than many

1. Cf. *Comédies et Proverbes*, ed. Gastinel, I, 260.
2. See *Histoire de l'art dramatique en France depuis vingt ans* (Paris, 1858–59).

others that take up a whole evening. The emotion we feel is delicate, our intelligence is satisfied at the same time as our hearts; besides the poetry which bursts forth exquisitely, there is great art in its dramatic structure."[3]

Lireux's last comment is ironic: the performance he saw contained debilitating changes from the text Musset had published eighteen years before.[4] Let us imagine a naive member of that first audience, familiar with that text but not with the traditions of the Comédie-Française. He would have been dismayed at the single decor—"A square in front of Claudio's house"—instead of the seven in which the original was set ("A street in front of Claudio's house," "Coelio's house," "Claudio's garden," "A street," "Another street," "Claudio's house," "A cemetery"). He would have noted the disappearance of one of the play's sapid minor characters—Ciuta, the "go-between," replaced by a stock figure, Coelio's valet Pippo—and remarked that Claudio, Marianne's husband, had been transformed from judge into "podestat." The cast was also augmented by two hired killers and an inn waiter. As the play progressed, our first-nighter might have noted extensive reworking of the original text: scenes reshuffled, speeches moved from one scene to another, passages modified to reflect these changes and the unitary set, references to political and religious authorities deleted, transitions inserted to clarify the logic of the play. If our imaginary spectator was not already numbed by these changes, he would no doubt have been confused to see that the final scene followed immediately upon the preceding sequence of events, in the same public square, instead of occurring later, at Coelio's grave. He might be excused for sharing Gautier's view of the production as a mixed blessing: "Precisely what we seek in a play which was not written for the stage but which we would like to see there, is its absence of accustomed forms . . . *Les Caprices de Marianne* should have been played as is, with its four or five transformation scenes, and without cutting a single word from a text everyone knows by heart."[5]

3. Cited by Lyonnet, Les "Premières," p. 107.
4. *Revue des Deux Mondes* (May 15, 1833); *Un Spectacle dans un fauteuil* (1834).
5. *Histoire*, series 6, p. 241.

The 1851 Revisions: Language

Since this was the only one of Musset's major plays to be performed while he was alive—and revised by the author himself for production—it is of interest to see how this affected his existing work (as opposed to those he was writing for the stage during this period): how his "armchair drama" was modified to meet practical theater requirements. (We must also, inevitably, consider factors outside the author's will or control, such as the strictures of the censor and the suggestions of a reading committee imbued with the peculiar stage lore of the Comédie-Française: for a century it had been under attack as a bastion of theatrical reaction.) [6]

There can be little doubt, given the circumstances under which *Les Caprices de Marianne* was first produced, that the modified text which Maurice Allem chooses to publish in his complete edition of Musset and which several Musset scholars refer to in their studies [7] is not a "mature" version of some youthful sketch.

6. See Jean Richer's account of the phases *Les Caprices de Marianne* went through under the influence of the Censor's office: *Textes dramatiques inédits* (Paris, 1955), pp. 57–62. Here are the most pertinent passages from the Censor's report: "Taken in itself the subject of this comedy does not present anything injurious to stand in the way of its performance; but its details, and especially the general way in which the author has treated it, give it a shocking character. Claudio is a stupid and cruel judge who must be deceived, and who avenges himself by killing; Octave, a complaisant friend who becomes the agent of Coelio's seductions as if he were performing a good deed. Marianne listens to all these amorous seductions and finally decides to take a lover; it will be the man who brings back the scarf she hands to Octave. The crudeness of certain details, the manner in which Octave presents theories, unbecoming to say the least, concerning marriage and love, seems to us to make this work inadmissable. It could only be presented after such numerous changes that we do not feel capable of asking them of the author..."

7. *Théâtre complet.* Cf. also Frederick Tonge, *L'Art du dialogue dans les Comédies en prose d'Alfred de Musset. Etude de stylistique dramatique* (Paris, 1967), and Herbert S. Gochberg, *Stage of Dreams* (Geneva, 1967). Pierre and Françoise Gastinel's edition of the *Comédies et Proverbes*, to which I will generally refer in this study, like Philippe Van Tieghem's in the *Oeuvres complètes*, "l'Intégrale" is based

It is rather the work of a precociously diminished author under powerful internal and external pressures and not at liberty to achieve a truly creative revision. The series of debilitating ill- nesses dating back to 1840, the recurrent, increasing lethargy which sapped his creative vitality from about the same time, com- plicated by Musset's legendary abuse of alcohol, in 1851 had brought the poet to a plateau of sterility on which he was to re- main until his death in 1857. His election to the Academy in 1852 stands as an ironic monument to the poet's impotence henceforth: after *Carmosine* in 1850 (a last flash of Musset's diminished genius), he wrote nothing worthy of note.[8] How then might he have recaptured the creative heat in which *Les Caprices* had been written eighteen years prior, and relived the thrust of its language and movement? That would have been a difficult feat, with a work of such lyricism, even for a more robust and durable talent than his. When we examine the two texts, the weakening effects of Musset's revision shed useful light on the unique qualities of the original version.

The essential lines of the plot are the same in both versions. In the original, the action takes place in Naples, at some un- specified time. Coelio, despite his serenades and the efforts of Ciuta, the go-between, has received no encouragement from the beautiful Marianne, wife of judge Claudio. Indeed, she does not even seem aware of his existence. In desperation, Coelio asks the aid of Octave, his charming, dissipated friend (by chance Clau- dio's cousin), who confirms Ciuta's judgment: the lady is a prude, too devout to deceive her stupid spouse. Octave promises none- theless to use his winy eloquence in Coelio's behalf. He tries to calm the latter's fears, fostered in Coelio by his mother's tale of a similar intervention and subsequent betrayal she unwittingly caused in her youth: Hermia married the spokesman, and her dis- appointed suitor committed suicide. In a series of fiery encounters, Octave succeeds in arousing Marianne's interest: in himself. At first indignant at the idea that she should yield to the first suitor

on the 1840 edition of Musset's *Comédies et Proverbes*, "the last one the author corrected before thinking of performance."

8. See Gastinel, *Le Romantisme d'Alfred de Musset* (Rouen, 1933), pp. 622–24.

who sighs for her, she later directs her attack at Octave's life of easy pleasures. Marianne soon stirs the embers of passion in the young rake. But Octave has also aroused the jealousy of Claudio. The latter's demand that Marianne stop speaking to her cousin prompts her, in a fit of pique, to issue an invitation to anyone—except the tiresome Coelio—whom Octave might send to her house that evening. Despite the evident come-on, Octave passes the scarf which Marianne has given him as a token to Coelio, who goes off to his rendezvous more dazed than elated. But a note comes for Octave from Marianne: stay away, Claudio and his servant Tibia will kill whoever enters the garden. Octave arrives too late to prevent Coelio from hearing Marianne call out from her window: "Go away, Octave, it's a trap . . . I'll meet you in church tomorrow . . ." Coelio rushes to his death, convinced that Octave has betrayed him. In an epilogue at Coelio's grave, Octave mourns his better self, the gentle, loving Coelio, and rejects Marianne's last advances: "I don't love you, Marianne; it was Coelio who loved you."

Even from this condensed synopsis, it can be seen that the action of *Marianne* is simple and, to a point, familiar. Although commentators have remarked on the comparative lack of specific literary sources for its plot, certain figures and devices—the bashful lover, the spokesman invited to speak for himself, the doltish husband, the capricious lady—are all reminiscent of a variety of models, chiefly Boccaccio, Shakespeare, and Italian and Spanish Renaissance comedy. Indeed, the Italian setting, the figure of Ciuta, the references to Carnival, and a host of other details make it evident that Musset was seeking a stylized, traditional comedy atmosphere, as he was later to do in *Fantasio* and in the first scenes of *On ne badine pas avec l'amour*.[9] *Les Caprices de Marianne* seems to fit the category of Renaissance love comedy, with its extolling of extramarital affairs, its mocking of the cuckolded husband (cf., on the contrary, *André del Sarto*), and its praise, through the voice of Octave, of what Verlaine calls "la vie opportune." It is surprising to see Musset reviving this particular

9. Musset, for reasons I will examine more fully later, emphasizes the temporal and geographical references in his 1851 version of *Marianne*.

type of theater in the midst of the Romantic "revolution," with its emphasis on new forms even when the matter treated was historical; and it is hard to imagine how he might make something fresh and modern enough out of it to justify Lireux's tribute to its originality or Gautier's reference to the "absence of accustomed forms."

Part of the explanation lies in the play's treatment of contemporary social themes: the problem of ennui, the relationship of the individual to society and the latter's pressures for conformity, the cold hypocrisy of institutional justice, the faults of convent education for women (George Sand was to open the poet's eyes further on this theme), and, particularly, the inequities of woman's place in society—one of the liveliest themes of nineteenth-century literature. Along with the author's mocking references to the Church, these account for a good part of the censors' objections, as we might infer even from a hasty first listing of the cuts and changes Musset made in the 1851 version: its action is situated in Naples "during the reign of François Ier" rather than at the unspecified time Musset ascribes to *Fantasio* and *On ne badine pas avec l'amour* in order to avoid the possibility of seeing contemporary political references.[10] For similar reasons Claudio is labeled a "podestat" (the meaning of which is somewhat vague for the 1850 spectator), to obviate any semblance of criticism of the contemporary judicial system. Tibia's line, "A death sentence is a magnificent thing to read aloud," becomes less pointed when Claudio's wistful comeback is changed to "It's not the podestat who reads it; it's the clerk":[11] Claudio's rank becomes part

10. A continuing polemic relative to productions of *Marianne* has precisely to do with the era it should be set in. A revival at the Odéon in 1922 opted for 1830's costumes. Gaston Baty, in his noted 1936 production, used a mixture of eighteenth and nineteenth century stylized decors, deliberately avoiding period realism; the Comédie-Française has tended to stay within the temporal frame of reference of its 1851 production, although it finally rehabilitated the 1840 text.

11. Gastinel, p. 143; Allem, p. 242. This particular series of modifications is among the most arbitrary and superficial: it consists of avoiding the word "judge," as in II, 1 (Gastinel, p. 153; II, 6, in Allem, p. 257), where it is replaced by "spouse," although the remainder of the

of a long-dead political system. One of Musset's most marked divergences from the aesthetics of the Cénacle concerned his habitual avoidance of "local color." While the theoreticians of French Romanticism were expounding historical realism, Pierre Nordon speaks of "Musset's lack of curiosity concerning geography or topography."[12] The author's letters to his uncle, Stephen Desherbiers, as early as 1830 when Musset was the darling of the Cénacle, show how long standing this indifference was. In the 1833 text of *Marianne*, the absence of physical or temporal localization lent the play a sort of universality, and by implication a contemporary relevancy. The revised version is both a recantation and an evasion.

Not even "evasion" can be claimed for the fate of Musset's barbed references to the Catholic church: they were simply dropped from the 1851 text. Thus Ciuta's characterization of Marianne as "prouder and more devout than ever" (Gastinel, p. 124) disappears with the old woman herself; Octave's caricature, "She's a skinny puppet who mumbles endless *Ave's*," has its ending modified to "who always does what she pleases, like a spoiled child." Most peculiar of all is the author's excision of the references to vespers in the first scene of act two (Gastinel, pp. 147, 151, 156). In the original text, the ringing of the bells serves multiple purposes: as action, accompanying Marianne's accustomed attendance at church services which enables her to meet Octave on the way out and back; as an atmospheric device, announcing the transition from daytime to evening, leading to the dark garden in which Coelio will be killed; and as a persistent moral echo revealing Octave's spiritual unrest and solitude: as he drinks his wine, he cries out "Ding! ding! What a bore those vespers are! Am I supposed to go to sleep? I feel as if I've turned to stone," and later, "Oh! those damned bells! when will they stop driving me into the earth?"—just before their abrupt silence announces Marianne's return from services. It is evident from this

---

exchange of insults between Octave and Claudio refers repeatedly to the court of law.

12. "Alfred de Musset et l'Angleterre," *Les Lettres Romanes*, 21 (1967), p. 42.

sequence and its association with the progress in Octave and Marianne's relationship that these religious references were not simply sidelong darts, but are connected with deeper themes of the play. Their disappearance weakens the originality, the fresh irreverence, of the work by cutting it off from contact with its temporal and spiritual environment. Musset's art, especially in his drama, attains its highest degree of personality in the dialectic of conflicting tendencies: the traditional and contemporary, the universal and concrete—or the classical and romantic, to put it in terms of the polemics of his time. The deletion of contemporary points of reference is a first step in the general unbalancing of *Les Caprices de Marianne*.

A similar effect, closer still to the heart of the play, is wrought by the bowdlerizing of its language. The transformation ("desexing") of Ciuta into Pippo gives an initial hint of what is to come. The references to Octave as a drunkard are carefully pruned: the subject was a tender one for Musset in 1851, as he was mapping his entry into the Academy. Above all, Musset systematically expurgated the amorous language of the play, ridding it of its explicit sensuality. Coelio, whose language remains on a fairly Platonic level even in the original, loses one of his few physical descriptions of Marianne and a troublesome reference to libertinism: "Isn't it an old saw among libertines that all women are alike? Why are so few loves alike? In truth, I couldn't love that woman as you would, Octave, or as I would love another. Yet what does it all amount to? Two blue eyes, two ruby lips, a white dress, and two white hands" (I, 1; Gastinel, p. 131). The innocuousness of the speech makes its disappearance more striking; so, too, for a reference to Coelio's inability to scale imaginary walls and reach his beloved's bedroom.

It is in the crucial series of four scenes between Octave and Marianne (excluding the final one in the cemetery) that we experience the real effect of Musset's cuts. The first encounter (Gastinel, I, 1, p. 133; Allem, I, 5, p. 236) shows the least damage, since their dialogue is scarcely engaged. But the process is initiated: love no longer "sucks" its nourishment, like a bee, from the flower of pain, but "draws" it (Gastinel, p. 134; Allem p. 238). A pettish exchange near the end of the scene disappears:

"*Marianne*—Why shouldn't I love Claudio? He's my husband. *Octave*—Why shouldn't you love Coelio? He's your lover." (Gastinel, p. 137).

The next encounter (Gastinel, II, 1, p. 148; Allem, II, 4, p. 252), in which Marianne counterattacks in the name of honor and decency and vituperates the double standard, raises the temperature of the discussion: the revised text thereby suffers more extensively. After the excision of Marianne's ironic retort to Coelio's feigned indifference ("Just when I was going to give myself to him"), it is a series of images expressing the sensuality of woman that disappears. Octave's irreligious comparison of Marianne to "a kind of [reverse] Galatea, [who] will turn to marble in the depths of some church . . . and cannot help finding a respectable niche in a confessional" (Gastinel, p. 149); Marianne's metaphor of woman's virtue as a flower—"Before casting the dust of her cherished flower to the wind, its calix should be bathed with tears, brought to bloom by a few rays of the sun, opened gradually by a delicate hand"—evidently suggested meanings that were too frankly erotic for the public taste of the times. Similarly, Marianne, who lends herself to the sensual atmosphere created by Octave in the original text, has her sarcastic expression of the male view of women as sex objects blunted. "A moment's occupation, a fragile glass containing a drop of dew, which you bring to your lips and then toss away. A woman is a pleasure party! Couldn't you say, on meeting one: There's a beautiful night passing by?" (in which the reference to drink suggests Octave's other vice) becomes simply, "A moment's occupation, a vain shadow you pretend to love, for the pleasure of saying you're in love. A woman is an amusement! Couldn't you say, on meeting one: There's a beautiful whim passing by?" Here, as elsewhere, the metaphor is abstracted.

The third encounter (Gastinel, II, 1, p. 156; Allem, II, 8, p. 258) centers ambiguously about Marianne's attack on Octave's drinking habits, and expands into a discussion on good versus cheap wine and women: Musset thus had double reason to blunt his language. Here, in contrast to other parts of the play, Octave's drunkenness is too necessary to the action to be eliminated: Marianne, coming from vespers, finds him waiting in vain for his mistress Rosalinde, drowning his sorrows and loneliness. She teases Octave about his conflicting tastes in wine (Lacrima Cristi) and women (Rosalinde), and gets drawn—or is it she who draws Octave?—into some equivocal exchanges whose sensual heat quickly rises to a new level. Since the scene takes place under the arbor of an inn, it gives Claudio the chance to complain later of his wife's lack of concern for his station and her own dignity, and thus leads to Marianne's fit of temper and its tragic results. It reinforces as well the conflict between Octave's hedonism and Claudio's rigorous conformism. Musset's revisions reflect an ironic concern for linguistic decency, especially on the part of the virtuous Marianne. The word "mistress" disappears from her vocabulary as well as Octave's. Octave's amusing jibe about communicating his emptiness to his glass remains; but his irreverent reference to the "tears of Christ" contained in his wine is deleted. The greatest loss occurs in the passionate lyricism of Octave and Marianne's climactic exchange, built on the metaphor of the wine bottle as a woman. The revised text no longer contains Marianne's clear statement, with its religioerotic overtones: "Isn't a woman too a precious vessel, sealed like this crystal flagon? Doesn't she contain a vulgar or a divine inebriation, according to her strength and her worth? And aren't there among women the wine of the people and the tears of Christ?" Her reference to the "arms of a prostitute" in which Octave seeks pleasure (Gastinel, p. 158) disappears, as well her sarcastic wish that Rosalinde return to him that night. Octave's impassioned reply, praising the willingness of even the best-bred bottle (as compared with women of the same class), loses the bite of its references to convent education: "But see how she (the bottle, the woman) lets herself go! ["What a nice person she is": 1851]—I don't imagine she's had any education, she's without scruples; see what a sweet girl she is! A word was enough to bring her out of the convent ["cellar": 1851] . . ." The deletion of the adjective "virginal" describing the "crown" of wax sealing the cork continues this weakening process; and Octave's parting shot, implying Marianne's inferiority to the kind-hearted bottle, which in the original version is an emotional peak of the play, is defused by deletion of its sensual metaphors: "She [the bottle] knows she's good to drink, and made to be drunk . . . she [here the bunch of grapes] plies the courtisan's trade; she brushes the hand of the passerby; she displays the curves of her bosom in the sun's rays . . ." (Gastinel, p. 159). The specific nature of her consolation to the passerby, who "lies down" to enjoy her in the original, is dulled by the use of the verb "rests" in 1851. This scene, which in the original rose to a remarkable erotic climax, benefits from all the ambiguity of Marianne's and Octave's mutual emotion: the real nature of their argument emerges from the lengthily developed metaphor of the bottle; Marianne's praise of virtue is transformed by Octave into a paean to generosity. She is caught more and more in the language which she herself has chosen to use (in what is evidently an unconscious prelude to surrender), and the scene ends abruptly in a kind of coitus interruptus, with Octave turning to enter the inn and Marianne well into the curve of rage which, further provoked by her husband's threats, will lead her to invite Octave to a rendezvous.

That invitation (Gastinel, II, 3, p. 165; Allem, II, 11, p. 263) loses its point when Marianne substitutes "a gallant" ("cavalier servant") for the original "lover . . . or at least a gallant," in which the second term is evidently a nervous correction that Marianne subsequently drops. The 1851 text keeps substituting further euphemisms: "Sigisbé," "Patito." In the faded context of the revised version it is no doubt daring for the young woman to decide, recklessly, to take a "patito." But it vitiates the explicit rise of passion and its consequences which the rhythm of the original text builds up. The shock of the play's ending becomes unreasonable and arbitrary, without the erotic tension that prepares it.

The 1851 Revisions: Structure

Examining the changes Musset made in the play's structure, we find a different sort of vitiation. Most of them result from the need to adapt the work from its freely shifting sequence of settings to the classical unitary set used by the Comédie-Française (at least in comedies: the Romantics had managed to get some of their dramas staged in multiple sets, though avoiding transformation scenes). The effect of this classical influence is not only apparent in the reduction of the decor to a single, "abstract" public square, with Claudio's house and the inn as its principal loci; it is also visible in the 1851 text (published in 1853), where the nine scenes of the original are fragmented into thirty-two. Three of these, of slight importance, are additions to the text, principally transitions dictated by the unitary set (I, 7; II, 3 and 19). The rest of the divisions correspond to classical theatrical practice: each change in on-stage characters initiates a new scene.

Beyond the typographical aspects of this modification, there is a deeper effect. Musset originally visualized his action as taking place in a number of locations which form blocks of development. If we examine the structure of the 1833 version, as published in 1840, we can make several observations about the organization of the first act. Even at first glance, we see that the three scenes are not at all equal in length, or similarly constructed. Their form is evidently not dictated by architectural symmetry or external criteria, as we might expect regular scene divisions to be; they reflect an internal necessity. The number of characters in each varies: six in the first scene (all the major figures except Hermia), two in the second (Coelio and Hermia), three in the third (Marianne, Claudio, and Tibia). The length of the three scenes follows the same proportions, the first almost twice as long as the other two together. The number of entrances and exits shows a similar pattern. This may be said as well about not only the amount of exposition or action in each scene, but also its density and rhythm: most of the play's themes are announced in the first scene, with the exception of the most important one— Marianne's "capriciousness," which will be the active principle of the second act. Scene 2, on the other hand, provides us with nothing more than a glimpse at Coelio's family background (with some tantalizing quasi-Freudian hints at the sources of his character); scene 3 develops only the growth of Claudio's suspicions, and Marianne's willful character.

Taken in relation to each other and in respect to their internal organization, these scenes reveal considerable structural ingenuity. Scene 1 opens and closes on Marianne under "attack," first from Ciuta, then from Octave. The supposed beneficiary of their efforts, Coelio, wanders in and out without ever crossing Marianne's path (as he will continue to do until the final misapprehension), expressing alternate desire and despair. The dialogue of Coelio and Octave falls approximately in the middle of the scene. It emphasizes their difference of character, but its use of repetition and symmetry also underlines their spiritual kinship, as mirror images of the same soul in reaction to the world. The sense of symmetry is disturbed, however, by the distribution of time allotted Coelio and Octave: the former dominates the first half, then leaves; the latter appears at midscene; at the end he gives a first hint of being snared by Marianne in his apparent non sequitur: "I'll be damned! she does have beautiful eyes." A seemingly random discordant note is injected by the pseudorational dialogue of Claudio and Tibia. The scene is thus characterized by an initial static symmetry which gives way to a directional vector of action, and is interrupted by a grotesquely heterogeneous element. It gives the impression of a structural unit, a whole in itself, thanks to its interplay of static and kinetic elements.

The second scene is, significantly, an interior contained between two exteriors. Its otherness is emphasized by Hermia's isolation from the main action of the play: her role has nothing to do with this action but exists as it were on the plane of the heart and mind. Her story provides a cyclical myth for Coelio's destiny, as her relationship with him provides psychological depth to his character and behavior. The scene's difference is further underlined by the abrupt ending: there is no exit, no further action indicated after the last sentence of Hermia's tale: "The poor young man was found in his bedroom, pierced through and through by several sword-thrusts."[13] It stands thus as a parenthesis, but an intensely meaningful one, in the pattern of the play's action. The scene also gives a special stature to the character of Coelio: although Octave, in I, 1, and Marianne, in II, 1, directly reveal a certain depth of sentiment, neither benefits from the kind of psychological exploration which Musset gives to

13. Musset's 1851 correction of this latter detail is perhaps one of his few really felicitous modifications.

Coelio. This can be seen in his two important monologues (Gastinel, I, 1, p. 126; II, 2, p. 161), where he evokes his alienation from the world in space and time, as well as in his lengthy dialogue with Octave, in which he tells his friend of his woes. But it emerges in a way common to none of the other major characters in the scene with Hermia. To say that he is the only one who has a mother may seem absurd, but there is an important element in the statement whose significance we cannot ignore. Coelio's mother "explains" him mythically and psychologically, in a manner which distinguishes him from Octave and Marianne. Marianne, too, has a mother; but she exists only by allusion—and primarily as a mother-in-law to Claudio, thus another species entirely! (It is interesting to note that she performs the same function for Claudio, in a stock comic way, that André del Sarto's mother-in-law does in a more serious context: that of the husband's confidant and receiver of complaints.) For one thing, Hermia gives Coelio a past. (This aspect of his characterization is fleetingly echoed by Marianne who, in her sole monologue, after her dispute with Claudio [Gastinel, II, 3, p. 164], reveals her awareness of a pattern of destiny being fulfilled: see below, page 54.) Hermia is also connected with that peculiarly subjective relationship which Musset enjoyed with his most successful characters and plays, forming an affective link between Coelio and his author. Musset's attachment to his mother manifests itself in many forms: his quasi-incestuous relationship with George Sand, his lifelong bachelorhood, the governess who was later to replace his mother; the relationship of Lorenzaccio to his mother and his aunt, the figure of Brigitte Pierson in the *Confession d'un enfant du siècle*, and of Jacqueline in *le Chandelier*, the ambiguity of the Muse in the *Nuits*, etc. But the most significant aspect of Coelio's scene with Hermia is structural: it is a parenthesis, and Coelio alone in the play benefits from this moment of stasis. His character exists almost solely outside of time and space, outside of the action, until the moment of his only decisive act: his impetuous rush to meet death. We are aware from the beginning of Coelio's penchant toward death, his fascination with the idea of suicide, which is the other face of his futile passion for Marianne. But this would be mere talk and would not commit the character to his destiny without the symbolic reinforcement given to Coelio by Musset's use of the metaphorical monologue and the dramatic parenthesis.

The third scene of Act I is a reversal of the effect achieved in the preceding one. Not only are we outdoors again, but we are in the presence of the play's least internalized characters, Claudio and Tibia. Their discussion, although superficially connected with love and the play's protagonists, is the very contradiction of psychological exposition. It is pure verbal action, shorn of deeper causality than the play of word associations and definitely not Freudian. Maurice Donnay showed striking prescience when, years before Ionesco's *Bald Soprano* put the language manual in dramatic vogue, he said of Claudio and Tibia's dialogues: "Wouldn't you think they were drawn from a French-Neapolitan conversation manual, in the time of the Renaissance, if such a thing had existed? . . . 'Do you have the foreigner's umbrella? The grocer is at the consulate. The parrot has broken the photographer's clock.' Was Musset perhaps thinking of that?"[14] But their role in the play is not limited to comic relief, as the later argument between Claudio and Marianne and the climactic sequence of events prove. The jarring juxtaposition of Claudio and Tibia's conversation with the Coelio-Hermia scene is a rhythmic device. Its significance and effect are emphasized by additional structural or symbolic procedures: the abrupt ending of the preceding conversation, the dramatic shift from interior to exterior, and the foreshadowing of the play's climax by setting the scene in Claudio's garden, where Coelio will meet his violent death. It is therefore far from accidental that the conversation finds its haphazard way through the topic of the death sentence and manages to touch lightly on the killer whom Claudio has been toying with hiring. This scene may seem a virtuoso series of non sequiturs, but it is far from unrelated to either the action or the sentimental life of the protagonists. By having Marianne pass briefly through the middle of this scene, in a moment of anger which prevents her seeing what is on Claudio's mind (if the term can be used), Musset brilliantly orchestrates the fugal vector of alien

14. "Les Comédies de Musset," *Revue française* (June 22, 1924), 683.

forces rushing toward collision. The fact that the most sinister of these voices is also the most comic, calmly babbling about matters of deadly seriousness, merely adds to our sense of the main characters' isolation, their inability to understand or to make themselves understood. Musset manipulates this feeling by his careful organization of contrasts, interruptions, and rhythmic sequences.

Act I thus becomes, when examined in this light, not an improvised series of disparate scenes, as it seemed in the judgments of contemporaries accustomed to an entirely different concept of dramatic construction (the linear movement of classical theater or the formulistic logic of the contemporary "pièce bien faite"), but a highly structured unity based on poetic, symbolic, and psychological associative principles. On the other hand, if we return to the uninterrupted string of scenes on an abstract stage locus in the revised version, we feel the justification of Jean Richer's observation concerning the two phases he had found in Musset's 1851 reworking: "Comparison of the two stage versions of *Caprices de Marianne* makes evident what may be called the principle of *temporal unity* of each act. Each set of tableaux forming the act is considered as a whole, within which the order of scenes, almost up to the dénouement, is unimportant."[15] If we define "scenes" as assemblies of characters, and the sequence as a series of encounters between various groups, then certainly the linear progression of the revised version can be considered of minor importance (especially in the exposition-heavy first act). Musset's repositioning of several scenes is evidence of this. The scene between Coelio and Hermia, for example, is moved to the end of the act, preceded by Claudio and Tibia's macabre conversation and Marianne's refusal to give Claudio her answer to Octave's advances. Since Coelio's threat to kill himself has been cut from the first scene (Gastinel, I, 1, p. 132; Allem, I, 4, p. 236), not only is the structural reinforcement of the scene lost, but its poignant relevancy to Coelio's state of mind is blunted. Our suspicion that this is a deliberate attenuation is confirmed by the words of consolation appended to Hermia's story, to soften the brutality of its conclusion: "Don't think of my misfortunes, they

15. *Textes dramatiques inédits*, p. xi.

are just memories. Yours touch me much more deeply. If you refuse to fight them, they have a long life ahead in your young heart. I won't ask you to confide in me, but I see them; and since you are moved by mine, come, let us try to help each other. A few old friends have come to the house, let's have a bit of distraction. Let's try to live, my child, and to look cheerfully together, I at the past, you at the future. —Come, Coelio, give me your hand" (Allem, II, 12, p. 248).

In the original version, even the sequence of subscenes within each major scene is marked by the search for balance and organic development. Musset thus reveals, in his period of youthful genius, an essentially Romantic, pre-Symbolist conception of artistic form as an integrated function of content, inseparable from it, and not as an abstract, generic, or traditional—"allotrious"—entity. Yet none of the other French Romantics went so far beyond mere doctrine or theory as did Musset. Hugo's definition of form in the 1826 edition of his *Odes et Ballades*, as a "New World forest" contrasted with a classical Le Nôtre garden, did not lead him to experiment much beyond the formal innovations of "Les Djinns." From a modern perspective, the enjambements, ternary alexandrines, and between-the-acts scene-shifts of his five-act verse drama do not seem to carry us a significant distance from classical French stage practice.

The second act of *Les Caprices de Marianne*, richer in action than the first, with more frequent scene-changes, provides further evidence of the deformation Musset wrought in 1851. Despite the immediately apparent differences between it and the first act (reminiscent of those between the two acts of *Fantasio*, we may note here), there are certain striking similarities of construction. The scenes themselves are irregular in length, distribution of character, and density. The first scene is once again the longest by far and the most complex in terms of action, entrances and exits, etc. It, too, is followed by a short scene involving Coelio, who reveals his torment and hopelessness. The following scene, like the third scene of act I, features a dispute between Marianne and Claudio. But from that point on, the action takes its inexorable direction toward the tragic climax, and the construction loses its parallelism. Even within the first group of scenes, certain significant variations are worthy of note: it is Octave, and not Coelio, whom we discover with Ciuta at the opening of the act: Octave underlines this substitution in a speech comparing himself to a gambler playing with his friend's stakes, and ruining him. It is Octave who takes the initiative in the struggle for Marianne, which Coelio is ready to abandon. The scene is once again marked by a meeting between Octave and Marianne, but the rhythm of their encounters is accelerated, and the second time it is Marianne who seems to be seeking out Octave, not the contrary. The short second scene involves Coelio with Ciuta (and not Hermia, who has disappeared from the action). Once again it centers about a foreboding of betrayal—but this time it is the woman who presses the point, and Coelio who ignores it. The third-scene interview between Marianne and Claudio is a head-on encounter, without the reticences and mysteries of the earlier one: Claudio has progressed from confusion and indecision to direct menace, and Marianne from virtuous indignation to pointed defiance. Musset to this point has made excellent use of the expressive possibilities of variation from a repeated pattern.

From here on, the play takes a new direction. It is Marianne who calls the cards, her resentment against Claudio giving pretext to the stifled passion that underlies her prudishness (this transfer of dominance connected with a loss of virtue is one of several interesting points of resemblance to Machiavelli's *Mandragola*). The rest of scene 3, following Claudio's exit (with Marianne remaining on stage this time), is a series of impulsive moves on her part, involving a considerable amount of message-sending, change of mind, and retraction—culminating in her final misdirected message to Coelio. Marianne sends for Octave, orders him to find her a lover, gives him a token to send with his candidate (an evident fiction); Octave goes to get Coelio, sends him off with the scarf, orders dinner to be brought for himself in Coelio's house (an ironic substitution); a servant brings the warning letter from Marianne; Marianne calls out to Coelio, thinking he is Octave, and tells him to meet her the next day. It is striking how much of this action takes the form of communication (and noncommunication) at a distance, through third parties, by tokens or symbols, through windows in the dark.

When we add the final mysterious disappearance of Coelio's body, it is evident that Musset constructed the dramatic action of the play's climactic scenes on the basis of a traditional device employed in an original way, in much the same manner as his use of symmetry and parallelism earlier in the play.

This latter part of the play takes place in three separate settings: Claudio's house,[16] Coelio's house, and Claudio's garden. The introduction of hiatuses in the action, and changes of locus, contributes powerfully to the confused, nervous activity which the criss-crossing of messages creates. Octave and Marianne, after two encounters by the inn (with their first transfer of initiative), meet in Claudio's house—this time at Marianne's open instigation. Coelio finally leaves the haven of his home, and the neutral ground of the various streets on which we have met him, to "scale the walls" from which he has hitherto retreated. Octave settles comfortably into Coelio's digs just as the news of his unwitting betrayal is about to descend on him. Ciuta warns Coelio of her mistaken (but finally justified) suspicions concerning Octave and Marianne on an unidentified street, in a scene which further disorients us by its brevity. After all this feverish and misdirected activity, the final scene of the play transfers us outside the previous frame of physical and temporal reference to one where Octave's and Coelio's relationship with each other and with Marianne can take on its true perspective *sub specie aeternitatis*.

None of the foregoing holds true for the revised version of the act. The apparent fragmentation of its structure, created by the division of six scenes into twenty, is a typographical illusion: in fact the scenes follow on one another in linear fashion, all the characters in succession coming through the neutral ground of the public square (against all logic, as Mme. Dussanne demonstrates in her comments on the play).[17] Leaving aside the evident difficulty for Marianne of overturning her chairs in the street, there is no progression in the series of interviews leading to her

16. Marianne refers to it, though, as "this garden" in the original version (Gastinel, p. 164); Musset corrected it to "here" in 1851 (Allem, p. 263).

17. See "Les Héroïnes de Musset. II. La Capricieuse: Marianne." *Revue hebdomadaire* (March 26, 1932), pp. 421–40.

change of heart; Coelio and Octave's relationship remains on the same plane, without the transfer of roles at the former's home. The rhythm of the entire play, but particularly the latter part, is far too regular, too standardized. It loses its breathlessness, its sense of teetering on the brink of a precipice.

When we examine the changes Musset effected within the context of this new scenic distribution, the impression of regularization—and consequent weakening—is confirmed. One of the most striking of the changes is an important addition to the text at the beginning of the second act (in II, 1 of the original; II, 2 of the 1851 version). The inserted passage, which has interested Musset scholars because of the light it sheds on his literary kinships, seems strangely out of place in the context. It is an extended quotation from Leopardi, whom Musset had discovered since first writing the play.[18] Finding in *Amore e morte* a sentiment which seemed to justify Coelio's thoughts of suicide, Musset simply has him *read* the apposite quotation (translated into French) at length. (Conscious of the awkwardness, he has Octave break into the reading with two sarcastic remarks.) Thus Coelio, instead of appearing mysteriously, changing his mind without conviction, then disappearing again, takes the trouble to "explain" himself by literary allusion. Adding to this clarification, evidently to make sure that all the i's are dotted, Musset then proceeds to transfer a monologue from scene 2 of the original text (Gastinel, p. 161; Allem, p. 251), which Coelio delivers immediately after his refusal to heed Ciuta's warning: he speaks of his nostalgia for the days of chivalry, when he would have worn Marianne's colors (as he is ironically to do just before his death). Coelio thus in the 1851 text organizes a rationale for his behavior, a philosophy of love and death, so that Octave can understand him fully before his graveside eulogy (which oddly enough will be given in the street, immediately after Coelio's death). The awkwardness of the Leopardi quotation, followed immediately by the misplaced reflection on time, makes this scene one of the play's worst victims of adaptation to the stage.

The fact that Musset made another transposition directly after this one gives evidence that he was seeking a more regular distri-

18. Cf. Allem edition, pp. 1334–35.

bution of encounters and action throughout the play. Thus he has Octave utter his promise to find a kinder-hearted Marianne for Coelio right after the Leopardi-chivalry sequence. This creates a single, longer, more logically constructed contact between the characters: Coelio takes on a greater degree of physical and psychological "solidity," avoids his brief return to the scene (with Ciuta) in II, 2, and will come back only in time for Octave to hand him Marianne's scarf. Such a distribution spared Delaunay the ridicule of wandering aimlessly in and out, changing his mind (or having the play's shifting sets come to find him). It must have satisfied the traditionalists among the *sociétaires* of the Comédie-Française; and it served the additional function of eliminating one of Ciuta-Pippo's embarrassing appearances. But its opposition to the spirit of the play's original structure is clear, and it obviously represents a practical measure in the name of facility and regularity, not an improvement.

From that point on, aside from the disappearance of Ciuta's warning to Coelio, the excisions which have been discussed earlier, and the reduction of the action to a single setting, the basic structure of the act remains largely unchanged until the final scenes. It is from the moment when Octave gives Marianne's scarf to Coelio and sends him off to his rendezvous that the author began to operate in earnest: II, 4 of the original, II, 14 of the 1851 text (Gastinel, p. 170; Allem, p. 268). The warning note which Marianne sends to Octave can no longer be justified when all the action takes place on the street: it is replaced by a scene in which Marianne overhears Claudio's and Tibia's machinations (also on the street). She thus warns her supposed lover only at the moment when Coelio, who has meanwhile left the stage for some unexplained reason, reappears for his rendezvous. Coelio, imagining himself betrayed, plunges into the garden as in the original. Octave, unwarned, ambles out of the inn, having evidently finished his dinner; he reflects at this point on his generosity, and on the fickleness of fate and women (as in II, 4 of the original). Hearing suspicious noises from Claudio's garden and Coelio's muffled cry for help, he tries to break in, but is delayed by Claudio until Coelio's body can be hidden. Marianne ventures out onto the street from the house, voicing her fear that Octave has been ambushed. But he reappears from the garden, brandishing his sword and still looking around for his friend's body. He explains to Marianne that Coelio is dead, and that he wishes, oddly enough, to remain there in the street in vigil for his friend. In answer to Marianne's questions about Coelio and her pointed suggestions, Octave eulogizes his friend's constancy and devotion, accuses himself of being a coward and a heartless rake, bids farewell to youth and happiness, and rejects Marianne's offer of love (as in the original text). A feeling of randomness, of arbitrary encounters and events, dominates the revised version's final scenes: it is due no doubt to the need for having all the characters and all the action converge on the neutral ground of the street. They lose the justification which the specific sets lent in the original. Instead of chaotic, misdirected *intentions* being crossed by a psychological and material opposition of forces, the play ends on this note of dramatic arbitrariness, typified by Marianne's overhearing of Claudio, the absence of the letter, Octave's exit from the inn, the prompt eulogy in the street. Musset must have regretted the loss of his cemetery and the perspective it lent: he has Octave refer to a monument which he will erect to Coelio's memory, an alabaster urn covered by a shroud just like the one found on stage in the closing scene of the original (Gastinel, II, 6, p. 174; Allem, II, 20, p. 273).

The Solitude of Lovers

It is perhaps unorthodox, in a study of this sort, to begin with the comparative analysis of two versions of a work, before attempting to come to grips with its essential qualities. But in the present case we are dealing with an exceptional phenomenon: a play considerably modified by a diminished author, under anti-creative conditions, years after its conception. This particular set of circumstances does not apply to *Fantasio* and *Lorenzaccio*, which underwent modification by alien hands before their production—the former in the well-intentioned and ill-advised performance version of the poet's brother, Paul, the latter in the deformed version executed (the term is apt) by Armand d'Artois for Sarah Bernhardt. A comparable case might be adduced for Paul Claudel's *L'Annonce faite à Marie*, whose successive transformations shed light on the evolution of its author's talent and theatrical craft. There is a significant difference, however: the several versions of *L'Annonce* testify to Claudel's development but can be regarded as progressive, self-sufficient manifestations of his genius.

Les Caprices de Marianne seems rather a case study in the psychopathology of literary creation. We must, of course, use these terms with some chariness. From one point of view, it is easy to see the 1851 revisions as a cancerous growth invading the work's system, effacing its youthful beauty and sapping its vitality. If, on the other hand, we consider the play's spiritual "message," a case might be made that Musset's drunken Octave, delicate Coelio, and troubled Marianne, in their struggle with society, fate, and one another represent a sickly flowering, like many of their Romantic contemporaries, and that Musset's later revisions were a surgical operation intended to restore the balance of health, to correct some of the spiritual deformities the work was born with.

One is inevitably reminded, however, of the anecdote which ends: "Unfortunately, the patient died." Whatever the work's spiritual weaknesses, however symptomatic it may be of its author's nascent psychological and physical problems, the 1833 text of *Les Caprices de Marianne* is, unlike the revised version, a sound piece of dramaturgy, deserving the long life it has earned in the French theater, and indeed further and wider life on the stages of other countries. Its special qualities, typical of Musset's best works, are its profound integration of form and meaning, its sparkling repartee, a strikingly original mixture of wit and poetry, and the author's penetrating analysis of the conflicting forces in himself and in those who, like himself, experience the pleasures and torments of youth.

The personal side of the work has received the most attention since the time of its creation. It is literary commonplace, in French criticism, to refer to the subjective nature of Musset's great heroes, their reflection of his public and private life. No author's sentimental history has provided so much material for other writers: the roster includes the poet's brother Paul's *Lui et elle*; his mistress, George Sand's *Elle et lui*; poetess—and available Muse—Louise Colet's *Lui*(!); and Charles Maurras' *Les Amants de Venise*. Musset's own *Confession d'un enfant du siècle* is a transparent exploitation of the events surrounding his affair with George Sand, roughly contemporary with the creation of his first theatrical works. Critics have never tired of citing the author's letters to Sand, both before and after the "drame de Venise," which claim that Coelio and Octave are the two faces of Musset himself.[19] Paul de Musset points out the reflections of his brother's personal life among the characters and events of *Les Caprices de Marianne*: Coelio and Octave as the two poles of his personality, Hermia as the portrait of their mother, Marianne as the quintessence of all the capricious women he had known.[20]

Even the most "objective" authors, of course, nourish their literary creation on personal material: witness the celebrated phrase of Flaubert, "Madame Bovary is myself." Musset never undertook the systematic depersonalization that characterizes Flaubert's work to an almost pathological degree: they were at opposite poles of that particular creative spectrum. Flaubert's correspondence with Louise Colet demonstrates how much he despised Musset's style of writing and living. In his opinion (prejudiced, for complex reasons not excluding the brief affair between Musset and Mme. Colet) Musset was the model of the despised Romantic artist who confused life and art, personal and creative emotion. Musset, for the intensely autocritical Flaubert, was typed as the facile poet, offering his flawed works to public view without shame or literary scruple. This attitude was shared, it must be said, by Baudelaire, the Parnassians, Rimbaud—several generations of poets who paradoxically admired Musset's great admirer, Gautier. Among the important artists of this generation, only Verlaine, whose personality and career resemble Musset's in so many curious ways, returned sympathetically to the themes and poetics of his predecessor.

19. See *Correspondance* (1827–1857), collected and annotated by Léon Séché (Paris, 1907), July 1833 and May 10, 1834.
20. *Alfred de Musset, sa vie, son oeuvre* (Paris, 1877), pp. 116–17.

But even Musset's admirers misunderstood the nature of his work in thinking of it as biographical transposition. The secret of its success lies not in the depth of emotional experience from which it is supposed to stem, but in the instinctive richness and complexity of the seemingly off-hand artistic process engaged in by Musset. It is easy to talk of Octave and Coelio as the two facets of the author's personality, for example: examination of *Les Caprices de Marianne* shows how artfully Musset creates two separate personalities out of this raw material. I will not undertake here to discuss the prevalent theme of the *double*, which emerged strikingly in the attempts of German and French Romantic literature to plumb the depths of the irrational in man; this particular obsession, so remarkable in the works of Gérard de Nerval, is also given notable literary treatment in Musset's *Nuit de décembre*, and recurs throughout the works of his artistic maturity. Although there can be no doubt that Octave and Coelio reflect to some degree this product of both *Zeitgeist* and personal experience, they stand more fully as transformations of a common theme into artistic reality, as original realizations of a literary commonplace in the realm of the universal and enduring.

What makes Octave and Coelio interesting is the psychological and spiritual dialectic embodied by their characters in the action of the play and in their conjunction with Marianne. We are struck first by the interweaving of resemblances and differences between the two male protagonists. They are youthful and handsome, they are idle members of the "Neapolitan" bourgeoisie. They are friends: Octave offers his services to Coelio as readily as if he were performing them for himself—more readily, perhaps, since Coelio's yearnings, if Octave ever knew them, are now dead in himself, the object only of an ironic nostalgia. It does not matter that Octave tempers his offer with humorous self-depreciation: "Do you want money? I haven't any more. Do you want advice? I'm drunk. Do you want my sword? Here's a slap-stick. Speak, speak, I'm entirely at your disposition." (Gastinel, p. 128). That is mainly a question of style and personality. Through the play, the sense of identification will be reinforced: witness the speech in which Octave compares himself to a gambler, and the exchange of places in the penultimate scenes of the original version. Octave never questions the validity of his friend's desires, or utters scruples. He identifies himself with Coelio's interests to the point of a confusion upon which Marianne knowingly comments (Gastinel, II, 3, p. 167).

Musset underlines this identity from the first scenes between his two heroes. As in the later *On ne badine pas avec l'amour* (and earlier, in *A Quoi rêvent les jeunes filles*), he makes extensive use of repetition and variation in the opening scenes to create the feeling of kinship. The device, by its evident artifice, is effective in creating the mood of gentle irony which distinguishes Musset's sentimental comedies. It is a form of aesthetic distancing, which confirms our judgment of Musset's art. In the first encounter of Octave and Coelio, their speeches are syntactical echoes of each other:

> *Coelio:* Octave, you fool! your cheeks are plastered with rouge! —Where did you get that outfit! Aren't you ashamed, in broad daylight?
>
> *Octave:* Coelio, you fool! Your cheeks are plastered with white —Where did you get that great black coat? Aren't you ashamed, in the midst of Carnival?
>
> *Coelio:* What a life you lead! Either you're drunk, or I am.
>
> *Octave:* Either you're in love, or I am.
>
> *Coelio:* More than ever, with the beautiful Marianne.
>
> *Octave:* More than ever, with Cyprus wine.
>
> *Coelio:* I was on my way to your house when I met you.
>
> *Octave:* I was on my way to my house, too. How is it doing? I haven't seen it for a week.
>
> (I, 1)

This may certainly pass as affectionate banter among friends: its stylized artifice is endowed by the context with a validating realism. But it puts such realism on a highly crafted plane. This is idealized banter, refined and polished by the author. Similarly, the language in which the two characters reveal themselves is a lyrical, stylized prose. Here, too, we see Musset's concern for symmetry: Octave and Coelio both introduce themselves by means of extended metaphors representing their spiritual state. To avoid monotony, the author varies the circumstances under which they are uttered: Coelio's as a monologue preceding Octave's entrance, Octave's as a reply to Coelio's criticism of his life-style. But the proximity of the two speeches and the resemblance of their basic images (means of locomotion representing a way of passing through life, emphasis on the subject's isolation), make us feel the speeches as parallel and complementary.

Coelio: Woe to him who, in the midst of youth, yields himself to a hopeless love! Woe to him who surrenders to sweet reverie, not knowing where his illusion will lead him, or whether he may be requited! Comfortably lying in his bark, he drifts gradually away from the shore; he sees in the distance enchanted plains, green pastures and the dim mirage of his Eldorado. The winds carry him off in silence, and, when reality reawakens him, he is as far from the goal he longs for as he is from the shore he has left; he can neither pursue his journey nor retrace his steps.

(I, 1, p. 126)

Octave: Imagine a tight-rope dancer, in silver slippers, his balance-pole clutched in his fist, suspended between heaven and earth; to the left and to the right, little old wizened figures, pale, emaciated phantoms, nimble creditors, parents, and courtiers, a whole legion of monsters, hanging on to his coat-tails and tugging on all sides to make him lose his balance: sententious phrases, gilded proverbs gallop round him; a cloud of sinister predictions blinds him with its black wings. He holds to his airy course, from east to west. If he looks down, his head spins; if he looks up, he loses his footing. He goes more swiftly than the wind, and all the hands grasping at him won't make him spill a drop of the joyous cup he bears in his own. There's my life, my dear friend: there is my faithful image for you to see.

(I, 1, p. 128).

Within the parallelism of intention and meaning, the form of the two images is also congruous: the lone figure, its movement, the external forces acting upon it, the sense of dizziness and precariousness, the goal struggled for in vain. Syntactically, the series of periods developing the two basic images are quite similar; so is their essentially Romantic use of epithets for subjective coloration ("sweet rêverie," "enchanted plains," "green pastures," "pale mirage"; "little old wizened figures," "pale and emaciated phantoms," "nimble creditors," "sinister predictions," "airy course," "joyous cup"). These aesthetic devices coupled with the characterization of the two friends leave no doubt in our mind that Coelio and Octave are intimately related, by more than mere friendship: they are manifestations of the same spirit.

But Octave and Coelio are also two distinct personalities; otherwise they would share in the mechanical nature which characterizes Musset's grotesque figures, as we shall see. The symmetries which serve to inform us of their kinship paradoxically make us conscious at the same time of their differences: they create a relationship upon which to base contrasts. The echo-phrases of Octave's and Coelio's first encounter are built on contradiction: red–white, Carnival regalia–black coat, drunk–in love, Marianne–wine. (The banter, it is true, ends on a note of resolution: both Coelio and Octave were heading for the latter's house as, curiously, they will end up in Coelio's, just before the denouement).

Similarly, when we analyze the two extended metaphors, we are struck by the contrasts reinforced by their parallelism. Coelio is borne "comfortably" on a watery medium symbolic of life as a passive state; the drifting boat denotes absence of will, at least in any effective sense, and the external figures (shore, plains, mirage) are frustrating by their distance or absence. The spiritual movement characteristic of the image might be termed centrifugal, moving away from the focus of will and desire, toward oblivion.

Octave's image, on the other hand, is centripetal: his ropedancer is struggling, by a powerful tension of his will, to avoid being torn from the path which he is doggedly following. Instead of sinking into a watery medium, he clings to a precarious, airy perch; his image of life is not the drifting flow of the boat but the inexorable line of the sun's path from east to west, from birth to death. He is not gazing at distant, fleeting goals but focusing on the "wine of life" in his cup. The winds do not carry him with them; rather he struggles to escape from the dark clouds that envelop him, and he outstrips the winds in his hedonistic flight. We may assume that he will thus only arrive more quickly where they were pushing him.

Similarly, when Octave seems to agree with his friend, in a subsequent passage of the same scene, we are once again made conscious of their divergences. Coelio tries to express to Octave the fear and trembling that overwhelm him when he sees Marianne: a nightmarish sentiment that prevents his speaking or acting effectively. Octave replies that he has had the same feeling when hunting in the depths of the forest, upon first catching sight of the doe he is about to shoot. Octave's emotion is that of a sensual predator, momentarily caught in the ambiguous ecstasy of the kill; Coelio's that of the prey, the victim he cannot help becoming in the struggle of the other characters' wills.

In essence, the play is a translation into terms of an action of the basic dialectic presented here: thesis (kinship, love), antithesis (difference, misunderstanding), synthesis (betrayal, solitude, death). It may be illustrated by a considerable number of thematic variants, which focus about the theme of isolation and noncommunication. Coelio loves Marianne to the point of despair but is incapable of saying or doing anything useful in his own behalf; Octave admires Marianne's beauty and sympathizes with his friend enough to speak the language of love persuasively, but he is incapable of loving Marianne. Marianne, the "prude," remains impervious to the mute, faithful love of Coelio but would yield to the eloquence of an empty-hearted rake speaking on another's behalf. Coelio is most suspicious of Octave when the latter is most disinterestedly ready to serve his cause, and suspects him least (despite Ciuta's only half-mistaken warning) when Octave's activities for him are most equivocal. Claudio's suspicion of his wife's infidelity, which leads to his ambush of Coelio (whom Marianne doesn't love), is awakened when she angrily complains of Octave's assiduities and asks him to take steps to protect her; Marianne is stung to retaliation by her husband's explicit prohibition. Coelio goes off to his rendezvous with death armed with an invitation and a token intended for Octave, who has yielded his place to his friend; Marianne's last warning, intended to save Octave, impels Coelio to plunge into the ambush. The basic pattern in these and numerous other examples which might be cited is: will to communicate—barrier to communication—misunderstanding and betrayal.

Coelio states the theme of isolation in one of those eloquent images he is capable of only when Marianne is not present: "Every man walks enveloped in a transparent web that covers him from head to feet: he imagines he sees woods and rivers, divine visages; and before his eyes all Nature is tinged with the infinite shadings of his magical fabric" (I, 1, p. 131). This lovely metaphor of the imagination ends in a cry for help to Octave; coming soon after Octave's remarks concerning the hunter and the doe, it ironically reinforces the feeling of noncommunication and miscommunication between the two friends, who evidently see life and each other through very different webs. Coelio, giving his life into Octave's hands, poignantly utters an appeal that his friend not betray him: he is like a blind man, afraid of stepping into an abyss, suspicious of the stranger who has offered to guide him. This image of the web, imprisoning men in their own subjectivity and forming a barrier to objective understanding of others and of the world, is developed further in *Fantasio*, as we shall see. In the context of *Marianne*, it constitutes an ambivalent symbol: on the one hand, this is Coelio's crowning quality as a sensitive man, the gift of imaginative vision which makes him a poet and a lover. The excised speech about the physical qualities of women, to which reference has already been made, expresses that clearly in the 1833 version: "In truth, I couldn't love that woman as you would, Octave, or as I would another. And yet what does it all amount to? Two blue eyes, two ruby lips, a white dress, and two white hands . . . Reality is just a shadow. Call what makes it divine imagination or folly . . ." (I, 1, p. 131). Yet Coelio's inability to deal with Marianne as a "real" person dooms his love from the start to futility, and Coelio to despair. His gift of vision hinders him from acting on his own behalf: this "poet" needs a "spokesman," and betrayal has already begun.

Similar failures of communication, stemming from the characters' isolation within their individualities, mark each turn of the action leading to Coelio's death and Octave's abandonment of Marianne. Despite his good will, Octave is unable to speak for his friend: in part because of what he is, in part because of what Marianne is. He only really understands his friend at the end, by his gravestone, and that understanding reveals to him his own emptiness, his irreparable loss. Octave cannot love the living Marianne, because he has failed the dead Coelio, and thus himself. But the die was cast from the beginning: Octave was only able to speak to Marianne because his soul was already dead, drowned in wine: "My drunkenness and I, dear Coelio, are too fond of each other for us ever to squabble; she does my will as I do hers. Have no fear; only a school boy on holiday gets drunk at the festive table, loses his head and struggles with his wine; it's my very nature to be drunk; my way of thinking is to let myself go, and I would talk to the king at this moment, as I'm going to talk to your lady fair" (I, 1, p. 133).

Marianne, as we have seen, is unable to understand Coelio, who succeeds in receiving from her lips only words intended for another, in the final minutes of the play. But she also twists Octave's meaning, or his intentions, to suit her own particular vision. Paradoxically, although Marianne is the most active force in the complications of the plot, she is the least free of all the major characters. Once Coelio has surrendered the initiative to Octave, he is at liberty to wander about alone, to change his mind (without effect or consequence), to avoid the field of action until he chooses his destruction. Octave is acting as an independent agent, disinterestedly (at least in principle): unlike Coelio, who has already lost everything from the start, he has nothing at all to lose. But Marianne, as a woman, is a veritable prisoner—of her marriage to a clod, and thus of one of her society's most rigid institutions; of her convent education, which has betrayed her into the hands of a husband without the knowledge or the means to fulfill her emotional needs; of the need to act in retaliation to her jailer, whom she despises and who nonetheless determines her acts even by reaction. The conflict of desires and scruples within her prevents her from accepting the man who really loves her (if there is real love in the play), and thrusts her into the arms of Octave. She herself feels the plaything of forces outside her, as she reflects at the moment of taking her final plunge, inviting Octave into the house: "Ah! so this is the beginning? I was warned of this.—I knew it. —I expected it." A sense of destiny weighs on her, as it does on Coelio and Octave, and it is an absurd destiny: "Divine justice," says Octave, "holds a scale in its hands. The scale is perfectly just, but all the weights are hollow . . . All human acts swing up and down, according to these capricious weights" (II, 4, p. 170). More than "divine justice," which is felt by its absence from the works of Musset rather than any active role in his characters' fate, it is the protagonists themselves, in their isolation from each other and their yearning for each other, who precipitate the inexorable sequence of mistakes. The rest can only be ascribed to chance, a goddess who takes no interest whatever in the events she brings about, favorable or not.

The absurd dialogues of Claudio and Tibia, far from being mere comic interludes or even criticism of the institutional spirit which the judge represents, can thus be seen as an essential part of this theme of noncommunication. It is not by accident or an arbitrary turning of the tables that the two puppet figures are the instrument of Coelio's fate (as of Octave's and Marianne's). Claudio and Tibia are caricatures, it is true. They are parodies of certain human emotions and ideas such as fidelity, jealousy, revenge, justice, righteous indignation, suspicion. Claudio's cliché-ridden language exaggerates to the point of deformity the emotional and physical realities it is meant to convey. "It's raining guitars and go-betweens" (I, 1), "My wife is a treasure of purity" (I, 2), "One of my relatives is one of your lovers" (II, 3), "Either you'll understand the unsuitability of stopping under a bower, or you'll force me to a violence repugnant to my cloth" (ibid.). The words lose their connection with reality, and Claudio's expression takes on an abstractness that is the opposite of life. So does his thought, if so it may be termed: Claudio's conversations with Tibia have but a dim resemblance to logic or common sense. In an exchange such as the following only the barest skeleton of logical causality is present, an association of purely linguistic elements in juxtaposition which nevertheless keeps leading us back to adultery and death.

Claudio: You're right, my wife is a treasure of purity. What more can I say? She's a solid virtue.

Tibia: You think so, sir?

Claudio: Can she help it if people sing under her window? The signs of impatience she evidences inside are the result of her character. Did you notice that her mother, when I struck that chord, was right away in agreement with me?

Tibia: Concerning what?

Claudio: Concerning their singing under her window.

Tibia: There's nothing wrong with singing, I'm always humming myself.

Claudio: But it's difficult to sing well.

Tibia: Difficult for you and me who, not having been given a voice by nature, have never developed it. But look how those theater actors manage.

Claudio: Those people spend their life on the stage.

Tibia: How much do you think they get a year?

Claudio: Who? Justices of the peace?

Tibia: No, singers.

Claudio: I haven't the slightest idea. —A justice of the peace gets a third of my stipend. Counsellors get half.

Tibia: If I were a judge in the royal court, and my wife had lovers, I'd sentence them myself.

Claudio: To how many years hard labor?

Tibia: To death. A death sentence is a marvelous thing to read aloud.

Claudio: It's not the judge who reads it, it's the clerk.

Tibia: The clerk of your court has a pretty wife.

Claudio: No, it's the chief justice who has a pretty wife. I had supper with them yesterday.

Tibia: The clerk does too! The killer who's coming tonight is the lover of the clerk's wife.

Claudio: What killer?
Tibia: The one you asked for.
Claudio: It's no use his coming after what I just told you.
Tibia: About what?
Claudio: About my wife.
Tibia: Here she comes herself . . .

(I, 3, pp. 143–144)

A game of verbal hop-scotch, but a sinister, lethal one. Claudio and Tibia are comical puppets, uniforms stuffed with gears and slogans instead of hearts and ideas. Yet the results of their mechanical action are as real as the protagonists' frantic struggle to find love, and they intersect at the point of death. At the hands of these automatons, death is somehow more horrible than the stab of a lover's dagger in passion. We are still laughing at their ineptitude when we realize with a start that a murder has taken place.

In the dialectic of the action, then, Claudio and Tibia (who must always be thought of as a pair) are the antithesis of Coelio, Octave, and Marianne. They represent a mechanistic imitation of life, which is life's antipode *because* it is imitation, not self-creating experience. Claudio's language and his "thoughts" are pure form, as Octave points out in his virtuoso duel of insults with him (II, 1, p. 152): "You're a magistrate who has beautiful forms . . . of language. Your wig is full of eloquence, and your legs are two charming parentheses." As in Octave's first-act portrait of his enemies, words and beings exchange their meaning until both lose their identity and become abstract: Octave saw himself harassed by platitudes turned into creatures; Claudio is transformed into the symbols of speech. His world, the world of sentences (in two senses) and formulae, is at odds with the world of sentiment in which the three protagonists live. All the commonplaces of society, the self-perpetuating givens of human institutions, culminate in this perfect civil servant whose only desire is "to let the punishment fit the crime." His level of existence is so irrelevant to the protagonists' that he might come from a different world, be a character from another, very different play:

commedia dell'arte or Guignol. But there he is, and the other characters must finally reckon with his existence and his influence on theirs.

For, on another plane, Claudio is not so alien to Coelio, Octave, and Marianne as he might seem. His jealousy and possessiveness are exaggerated to the point of grotesqueness, but they are still the attributes of passion. He may be as different from Marianne as a comic-strip character is from a live actor; he is still her husband. And his climactic act of murder is not the arbitrary action of a *diabolus ex machina*, appearing in time to end the drama: it and he are the logical symbolic representation of Coelio's fate, and Octave's and Marianne's. His simulacrum of communication with Tibia is a parody of the protagonists' mis- and noncommunication. His envelopment in the forms and costume of his social function is the caricature of their isolation within their subjective natures, and their ineluctable determination by past history (Octave's surrender to debauchery, Coelio's mythic sense of predestination, Marianne's education and marriage). Claudio's crazy act of vengeance is merely the realization of what Coelio expected all along: death without satisfaction of his love. And Coelio's death reveals to Octave what he must have known all along: that he himself is dead to the world, to friendship and to love, because he has withdrawn into wine and easy pleasures rather than accept the suffering that Coelio has undergone for his passion. Claudio *is* destiny, in all its capriciousness and absurdity.

Les Caprices de Marianne is a curiously pessimistic, almost nihilistic "comedy." It is certainly not comedy in the classical French sense, meant to correct morals and manners through laughter, to analyze social or psychological types. It has the superficial attributes of both comedy of manners and *commedia dell'arte*: their language, devices and characters. Yet it resembles tragedy not only in the catastrophe of its ending but in the structure of its action. Its vicissitudes are not a series of temporary obstacles to the accomplishment of its protagonists' aims, or a sequence of trials to be overcome. They are an inexorable chain of steps toward unhappiness and death, and toward anticlimactic, tardy recognition of destiny. Marianne's, Octave's, and Coelio's sense of helplessness in the face of superior forces is one side of this. Another is the peculiar concept of time represented by each of the protagonists, and reflected in the play's structure.

Time: the "Deadly Enemy"

Coelio knows he will die of love from the beginning of the play. In his first exchange with Ciuta, he exclaims, "Ah! unfortunate wretch that I am, I have nothing left but to die." To Octave, in the same scene, he says, "I'll either succeed or I'll kill myself"; later, again to Octave, "Tell her [Marianne] that to betray me is to kill me, and my life is in her eyes." Nothing really changes in Coelio's attitude throughout the play: he fluctuates, yet without any meaningful pattern, and when Octave finally pushes him out the door toward Marianne's house, there is no visible sign of hope or desire on Coelio's part. Coelio is as far outside of the play's action, in his way, as Claudio is in his. He is being carried along by events remote from his will, as he states in the boat-monologue. For Coelio is out of time: out of the "objective" time of the play's events, in any case, and in a fabulous time of his own. He sees himself as a man from another time, one who would have been at home in the age of chivalry:

> Ah! if only I had been born in the time of tourneys and battles! If it had been granted to me to wear Marianne's colors and stain them with my blood! If I had only been given a rival to fight with, an entire army to challenge! If only the sacrifice of my life might be of use to her! I know how to act, but I cannot talk. My tongue won't serve my heart, and I'll die without making myself understood, like a mute in prison. (II, 2, p. 161)

We cannot, of course, accept Coelio's estimate of himself as a man of action, any more than we can believe that he would really have been at home in some other era. His error is part of his being "out of time." Coelio cannot exist in the present—in *any* present. There would always be some legendary time that would be his, because *it* is a myth of the past. In the same way, Hermia's story of her youth, associated with the circumstances of Coelio's birth, provides a cyclical myth which binds Coelio because of what *he* is (not because of what *it* is). Coelio can finally enter the action of the play only at the moment of his betrayal and death, which he has expected all along. His one true present moment comes at that instant when the present becomes eternal and null. He has never been able to accept the idea of passage, the flow of time and of man through time, or of man's participation in time through action. That, too, he reveals to Octave in the scene of their first encounter:

> I lack the calm, the gentle carefreeness that makes life a mirror on which every object is painted for an instant, and over which everything glides. For me, a debt is a remorse. Love, which people like you take as a pastime, upsets my whole life . . . What delight I feel at moonrise, under those little trees across the square, leading my modest group of musicians, marking the beat myself, listening to them sing the praise of Marianne's beauty! She's never appeared at her window; she's never come and leaned her charming head against the blinds.   (I, 1, p. 129)

Coelio's love is timeless, too; not just "eternal," as in the sonnets, but an endless repetition of the same inconsequential serenade beneath an empty window in the moonlight. There was never any reason to believe Marianne ever would appear. Even in his brief moment of apparent triumph, Coelio is like those other moonstruck lovers, in Verlaine's "Clair de Lune," who "seem not to believe in their good fortune."

As much as Coelio's "moment," his present, is rendered impossible by the confrontation with the eternity he is always expecting, Octave's present is so all-absorbing that it precludes any meaningful duration. His images of the tightrope walker and of the hunter both represent that. The tightrope walker, because he is intent on maintaining his precarious balance, protecting the cup of momentary pleasure into which he projects all his consciousness. Parents, liabilities, "the wisdom of the ages" tug at him in vain as he steps gingerly, endlessly along his linear path from birth to death. There is room for no one else on the wire, and Octave can look neither forward toward a goal nor back toward his origins and lost dreams. And like the hunter, he is caught in the delicious expectation of his kill, frozen for a moment in pleasure before destroying the object of his desire. We know that Octave is an involuntary killer even before he sends Coelio to his death: each of his moments kills its predecessor, he has destroyed his soul in the search for instant pleasure and forgetfulness. His debauchery has the appearance of life, just as his drinking and his whoring have the appearance of exaltation and love. That is what attracts Marianne: Don Juan has always fascinated dissatisfied women. But we know Octave has died long before the scene in which he admits it, in the cemetery. He has a brief inkling in the vesper-bells scene, as he cries out, "When will they stop driving me into the earth!" Like Coelio, Octave is awaiting the moment of his death throughout the entire play; he only *seems* to be behaving more effectively, less passively than his friend. The difference is that Octave's will be a living death, strangely reminiscent of Musset's own after the demise of his talent: the play is prescient.

Marianne, through a complex interplay of forces characteristic of Musset's best work, participates in both Coelio's and Octave's time concept, but paradoxically is unable to enjoy the fruits of either. Like her sister in *On ne badine pas avec l'amour*, the virginal Camille, she thirsts for the eternal, the ideal. At the same time the forces of life, of sensual desire within her fight in the name of the moment's pleasure. But unlike Camille, she is a married woman, and married to a sinister clown: she knows the lie hidden behind the words honor and fidelity. She is being swept away by internal forces beyond her control, even as her sarcasm defends the conjugal virtues against Octave's attack:

> *Marianne:* Aren't virtue and faithfulness terribly ridiculous things? And a young girl's upbringing, the pride of a heart which imagined it was worth something, that before casting the dust of its cherished flower to the wind, it should be bathed in tears, brought to bloom by a few rays

of the sun, opened gradually by a delicate
hand? . . . After all, what is a woman? A moment's occupation, a fragile cup containing
a drop of dew, which you bring to your lips and
then toss away. A woman is a pleasure party!
Couldn't you say when you meet one: There's a
beautiful night passing by? And wouldn't a
man have to be a great schoolboy in such
matters, to lower his eyes before her and say
to himself: "There goes perhaps an entire life's
happiness," and let her pass by?

(II, 1, pp. 150–151)

Her image of the flower, spoken to Octave (and prefiguring
the metaphorical exchange in their next encounter), is so sensual
as to contradict the intended defense of ideal, eternal values. It
reminds us too clearly of that great body of Renaissance love
poetry evoking the fragile rose in defense of *carpe diem*. Marianne's language betrays her deeper feelings, as they emerge from
beneath the prudish exterior in the succeeding action of the play.

Thus on the one hand, Marianne's adherence to ideals like
those which Coelio himself lives for—enduring love, respect,
fidelity—places her in a dilemma: if she chooses honor and
fidelity, she cannot respond to Coelio's love (even granted that
she were so inclined). Musset suggests thereby that, by definition,
the ideal represented by Coelio is incapable of translation into
the world of the real. On the other hand, at the very moment she
extolls these virtues, she is already caught up in the inexorable
movement of her desire. Each of her scenes with Octave is marked
by increasingly sensual language, equivocally employed in defense of her ideals (which are gradually modified from the
honor of a woman to her relative quality, compared with such as
Rosalinde). Similarly, the rhythmic pressure of their encounters,
in terms of both frequency and heat, builds to an interrupted climax at the end of II, 1, and leads toward the rendezvous granted
at the end. We are made aware that Marianne, more than Octave,
is caught in another time-pattern, that of the irreversible drive
toward sensual fulfillment characteristic of the sex act. If she

seems to be determining all the action from Act II on, it is not because she is in command of herself and the situation but because she is the plaything of forces within her, beyond her control. That is the origin of her "caprices." Everything serves as a pretext for what Marianne has felt all along would happen, and Claudio's threats merely give her an opportunity for self-justification. It is difficult not to be reminded of Jean Anouilh's representation of the tragic impulse as the moment when everything becomes inevitable: when the trigger is pulled, or when two lovers stand naked before each other.[21] The association above is of course profoundly relevant: the traditional identification of the sex act and death informs the psychology of the characters, the dramatic action of the play, and the rhythmic structure underlying its temporal sequence. For Marianne, as for Coelio, the encounter between the idealizing tendency and the insistent demands of life can lead only to death—Coelio's "death and transfiguration," Octave's death in the midst of life. In the context of Musset's drama that is the tragic joke played by destiny upon the young: the destiny embodied by a hostile world (Claudio and the institutions he personifies) and the destiny which the protagonists bear within themselves, as part of their condition.

Our analysis of *Les Caprices de Marianne* must, however, take account of an element that has always caused some perplexity: the final scene of the play. As we have noted, Musset himself evidenced doubts about it in his 1851 version, when he attempted to integrate the scene temporally and scenically into the action by placing it immediately after the murder of Coelio and transferring it from the cemetery to the public square. The scene is far more suitable and more effective, however, as it was originally written. It becomes a true epilogue, separated in time and space from the action upon which it comments and which it defines. Octave dominates the scene, with Marianne reduced to the role of a *figurant*: she is there only to provide a few articulations in what is essentially Octave's monologue. The latter is an elegy, a poem of mourning in honor of Coelio which becomes a meditation on universal death, the passage of all things in the order of the

21. *Antigone*, in *Nouvelles Pièces noires* (Paris, 1958), p. 161.

world. The play must be understood in the light of this final elegiac perspective, which typifies Musset's dramas: rather than comedies or tragedies in the usual sense, these works are elegies, mourning the inevitable destruction of all that is young and beautiful, and singing its praises at the same time. Octave speaks of Coelio as the better part of himself, the only one capable of love: the expression "he alone" recurs as an echoing motif to Octave's proud but resigned "I alone knew him," and the repeated "adieu" which concludes the scene. The play's meaning takes form in this funeral oration. Coelio, the sole true lover, had to die by the very nature of his love. Octave could not help betraying him: his was the voice of sensuality, appealing to Marianne's thirst for pleasure. Octave can fully appreciate Coelio's worth only now that he has died, and taken Octave's soul and hope with him. The latter's anguished cry, "I'm a coward; his death is not avenged," is a statement of the spiritual impasse in which he finds himself: he can do nothing for his friend against a Claudio too old to fight, whose death would be meaningless; and nothing for himself or for Marianne in the knowledge of his emptiness.

Here, as subsequently in *Fantasio*, Musset demonstrates his use of the symbolic resources of dramatic form. *Marianne* is a two-act comedy incorporating an epilogue in its second act. The author thus avoids the natural sense of resolution which seems inherent in the three-act form—a resolution in terms of reality, either of manners or of character—and yet provides a kind of resolution which is not really one, since it takes place beyond life at the crossroads of Coelio's tomb. There, paradoxically, Coelio finds life, or a meaning to his life—too late for action— and Octave finds death, or life deprived of meaning; Marianne is abandoned between the two erstwhile lovers, left in the hands of her puppetlike, murderous husband. The form is a curious open end, after the apparently normal exposition of the play's beginning and the accelerating vicissitudes of its second act: we are left with a conclusion that traditional comedy would not lead us to expect—although, as we have seen, it was not without warning from the very beginning. No doubt this explains the uneasiness which *Marianne* has evoked in audiences and critics from its first production, and the mixed reactions it continues to elicit to our day. This stylized, "traditional" comedy which seems to owe so much to the generations of its predecessors and so little to the literary movement of its time is in fact an original and indefinable dramatic masterpiece.

Fantasio, Act II, Scene 1. Comédie-Française:
Mony Dalmès (Elsbeth), Julien Bertheau (Fantasio).
Courtesy of Agence de Presse Bernand, Paris.

Chapter 4 Fantasio:

The Paradise of Chance

"Of all Alfred de Musset's plays, *Fantasio* is the last that should have been carried from the book to the stage. This brilliant, desperate man, who seems moreover to be the incarnation of the poet, has nothing interesting or dramatic about him. Disgusted with the world, with others and with himself, he no longer either loves or admires anything, and he derides everything that is grand, noble, and beautiful; he is indeed quite a disagreeable character ... For all the cuts, reworkings or entirely new ending that were imposed on the play, it was listened to only with respect, and after its performance this singular whim of the poet returned to the pages of its book, where it is far more at home."[1] This harsh judgment by one of the Comédie-Française's chroniclers—contemporary with *Fantasio*'s posthumous premier in 1866, thirty-three years after its publication—is echoed by no less an authority than the actor who created its title role, Delaunay, for many years Musset's principal interpreter. He referred to it as "Musset's strange and almost unplayable comedy."[2] Posterity seems almost to have pronounced a final confirmation: *Fantasio* has remained the least performed of Musset's major comedies. Only *Lorenzaccio*, a totally different sort of enterprise, has been subjected to greater neglect in the theater—a neglect which recent years have begun to remedy.

Yet this strange comedy, in which biographers and commen-

1. G. d'Heylli, *Journal intime de la Comédie-Française*, pp. 461–62, cited by Lyonnet, *Les "Premières,"* pp. 155–56.
2. *Souvenirs de Delaunay*, p. 181, cited by Lyonnet, p. 148.

tators have seen the poet's closest representation of himself in the character of the hero, exerts a deep fascination even on those who depreciate it. Francisque Sarcey, who did not admire Musset's heroes, wrote: "I don't much like *Fantasio*, and his fine, contorted wit. But look at that first scene, where he is talking with his three friends [*sic*]. How well it is constructed! How completely in place every word is! How we feel ourselves carried along, from beginning to end of this conversation, by a grand dramatic sweep."[3] And Jean Starobinski does not hesitate to call *Fantasio* a masterpiece, "perhaps the only great French work in which we find the equivalent of what the Germans have designated under the name of romantic irony."[4]

Fantasio is a play that seems to generate misunderstandings. One of the fundamental ones can perhaps be elucidated in part here. The play's detractors, in general—those who speak of its structural flaws or its formlessness—tend to have in mind the reworking which Paul de Musset undertook for the play's premiere: a reworking whose aim, paradoxically enough, was to "regularize" the piece, giving it a more normal plot and formal resolution. More than any of its companions, *Fantasio* was felt to be ill-adapted to the stage in its original form, a kind of "barely-finished sketch" (in Sarcey's words) whose irregularity was the result of carelessness rather than any higher plan. Thus when the play first appeared at the Comédie-Française seven years after the author's death, it was in a form supposedly dictated by Paul's conversations *in extremis* with Alfred: three acts instead of two, the order of its scenes somewhat scrambled, and with an ending in which the original's troubling ambiguity was replaced by a quasi-certainty of love between hero and heroine. The poet's brother had even ghost-written a number of "clarifying" transitions, and inserted a bit of irrelevant material from Alfred's lyric poetry.[5]

The play's defenders, on the other hand, have had in mind either the original printed text (as in the case of Musset's loyal,

3. *Quarante Ans de théâtre* (Paris 1900–02), IV, 269.
4. "Note sur un bouffon romantique," *Cahiers du Sud*, 61 (1966), 271.
5. See Alfred de Musset, *Oeuvres complètes*, ed. Gastinel, I, 273–81.

patient advocate Gautier) or the productions of this text which finally reached the stage fifty or more years after the premiere. *Fantasio* had meanwhile disappeared from public view following the tepid success of 1866. When it was revived for the first time in the *Urtext*, in 1911 at the Théâtre des Arts, one reviewer at least was struck by its structural integrity. "People generally see in [Musset] only the bubbling wit, banter and youthfulness floating on the surface of his theater; they fail to recognize the robust genius, the understanding of the heart, the humanity, in sum, which are concealed within it. People agree that nothing is more graceful, more delicate—nasty tongues add, more 'well-written' —than these legendary dramas; but only to avoid admiring their solid, enduring structure."[6]

It was only in 1925, sixty years after its premiere, that *Fantasio* returned to the stage of the Comédie-Française in Musset's unmodified text. That was the occasion of a triumph, abetted no doubt by the exceptional talents of a group of young interpreters soon to become leading stars: Pierre Fresnay (Fantasio), Marie Bell (Elsbeth), and Pierre Bertin (the Prince). Asté d'Esparbès was prompted to write: "One asks with amazement how this little masterpiece of a *Fantasio* could remain for almost sixty years in silence and neglect! It is a jewel."[7]

In much the same way that *Fantasio's* stage career rests on a false start, successive critical appreciations of the play seem to be founded on a series of irrelevancies which for a long time left many basic questions unanswered, and indeed unasked. If criticism of this play, like that of much of Musset's work in all genres, concentrated on questions of biography or history, part of the fault was Musset's own: is he not supposed to have refused to give the role of Fantasio to the actor Brindeau, according to legend, because "Fantasio is myself; you don't look enough like me"?[8] Similarly, if extensive attention has been given to the literary sources of the play, that is because *Fantasio*, like so much

6. Alfred de Tarde, February 19, 1912, Fonds Rondel, Bibliothèque de l'Arsenal.

7. *Comoedia*, August 23, 1925, Fonds Rondel.

8. Claude Schnerb, "Fantasio ou la destruction d'un mythe," *L'Illustre Théâtre* (spring 1955), pp. 24–25.

of Musset's work, is riddled with visible evidences of his tastes and passions. Jean Giraud and Marjorie Shaw demonstrated, for example, the precise debt the play owes to Hoffmann, Richter, and Heine, on the one hand, and to Carmontelle and George Sand, on the other:[9] French source criticism has enjoyed particular success with Musset's theater. Such studies, giving us an insight into the workings of a brilliantly absorbent mind, have been of great usefulness to serious readers of Musset. But in spite of these critics' repeated assertion of the originality of Musset's genius, they may very well have created an unfortunate image of inspired plagiarism.

The remarkable resurgence of critical interest in Musset's theater during recent years has affected *Fantasio* somewhat less than its companion pieces. The play, because of its brevity and its apparent whimsy, has rarely been the object of monographic studies. But several critics have touched on it in its larger context, and revealed the deep seriousness beneath its provocative surface.[10] They have helped to define *Fantasio*'s place in the evolution of Musset's theater: in the overall configuration of his alter-ego heroes and their masks, in the demographic analysis of his puppet-world, in the development of the peculiar philosophy which underlies the plays' dramatic structure.

What remains to demonstrate, however, is that, far from being a grab-bag of *bons mots*, free association metaphors, and paradoxes set in a sentimentally pathetic autobiographical plot ma-

9. Giraud, "Alfred de Musset et trois romantiques allemands," *Revue d'Histoire Littéraire*, 18 (1911), 297–334; 19 (1912), 341–75. Shaw, "A Propos du 'Fantasio' d'Alfred de Musset," *RHL*, 55 (1955), 319–28; "Deux Essais sur les comédies d'Alfred de Musset," *Revue des Sciences Humaines*, fascicle 93 (1959), 47–76.

10. Cf. particularly Philippe Van Tieghem, "L'Evolution du théâtre de Musset des débuts à *Lorenzaccio*," *Revue d'Histoire du Théâtre*, 4 (1952), 261–75; Bernard Masson, "Le Masque, le double et la personne dans quelques Comédies et Proverbes," *Revue des Sciences Humaines*, fascicle 108 (October–December 1962), 551–71; Robert Mauzi, "Les Fantoches d'Alfred de Musset," *Revue d'Histoire Littéraire*, 66 (1966), 257–83; and Starobinski, "Note sur un bouffon romantique," pp. 270, 272.

trix, *Fantasio*, like all of Musset's major dramas, possesses a tightly composed and carefully organized plot structure of a most original sort, based on a fusing of linguistic play, fantasy, and characterization. It is certain that Musset's enduring success as a dramatic author is due in great part to this organic cohesion; but the unity which audiences and players have experienced in performance needs more intensive analysis.

Fantasio is a comedy in two rather unequal acts. The first is divided into three scenes (to the second's seven), and it is characterized by considerably less dramatic action than the second. Indeed, the entire second scene of the first act, which occupies all but six pages of the Gastinel edition, is marked by an absence of event and by a length of "philosophical" dialogue which is in contrast to the rapid changes of scene and the sudden events of the second act. Its two-act form is in itself worthy of attention. If Paul de Musset, in tampering with Alfred's original, transformed *Fantasio* into a play in three acts at the expense of the most elementary proportion (his third act consisting essentially of the original's final scene), it was evidently because the original division did not correspond to his idea of a properly constructed play. It is true, of course, that Musset used this form on other occasions, notably in *Les Caprices de Marianne*. But the three-act division is more traditional, and with reason: as in the five acts of neoclassical tragedy, the uneven number seems to complete a cycle, to put a definitive end to the sequence of events. The aesthetic universality of this feeling finds its analogue in musical form: the *aria da capo* and sonata are trinary. In a negative sense, banal though the example may be, Schubert's unfinished Symphony illustrates the sense of incompleteness given by binary division.

But a closer analogy, literarily and generically, can justify the binary division of *Fantasio* on aesthetic grounds: Samuel Beckett's *En attendant Godot*, in which the division into two acts clearly represents the play's philosophical "form," communicates a sense of openness at the end, suggesting endless future repetitions of the two days' tragicomic nonevents. *Fantasio*, too, is an open-ended play, implying an end which is not a conclusion, but at once a beginning and the continuation of a repetitious cycle. The moral and aesthetic justification for this will be seen in the examination of theme and resolution in the play.

The scene is Munich, the time unspecified. The King of Bavaria confesses to Rutten, his secretary, that he has doubts concerning the marriage he has contracted for political reasons between his daughter Elsbeth and the Prince of Mantua, whom he has never met. The Prince's aide-de-camp, the obtuse Marinoni, is shown ineptly seeking information about Princess Elsbeth's reputation from three of her young subjects, Spark, Hartman, and Facio, who treat him with supercilious disdain. The youths are joined by their friend Fantasio, who is feeling too weary to join them in disrupting the festivities for the Princess' betrothal. Alone with Spark, Fantasio confesses his boredom with Munich and the world. Love and religion are dead; all his dreams—of art, travel, and adventure—have prematurely evaporated; his creditors are on his trail, and he can find no activity in life capable of stimulating him, except getting drunk . . . Suddenly a procession passes: the funeral of Saint-John, the King's jester. Fantasio, deciding to take Saint-John's place, goes off to find a suitable costume and disguise. Meanwhile, the Prince of Mantua, inadequately enlightened by Marinoni's inquiries (according to which Elsbeth is "melancholy, capricious, wildly joyful, submissive to her father's will, extremely fond of green peas"), decides on a daring venture: he will change costumes and roles with his aide-de-camp, in order to observe the Princess incognito and win her love!

The second act finds Elsbeth admitting to her governess that she is marrying the Prince out of obedience to her father. Fantasio appears in the garden, wearing the deforming disguise of her beloved Saint-John, and teases her about her coming wedding. His cryptic thrusts at arranged betrothals, blue tulips, and mechanical songbirds pique and yet fascinate Elsbeth. The Prince of Mantua's grotesque clumsiness in his borrowed role, coupled with the disguised Marinoni's distressing banality, succeed in upsetting Elsbeth's precarious control over her emotions. When Fantasio spies her weeping, he is moved to help her out of her predicament. From a vantage point in the King's pantry, where he has been drinking, he snatches the supposed Prince's royal wig with a fishhook and line, thereby unleashing the real Prince's contumacious wrath at this offense to his dignity. The Prince breaks off diplomatic relations with Bavaria and declares war. When Fantasio is put in prison for his deed, Elsbeth discovers him sleeping in his undisguised youth and beauty. In return for the service he has rendered her, Elsbeth gives Fantasio his freedom, permitting him to return as jester whenever he tires of the real world and finds his creditors unbearable.

From this summary it should be easy to see why Paul de Musset was concerned with regularizing the play. *Fantasio* is a remarkably free-wheeling combination of political satire, social commentary, fantasy, farce, and sentiment. Its numerous scene changes and its lack of what normally passes for a plot in legitimate theater tradition (there are elements of vaudeville or comic opera in it, however) give it an offhand, improvised air which goes even beyond the limits of "indirect progress" in Musset's other comedies. It seems almost like a small-scale *Lorenzaccio*.

The first act of *Fantasio*, in accordance with its peculiarly disproportionate and static form, is essentially expository. It presents, in the manner that Musset may have discovered in Shakespeare, an oddly disjointed sequence of three unequal scenes, linked by their general setting (a quasi-Illyrian city of Munich), and by their superficial plot relationship (the coming marriage and its preparation). But they are radically distinguished by their tone and by their groupings. The only character who plays a role in more than one of these scenes is Marinoni, a minor figure. Fantasio's friends, who dominate the opening pages of the second scene, disappear completely soon after his entrance, with the exception of Spark; all three are absent from the second act. Gastinel speaks of this tendency in Musset to separate his character groupings in successive scenes, rather than having them mingle on the stage.[11] It is true that he seemed to find two-character scenes more suited to his talent than crowded ones. But here there is a deeper reason, related to levels of characterization. Suffice to say that in the first act of *Fantasio* this kind of dramatic construction creates a sense of episodical disjunction which un-

11. *Le Romantisme d'Alfred de Musset*, p. 305.

derlines the central moral theme of the act: the discontinuity between internal and external experience at the root of the hero's unrest.

Critics have been tempted, in the context of the 1830's as well as our own sociologically oriented age, to put this unrest in sociopolitical terms. Gustave Lanson gave impetus to this interpretation when he demonstrated the links between *Fantasio* and contemporary history in a noted article.[12] Numerous analogies between the never-never land of Munich and Louis-Philippe's Paris could be extended from the play's basis in current events: the political marriage between Louis-Philippe's daughter, Louise d'Orléans, and Leopold I of Belgium. In recent times these social and political implications in *Fantasio* as in the rest of Musset's theater have been developed to an extreme by Marxist critics. For Henri Lefebvre, Fantasio's practical joke and his ironic self-degradation become a "heroic action" against the bourgeois order.[13] A less perceptive and intelligent writer, working in the context of East German socialist realism, goes so far as to see in Fantasio "the character with whom Musset wishes to mock the bourgeois world."[14] But his interpretation is based on a misreading of Musset's text (below, page 74). It is true that some of the play's thematic treatment of disjuncture is expressed in social terms, for example the contrast between the bourgeois king and his prestige-conscious future son-in-law or between Fantasio the commoner and Princess Elsbeth. Hartman, Facio, and Spark express their own unrest in terms far more in accordance with our standard idea of youthful revolt under Louis-Philippe's middle-class monarchy than with that of Munich at some unspecified era. Moreover, Fantasio's most concrete antagonist here in the first act is represented by the capitalistic body of his creditors!

Already in the first scene the King indicates by a metaphor that even he, representing the highest social level in the play, is subject to a malevolent and transcendent force: "Politics is a delicate spider-web, in which all too many poor mutilated flies flail about; I

---

12. "Mariage de Princesse. Vérité et fantaisie dans une comédie de Musset," *Revue de Paris* (March 1, 1913), 32–46.
13. *Alfred de Musset dramaturge* (Paris, 1955), p. 64.
14. Werner Bahner, *Alfred de Mussets Werk*, p. 78.

will not sacrifice my daughter's happiness to any interest." The image contains elements present in a number of other significant passages: human impotence at the hands of a powerful, evil force; physical immobility and destruction; disproportion between the two terms of the comparison (and a certain physical paradox represented by the adjective "delicate"); and finally, for the moment, its basis in the terminology of the insect realm. The comparison of political order, destiny, and impotence with insect life is further illustrated by the apparent non sequitur in Fantasio's suggestion to Spark: ("Let's imagine government coalitions; let's catch all the may-flies that pass around this candle, and put them in our pockets") (I, 2). We are reminded of the presence of an antagonistic force which transcends the merely social context. If, indeed, social obstacles and frustrations are part of this force, they are not all of it but merely symptomatic of a larger, cosmic disorder.

Seen in this light, Facio's characterization of Marinoni, ostensibly spying for the Bavarian authorities, as a "gobe-mouche" (a fly-catcher) could be both a familiar term for a gawker and a sinister echo of the insect images. This and related groups of comparisons found subsequently in the play may be seen as expressing the existential situation: man caught in a conflict between the strivings of individual will and his impotence in the face of cosmic forces and destiny; man trapped in himself, caught in a machine-like universe and constantly tempted into correspondingly mechanical reactions.

The conflict underlying Fantasio's sense of discontent with the world is too complex to be expressed in purely social terms. Look at his brilliant monologue of Act I, scene 2, where we find him underlining the spiritual and psychological barriers which prevent communication among men:

Fantasio: If only I could get out of my skin for an hour or two! If only I could be that gentleman going by!

Spark: That seems rather difficult to me.

Fantasio: That gentleman going by is charming; look: what a beautiful pair of silk breeches! What beautiful red flowers on his vest! His watch-fob

> swings against his paunch in counterpoint to the
> tails of his jacket, which twirl about his
> calves. I am sure that man has thousands of ideas
> in his head which are utterly foreign to me;
> his essence is peculiar to him. Alas! Everything
> that men say to each other is alike; the ideas they
> exchange are almost always the same in all their
> conversations; but inside all those isolated
> machines, what hidden recesses, what secret
> compartments! It's a whole world that everyone
> bears within him, an unknown world which
> lives and dies in silence. What solitudes, all these
> human bodies!

Bahner, studying this speech from his Marxist viewpoint, misinterprets its intent: "Fantasio wittily describes a bourgeois to his friend Spark with the words: 'That gentleman is charming . . . I am sure that man has thousands of ideas in his head which are utterly foreign to me. *His entire being seems peculiar to me.*' [Italics mine.] Fantasio will have nothing to do with this world, and is on a war footing with it."[15] The mistranslation throws the portrait into a new perspective, compatible with Bahner's literary and political philosophy: instead of Fantasio's half-plaintive, half-ironic fascination with the gentleman's isolation, which corresponds to his own, it becomes a simple caricature of the bourgeois. It is true that the isolation from man to man, from element to element of the social structure, is an essential factor. But the existential trap is the machine, the body itself, which is the locus of Fantasio's larger complaint against the universal order. The "gentleman going by" is humanly rich, a subject for ironic admiration and wistful conjecture—he is "charming"—because of the "thousands of ideas" generated by this complicated machine which carries him along. But the formalization of these ideas, doomed to banality, erects a barrier between men on the level of communication. And the machine itself is the barrier, the armor as well as the motor, the temporal generator of timeless ideas. "You call me your life, call me rather your soul, / For the

15. Ibid.

soul is immortal, and life is but a day," sings Fantasio, citing a "Portuguese romance." It is life itself, it is the body, which is the cause of his malaise, and of the death awaiting him.

In the broader context, then, Fantasio's primary conflict is between the internal world—the idea—and the external world of physical reality. The exposition of the first act and part of the development of the second provide us with the horns of a human dilemma on which Fantasio is suspended: the two possibilities of resolution to close the gap between man's physical nature and his spiritual desire and need for the ideal. Nowhere can this be better understood than in Musset's use of caricature in this play.

The function of the grotesques or *fantoches* in *Fantasio* can be best understood from this existential point of view. The conflict between Musset's "real" characters and his puppets, a less active element in *On ne badine pas avec l'amour*, here becomes a central dramatic force. The association between the grotesques and the above-mentioned images of insect life is not incidental or merely descriptive: it is a part of a larger metaphorical and thematic structure. At one pole of the conflict between the physical and the spiritual world we find a hypothetical resolution represented by the grotesques: total acceptance of the physical by man, resignation to the inexorable machine which isolates and kills us, implicit renunciation of the spiritual realm. The Prince of Mantua and his agent Marinoni are caricatures: they exist as characters on the level of pure physical action, or merely routine or mechanical psychological processes.[16] They have no real inner resources, and therefore no internal conflict. They have resolved their existential dilemma; or rather, through their total submission to the mechanical fatality of the world, they have cut the Gordian knot by never confronting the dilemma. Their nature can be defined as pure form, devoid of the human substance represented by internal, spiritual life.

Musset's intention to employ his grotesques not only as comic relief but as quasisymbolic representations of this particular pole of life can be clearly seen by examining the peculiar obsessions embodied by the Prince. One of our first encounters with him

16. For an excellent synthesis on Musset's *fantoches*, see Robert Mauzi, "Les Fantoches d'Alfred de Musset," pp. 257–83.

manifests the opposition between grotesque and true character. In Act I, scene 3, the Prince, obviously incapable of distinguishing between the improvised, intuitive, and gratuitous nature of manly friendship and the mechanical, automatic quality of court protocol, says to his aide-de-camp: "I name you my bosom friend; I know of no finer handwriting than yours in all my kingdom." The polar, symmetrical example of Fantasio's and Spark's conversation in the preceding scene serves further to emphasize this distance.

The symbolic importance of handwriting to the grotesques suggested in the above quotation, as a means of formalizing the spirit, can be seen as well in another speech of the Prince which underlines his submission to the world of form. Marinoni's chaotic attempts to define Elsbeth's (human) personality for the limited comprehension of his master lead the latter to say: "Write that down; I can't understand anything clearly unless it is written in a round Spenserian hand."

For the Prince the outward aspect, rank, or appearance of a character takes precedence over all other considerations. It is therefore not surprising that he should find the wornout theatrical device of exchanging costumes with his lowly aide-de-camp at the same time supremely new and shocking, and deliciously tempting. Nor that the most revolutionary aspect of the whole scheme is the exchange of clothing itself, for the appurtenances of royalty are more significant to him than even royal birth itself. That is why, to startle his aide-de-camp, he chooses to announce his plan in these terms: "What would you say, Marinoni, if you saw your master put on a simple olive-green suit?" The repetitions of this "olive-green suit" in subsequent scenes take on more and more comical overtones, because they are deeply in accord with the automatic basis of repetitive comedy. The farcical business of hesitation, repetition, and overemphasis connected with the Prince and Marinoni's constantly threatened reexchange of costumes carries it several degrees further. The Prince's costume becomes identified with a sort of destiny to which he feels himself to be comically subject in his actions.

If, however, we are tempted to explain the grotesque in terms of the social conflict between Philistines and Romantics, we have only to look at the delightful parody of Byronic or Hugolian romanticism offered by the Prince himself: "I am of obscure birth; my only possession is a name dreaded by the enemy; a pure and spotless heart beats under this modest uniform; I am a poor soldier riddled with bullets from head to toe; I haven't a farthing to my name; I am solitary and in exile from both my native land and my heavenly home, that is to say the paradise of my dreams; I haven't a woman's heart to press against my own; I am accursed, and silent" (II, 2). The Prince illustrates by this *morceau de bravoure* that the Romantic hero-accursed is just as susceptible of falling into the mechanical pattern as the meanest Louis-Philippian bureaucrat. The burlesque potential of Hernani's "force-qui-va" here lends itself readily to Musset's brand of caricature, through a pattern of repetition and exaggeration.

We can see from Musset's treatment of clothing in *Fantasio* that it is at the same time a symbol of the mechanical nature of man in his world (of form dominating substance) and a means to depersonalize the individual, clothes taking precedence over essence. The Prince's psychological disarray, his loss of control over the situation once he has quit the costume of his rank, are indices of this fact. The theme of depersonalization is further developed in the character of Elsbeth's governess, although she is treated more sympathetically than the Prince. In the camp of the *fantoches*, she would require classification under the subheading "banal." Her ridiculousness is exemplified best in her repeated attempts to classify the people around her in terms of preexisting characters, to normalize and depersonalize them in order to understand them. Thus the Prince is seen as "an Amadis of Gaul," Elsbeth as "a real paschal lamb," the adjective "real" underlining ironically the deformation taking place. Saint-John the jester was "a real Rigoletto," the King would have to be "a veritable Jephthe" to make his daughter marry the Prince, whose exchange of costumes with Marinoni is "a real fairy-tale"; the Prince himself is "a veritable Almaviva," and finally Fantasio, stripped of his deforming mask and costume in the final scene, is as beautiful as "a real infant Jesus," the term being a commonplace in French for a pretty baby. The governess, like the Prince, is a willing prisoner of the social order, historical precedent, and, in the final analysis, that triviality of the physical world with which Fantasio is struggling. It is not at all surprising, therefore, that the latter chooses the most trivial of the Prince's royal appurtenances, his wig, as the object of his crucial act of defiance in the second act. And the comic violence of the Prince's reaction to this offense against his dignity is no less expectable: "No, no! Let me unmask myself. It is time for me to burst forth. It won't go on this way. Blood and thunder! A royal wig on a fish-hook! Are we among savages, in the wastes of Siberia? Is anything civilized and proper left under the sun? I am foaming with wrath, and my eyes start from my very head!" (II, 6).

In the light of these extreme representations of submission to the mechanical order of the universe, we can better understand the nature of Fantasio's dilemma. It is true, as Gastinel says, that the dominant trait of Fantasio's character is "the feeling that adaptation between his heart and his times is impossible."[17] But that is only a partial truth. It is not only his own time which is at fault, but time itself. The paradox of "that gentleman going by," of a man made of this world by his body and isolated from communication with his fellow men by it, is too forcibly present in his mind for him to be able to accept Spark's phlegmatic well-being. Fantasio, borrowing from the *Pensées* of Jean-Paul Richter, compares himself to a diver in the midst of the vast ocean—but unlike Jean-Paul's "man absorbed by a profound thought," he has no diving-bell to save him: he is a latter-day Christ, grotesquely deformed in his self-image. For Musset suggests delicately, here and elsewhere, that Fantasio is a modern-day, comic Christ, symbol of a crucified generation.

In the first act of the play, Fantasio is on the verge of joining the *fantoches*. Or, more aptly, he is tempted in his desperation by the heresy of the mechanical. Why this state of events should reign is clearly indicated by a complex of images. Fantasio is the youth precociously old, he has "the month of May in his cheeks" and "the month of January in his heart" (I, 2). His internal landscape, in a series of paradoxical metaphors, is translated into the most tired and banal of natural landscapes. His head is like "an old chimney without a fire"; his brain, for which he uses the

17. *Le Romantisme d'Alfred de Musset*, p. 322.

crudely physical "cervelle" (a butcher's term) in a manner later imitated by Baudelaire ("Je te donne ces vers . . ."), is as well-trodden and familiar as the boring city of Munich: "This town is nothing compared to my brain. All its crannies are a hundred times more familiar; all the streets, all the holes in my imagination are a hundred times more worn out; I've walked in a hundred times more directions in this dilapidated brain of mine—I, its sole inhabitant!" (I, 2).

The horrid temptation to establish an identity between the internal and the external worlds is rendered more poignant by Fantasio's images of the latter. He expresses the wish that "this great, heavy sky were an immense cotton night-cap, to envelop this stupid city and its stupid inhabitants right up to their ears," to complete the process of invasion by the banal. Nature itself is "pitiful," the sunset is a "botched painting," no better than the ones Fantasio stopped drawing at age twelve. Fantasio seems to Spark to be "revenu de tout"—"back from everywhere" (a play on "je n'en reviens pas," "I can't get over it," thus "gotten over everything.") Like the Prince, he is now ready to be assimilated into the "real" world, even to the extent of turning toward his costume: "Let's stay here awhile talking of one thing and another, looking at our new clothes." Space and time, the essential facts and vectors of physical being, become his chief antagonists: "What a wretched thing man is! Not even to be able to jump out your window without breaking your legs! To have to play the violin ten years in order to become a decent musician! To learn in order to be a painter, to be a groom! To learn in order to make an omelet!"

Under these circumstances, the supreme temptation for Fantasio, weary of his struggle, is to submit himself totally to the overwhelming forces of time and mechanical destiny: "You know, Spark, I get an urge sometimes to sit on a railing, looking out at the river, and to start counting one, two, three, four, five, six, seven, and so on, to the day of my death."

Out of the first act's chaos of disillusionment emerges one remaining dream, which Fantasio expresses in a pictorial evocation that is one of the play's most celebrated passages: the "stirrupcup" (see below). The source of his monologue, in the

form of a tableau, has given rise to a fair amount of futile conjecture. The attempt to find a precise model in the work of
someone in the Mieris family seems based on a misreading of the
text. Fantasio, describing to Spark the woman he might love, if
he were still capable of loving, refers only in passing to the attraction of Mieris' women. Nor does it seem very important to
attribute the inspiration for this tableau to a picture by Hummel
described in Hoffman's *Artist's Life*, as does Jean Giraud, or to
Heinrich Heine, like Faguet.[18] The passage is of importance in
Musset's apparently careless dramatic and thematic structure for
other reasons.[19]

First of all, it is not a declaration of undirected love, an aspiration toward amatory fulfillment. Paul de Musset's transfer of this
passage to a hypothetical love scene between Fantasio and the
Princess in the second act is proof, if that is needed, of his misunderstanding of the play. Rather, it is a yet undefined aspiration
toward the only resolution possible in the spiritual stalemate of
the first act. It provides a thematic link between the two acts,
showing the lyric thrust of Fantasio's personality, which will lead
him haphazardly into the strange situation of the second act. This
tableau is a reply to nature's "botched painting" previously mentioned. It is doubly *réussi*: it evokes most vividly both a kind of
art which was in fashion at the time Musset was writing *Fantasio*,[20] and a saving ideal adapted to the hero and his time. The
apparent triviality of the scene evoked is a necessary element of
the salvation envisaged by Fantasio. The genre scene, dear to the
heart of a bourgeois public because it possesses no particular
moral grandeur or heroic stature, is indeed the only symbolic
form which Fantasio's future redemption can take.

Let us examine this evocation of a Flemish painting to see
briefly what elements the scene contains for future development
in the play's resolution.

What a fine thing the stirrup-cup is! A young woman on
her doorstep, the lighted fire you can glimpse across the

18. Giraud, "Alfred de Musset et trois romantiques allemands," p. 324.
19. See below, pp. 103–104, for discussion of another, similar tableau.
20. Cf. Auguste Brun, *Deux Proses de théâtre: Drame romantique,
Comédies et Proverbes* (Gap, 1954), p. 82.

room, supper ready, the children asleep; all the calm of the
peaceful and contemplative life in a corner of the picture!
And over there the man, still panting, but steady in the
saddle, who has ridden twenty leagues and still has thirty
to go; a swig of brandy, and farewell. The night is deep
down that way, a storm is brewing, the forest is full of
danger; the good woman watches him go for a while, then,
returning to her fire, she lets fall that sublime charity of
the poor: God protect him!   (I, 2)

What strikes us most is first of all the sense of precision, of
plastic definition, which this "dream" gives. Its sense of composition, of tonal values, gives it a pictorial reality which, if it does
not indeed spring from the author's experience of a given painting, at least conveys to us the feeling of vision long mulled and
carefully transposed into pictorial image.

But after this initial impression, we are struck by a certain all-
pervading ambiguity which manifests itself in a variety of ways.
First of all, in spite of those qualities which attach the passage
to the tableau genre (the lack of active verb forms, the use of
participles and of adjectives, the homogeneity of its description-
reinforced sentence structure and punctuation), it is not wholly
a tableau at all. The description oversteps the boundary of the
picture's time frame (its instantaneousness) at the end: the rider
departs and leaves the young woman alone. The sentiments
evoked, too, are imprecise or ambiguous: tranquility and anguish,
peace and danger, pity and boldness, balanced against each other
and intermingled. And these delicately equilibrated duads are
reflected in the chiaroscuro of the lighting. Where is the focal
point of the tableau: in the hearth or in the forest? What does
the young woman feel for the rider: admiration, pity, incipient
love (as the context of the passage would lead us to conjecture)?
What does the man feel? Steadfast resolve to continue on, nostalgia for the peace of the hearth, fear of the dangers confronting
him? The pathos of the children, the physical promise of the fire
and the dinner, the alcohol's momentary warmth and forgetfulness are all active elements as well, in the subtly shaded mood
which the tableau conjures up for us. Yet the end, ostensibly, is

a departure which destroys the delicate stasis the picture has created. Or does it? Do we not have a sensation of both having left, and having remained behind?

It is, then, a strikingly precise evocation of a certain quite special kind of sentiment, from a character who is shortly going to declare that "love no longer exists"! But its precision is not that of the character whose will must lead him in a highly defined direction. This tableau is our clue to the fact that the dramatic resolution of *Fantasio*, the realization of its hero's aspirations, will be neither in the direction of the pure ideal, which his disillusionment (plus a certain physical heaviness) no longer permits him to cherish, nor in the direction of the purely mechanical, which his intelligence bars to him. The resolution will take the form of the creation of a new paradise, in which his dilemma may be perpetually resolved afresh, in which one may have the fruits of both departing and staying. But Fantasio must first take his revenge on the two poles of his torment, must destroy them symbolically in order to construct his new freedom.

In one sense Fantasio's revenge on the physical world, on the mechanical universe which threatens him in the first act, is carried out by proxy. The flaws inherent in the mechanical nature of the grotesque, in confrontation with more human characters or aspirations, lead to self-destruction. The Prince of Mantua is trapped by his own desire to play with role and costume, to inspire love for himself and not his rank, as if he were a real person. Unable, because of his complete possession by the part he normally plays, to adapt himself to that of a subaltern, he passes the greater portion of the second act in the throes of indecision. And his inadaptation leads to scenes like that of Act II, scene 4, where he reproaches Marinoni for having treated him in public like the aide-de-camp he was pretending to be, and for daring to act out with the Princess the role Prince Marinoni was supposed to play, to the extent of giving him, the "real" Prince, orders! There is an elaborate pattern of reality and unreality, of the possible and the impossible, suggested here which reminds us that the favorite exclamation of Musset's grotesques, when confronted with the inhabitual, is "That is impossible!" The dewigging of the Prince is thus only the culmination of a revenge against the physical trap which destiny has set before Fantasio. The undoing of the Prince's dignity, in the form of his royal perruque, is symbolic action; but the temptation of the mechanical, we can see by the Prince's nonadaptation to the needs of his world and to his desires, leads to its own punishment. Destructive laughter is the inevitable retribution of the grotesque.

If Fantasio's acceptance of the role of jester permits him to undertake the Prince's defeat, however, it is also a form of revenge on himself. His adoption of a grotesque disguise is an act of symbolic destruction of his own manly physical beauty and dignity. The young man gives up the possibility of exciting love for his physical form and thereby takes revenge on that part of the idea which was associated with physical happiness and amorous satisfaction. The hump and the mask are one part of this revenge; the loss of identity through taking on an alien name is another.

Fantasio's adoption of the jester's role wreaks vengeance against the spiritual realm as well. From his first appearance in the castle garden, the new jester is primarily occupied with firing off as many quips and puns as possible: "It is so difficult sometimes to tell a witty quip from an inanity! The most important thing is to talk a lot; the worst pistol shot can hit the bulls-eye if he shoots seven hundred eighty shots a minute just as well as the most expert marksman who only shoots one or two well-aimed ones" (II, 1). Word play will be the means of sapping the intellectual order of the universe: "I'm in the midst of turning the universe upside down to put it into an acrostic," he says a little later on. The primary weapon is the *calembour*, the pun, which by its nature destroys the original sense of an expression and turns it at random into another path. For example, when the Princess accuses Fantasio in the same scene of overhearing her conversation with her governess and advises him to "mind his own ears," Fantasio turns the "sense" of her expression around: "Not my ears, but my tongue. You've got the wrong sense. There's a mistake in sense in your words." He reveals the systematic intent of his plays on words immediately thereafter: "A pun can console us for many a sorrow; and playing with words is as good a way as any to play with thoughts, actions, and beings."

In the fifth scene of Act II we begin to see that rapid-fire word play is not only a destructive weapon in response to the grotesques' "round Spenserian hand"—the antidote to the mechanical and formal being naturally enough the improvisational—but also a systematic means of combatting the deadly trap of mechanical causality. Fantasio engages the Princess' interest by his extravagant claims concerning a stuffed bird which sings like a nightingale, thanks to the clever mechanism within it. He proceeds to establish a parallel between the mechanical bird and the Princess, whose destiny prevents her from marrying the Prince of her choice, in the best democratic pattern, and who is compared with a mechanical doll.

> They have a little spring under the left arm, a pretty little
> spring of fine diamond, like a playboy's watch. The tutor or
> the governess winds the spring, and immediately you see the
> lips open with a most gracious smile; a charming cascade
> of honeyed words issues forth in a soft murmur, and all
> the social graces, like airy nymphs, begin to dance around
> on the tip of their toes, round about the marvelous fountain.
> The suitor opens his eyes wide in astonishment: the spec-
> tators whisper indulgently, and the father, filled with secret
> contentment, looks proudly down at the golden buckles
> on his shoes.   (II, 5)

I need not underline the fact that the speech is a close paraphrase of E. T. A. Hoffmann's *Coppelius*. Musset certainly makes no attempt to disguise his source by changes in detail. But what is central to the German story-teller's plot here is used as a metaphorical accessory to Fantasio's argument; the Princess, as far as he can know (given their spiritual isolation), is a willing puppet of mechanical destiny, in its political guise. Finally, when Elsbeth asks him how he dares to speak so boldly to her, how he manages to strike home with so many of his thrusts, and whether his remarks are really pointed or he is speaking only at random ("au hasard"), he replies: "Oh, at random: I direct many of my remarks at random. He's my closest confidant." The apparent playfulness of this remark should not mislead us: Fantasio is engaging in systematic word play, and at the same time underscoring an important theme of the second act, which is the primary resolution of his dilemma: that of "hasard," or chance.

Destructive or improvisatory word play is only one aspect of Fantasio's recourse to "hasard" in order to escape his destiny. In retrospect, he can see the sequence of events arising from his encounter with Saint-John's funeral procession first as the working of an obscure force which counteracts the mechanical boredom of the first act: "How unpredictable chance is! I had to get drunk, and encounter Saint-John's funeral, to take his costume and his place; in sum, I had to commit the greatest folly on earth, in order to see in a mirror the only two tears that this girl will ever shed on her bridal veil" (II, 3). Then, in the prison scene, it becomes the only credible equivalent of Providence, replacing beneficent divine direction of human affairs (with the help of a few drinks):

> I don't know whether Providence exists, but it's amusing
> to believe so. In any case, here is a poor little princess
> who was about to wed a filthy animal against all her better
> instincts, a country pedant on whose head chance happened
> to drop a crown, as Aeschylus' eagle dropped its turtle.
> All was ready: the candles were lit, the suitor's wig
> powdered, the poor little girl all confessed. She had dried
> the charming tears I saw her shed this morning. Nothing
> was left but three or four signs of the cross for her life-
> long unhappiness to be all in order. The fortune of two
> kingdoms, the peace of two populations were at stake; and
> I had to go and get the idea of disguising myself as a hunch-
> back, to come and get drunk again in our good king's
> pantry, and to hook his dear ally's wig on the end of a
> fishline! In truth, when I'm drunk, I think I have something
> superhuman about me. (II, 7)

The effect of alcohol is, of course, a wonderful aid to the free working of chance and random choice; perhaps it might take the place of baptism and grace in the new religion. Musset later seemed to think so. It is certain, in any case, that Fantasio has found the answer to his spiritual unrest of the first act. Even the Prince, his philosophical antagonist, recognizes the workings of

Providence in the peculiar chain of events leading to his dewigging. But he still attributes this Providence to a benign God who
supports the pretentions and desires of legitimate monarchs:
"Ah, there is a Providence! When God suddenly sent me the
idea of disguising myself, when the thought flashed through my
mind: 'I must disguise myself'—this fatal event was foreseen by
destiny" (II, 6). The parallelism of his words with those of Fantasio emphasizes the directly antithetical world views of the two
characters.

The importance of the idea of "hasard" to Musset as a dominant philosophical and literary theme can be judged by looking
forward to the beginning of his theatrical decline: to 1838 when,
under the influence of a neotragic revival inspired by the actress
Rachel, he was to write that classical tragedy, as the Greeks conceived it, was no longer possible and must be renewed on a different moral base. "What they called destiny or fatality no longer
exists for us. Christianity, on the one hand, and modern philosophy on the other, have altered everything: only Providence and
chance are left for us; neither of them is tragic. Providence would
only make for happy endings; and as for chance, if we take it as
an element of a theatrical work, that is precisely what produces
those formless dramas in which events happen without our knowing why, except in order to end the play."[21] (It sounds almost
like a specific abjuration of *Fantasio*!)

What does this signify in its larger perspective? That Musset
turned from the concept of chance, as well as from the free fantasy of his earlier comedies, in favor of the vain hope that a
return toward the past, toward more strictly and traditionally
defined forms, would renew his inspiration. But the attack itself
sheds light on the importance that "hasard" possessed for him
earlier, its connection with the idea of Providence as a possible
replacement for earlier metaphysical concepts. *Fantasio* represents a dramatic working-out of the idea that chance and Providence could even be identified with one another.

All that remains for Fantasio, then, is to establish the possi-

21. "De la tragédie," in *Oeuvres complètes en prose*, text established
and annotated by Maurice Allem et Paul-Courant, "Bibliothèque de la
Pléiade" (Paris, 1960), p. 910.

bility of a life constantly open to the beneficent workings of chance. The castle garden represents one such possibility. A profound change in his fortune and mood has come about through the act of swapping his clothes for the jester's and entering the royal household. For Fantasio, the castle represents from the beginning a paradoxical liberty. This should not surprise us, since the physical liberty of Act I was the locus of Fantasio's sense of spiritual imprisonment, giving rise to metaphors of mental strangulation in which the limits of the city became confused with the boundaries of his skull.[22] In his new cage he feels "as free as a bird." "The size of a palace or a room does not make a man more or less free. The body moves where it can, at times the imagination opens wings as broad as the heavens in a prison cell no bigger than a man's hand" (II, 5). Thus Musset's whimsical hero, like Julien Sorel, prefigures the alienation of Camus' Stranger—here, a Portrait of the Stranger as Young Clown. The prison cell in which he finds himself in the final scene seems far from unpleasant to him, if we are to judge by the exalted mood of his first speech (II, 7).

But if the palace has provided him with the setting and material for one random, amusing sequence of events, it is only a single place, lending a single chain of possibilities. The role of court jester is a privileged one in its constant opportunities for word play, comic action, and discovery. Even if Elsbeth pays off all his debts and permits him to stay on as her father's buffoon, however, Fantasio knows that he will be unable to stay with a single occupation: "In truth, if I were forced into it, I would jump out of the window and run away one of these days" (II, 7). Even his debts, it would seem, are necessary to his sense of precarious well-being.

Thus it is that the Princess suggests the natural locus of Fantasio's new-found freedom from mechanical destiny: the little garden in which she first found him picking flowers and uttering paradoxes. The garden is a new Paradise for both Fantasio and Elsbeth, the Adam and Eve of the religion of chance. There Fantasio will be able to put on his jester's costume and put off

22. This foreshadowing of Baudelaire's fourth "Spleen," in the *Fleurs du Mal*, is another of the numerous links between the two poets.

the cares of the real world. There the Princess will remain forever a maiden, thanks to Fantasio's defeat of the Prince of Mantua, forever almost on the verge of falling in love with her savior —but not quite. Fantasio from now on will have the possibility of entering and leaving as his fancy dictates, of destroying the troublesome predictability of the world outside by his word play. The garden will be for him a Paradise of Gidean *disponibilité*, of availability or freedom of choice, where not even the unexpected can become too predictable. The Princess' garden, between two worlds, with its unlocked door like the door of the prison which she opens at the end for Fantasio, provides the open end, dramatically and thematically, which marks the resolution of Fantasio's existential dilemma. His salvation rests on a perpetual and perpetually renewed evasion. This resolution requires the possibility of turning away from besetting problems, cyclically, in order to diminish their pressure: the garden is an eye in the cyclone of necessity, a calm refutation of the existence of problems.

Whether or not this thematic resolution is a satisfactory or even a durable one on the level of human experience can be of no particular interest to anyone but the moralist. What concerns us is the justness of Musset's resolution of dramatic and thematic tensions. In this sense *Fantasio* is a consistent literary whole, a most satisfying dramatic construction, and not just, to repeat Jules Lemaître's phrase, "the dreamiest of dreams." We have seen that the play makes use of all the resources of literary art in order to present its theme: the existential dilemma which confronts its disillusioned idealist-hero. Musset exploits an apparently static first-act structure in order to let us enter into the sense of frustration which characterizes Fantasio, and a highly imaged, "poetic" prose to let us know how he became that way. He uses metaphors of stagnation, of stifling, and of power imbalance (the insect images, the reversal of physical and spiritual world in terms of Munich, etc.) to make us feel his hero's discomfort and at the same time his aspiration toward something better. And he introduces characters on two levels of reality, his protagonists and his grotesques, in order to embody two alternative approaches to the problem of living in a world which threatens the spiritual existence of men by its mechanical fatality.

Then, in the second act, Musset evolves in most dramatic fashion a thematic resolution of this existential dilemma. The confrontation of the rigid grotesques and of the real characters on the battlefield of sentiment ends happily in the former's rout. Trapped by his own submission to habit and to role (symbolically represented for us by clothing and handwriting), competing for the "real" love of the Princess, the grotesque Prince must succumb to the assault on his wooden dignity represented by Fantasio's snatching of his wig. Fantasio himself, true to the authentic stalemate in his character represented by the dilemma in the first act, must find a resolution that evolves dialectically from the poles of internal and external reality: not through the fairy-tale love of the Princess, as Paul de Musset would have wished (and as we will find in Musset's later play, *Carmosine*), but through an espousal of chance, of *disponibilité*, which will permit him ad infinitum to find the paradoxical liberty of the castle (and his role as jester), and yet to escape into the outside world which will always tempt him.

It is then perhaps understandable and fitting that *Fantasio* should seem a kind of improvisation, since that is the resolution which its hero finds in the end. But this is a carefully planned "improvisation." Musset, like all great artists, exploits the implications and the possibilities of form, rather than accepting it as convention. Thus the two-act division, with its open end; the change in rhythm between the two acts; the apparent disjointedness of its movement from scene to scene, from set to set, from grouping to grouping: all enhance the development and resolution of theme and character which form the logical structure of the play. But nothing is more revealing of Musset's profound mastery of literary and dramatic resources than his original handling of character, in the confrontation between differing levels of reality and realization. It is here, in the clash between character and caricature, that we find best illustrated the existential theme of the play: out of the defeat of the grotesques' mechanical imitation of life comes the affirmation of freedom and improvisation as the only durable antidote to the mechanics of destiny.

On ne badine pas avec l'amour, Act I, Scene 5.
Théâtre National Populaire: Robert Arnoux (Blazius),
Georges Wilson (the Baron), Raymond Bour (Bridaine).
Courtesy of Agence de Presse Bernand, Paris.

Chapter 5 Multiplicity and Integrity in

On ne badine pas avec l'amour

Perdican, the son of a provincial baron, and Camille, the latter's niece, return to the chateau in which they spent their childhood. They have completed their education: Perdican at the Sorbonne, Camille in a convent. Accompanying them are their tutors, the bibulous cleric Master Blazius and the devout spinster Dame Pluche, whom a rustic chorus greets with ironic formality. The Baron has announced to his village curate, Master Bridaine, his decision that the two young people are to be married. He is therefore most irritated to observe that Camille greets her cousin with an affectation of prudish reserve. The reason soon becomes apparent: although Perdican is delighted to rediscover the joys and the friends of his boyhood, Camille has decided to renounce the world and take the veil. But the girl, apparently uncertain in her vocation,—and piqued by Perdican's good-natured resignation,—begins to play a double game: while Perdican consoles himself with a village girl, Rosette, Camille has the shocked Dame Pluche carry a note to him asking for a last rendezvous. There she puts aside her cold airs and questions her cousin on his Paris loves. In a scene of rising emotional tension, the two young people enunciate their opposed views on life. Camille, who has been the confidant of a nun with a story of unhappy marriage and a love affair before entering the convent, will embrace only an eternal lover to avoid the risk of disappointment. Perdican accuses her of refusing to live and, against Ca-

mille's vicarious disillusionment, proclaims a doctrine of passionate experience which transcends disappointment:

> Farewell, Camille, return to your convent, and when you
> hear those horrible tales which have poisoned your mind,
> answer them in these words: "All men are liars, unfaithful,
> false, prattling, hypocritical, fatuous and cowardly, despic-
> able and sensual; all women are fickle, scheming, vain,
> curious, and depraved; the world is a bottomless cesspool
> in which hideous monsters crawl and squirm on piles of
> muck; but there is one sublime and holy thing in the world:
> the union of two of these imperfect, horrible creatures.
> You are often deceived in love, often hurt and often un-
> happy; but you love, and when you are on the edge of the
> grave, you turn around to look back, and you say to
> yourself: "I have often suffered, I have been mistaken
> sometimes, but I have loved. It is I who have lived, and
> not a counterfeit being created by my vanity and my
> weariness."   (II, 5)

Despite their ostentatious farewell, Camille and Perdican begin
a duel of vanities before the startled, uncomprehending eyes of
the Baron, Dame Pluche, and Masters Blazius and Bridaine (who
are conducting a tragi-comic duel of their own for the place of
honor at the Baron's table). Rosette becomes the pawn in the
lovers' struggle. Upon intercepting a letter to Camille's confidant, Sister Louise, in which the girl boasts of breaking his
heart, Perdican asks Rosette to marry him, knowing that Camille
is concealed in some nearby shrubbery. Camille in turn tricks
him into confessing that he still loves her, after hiding Rosette
behind a curtain so that she may hear him. Camille's mockery
only makes Perdican more obstinate in his resolve to wed the
unfortunate Rosette, who is trapped between her love for Perdican, her doubts about the suitability of their match, and the taunts
of the other villagers. At the climax of their frantic skirmishing,
Perdican comes upon Camille in the castle chapel, praying for
guidance in the conflict which is rending her soul. He takes her
in his arms, and the two lovers are united in a moment of sincere

abandon. But a terrible cry is heard: it is Rosette who has once again overheard them, and whose heart has been broken by this renewed shock. The play ends abruptly with Camille's words: "She is dead. Farewell, Perdican!"

This curious play, which begins with an archly stylized set of apostrophes by the chorus to its comic characters and ends on a melodramatic cry of despair, is generally accepted as Musset's most typical and most popular dramatic work, despite its internal contradictions and its moments of grandiloquence.[1] Its success in the theater has been constant since the first performance at the Comédie-Française in 1861, in a bowdlerized version which defrocked Blazius and Bridaine and eliminated from the dialogue most of its unseemly or irreligious language. It was not until January 8, 1923, that the national theater finally reinstated the original text: another instance of the tenacity with which Musset's posthumous destiny dogged his work.

The unevenness which characterizes *On ne badine pas avec l'amour*—its stylistic shifts, the change in mood, certain psychological discontinuities in its protagonists—elicited doubts as to the veracity of Paul de Musset's claim that the play was written in its entirety following his brother's return from Venice in the spring of 1834. An earlier, versified treatment of the opening scene, dating from prior to the trip with George Sand (published posthumously by Paul in 1861), gave initial evidence that the work had actually been written in two stages. Henry Bidou declared in 1920 that the first two acts, in which comedy and satire dominate, must date from the earlier period, whereas the melodramatic third act was evidently a product of Musset's shattering experience with George Sand.[2] Pierre Gastinel modified this view, adopting Bidou's conjecture that a part of the second act might also be included in the later phase of creation. His theory, which is substantiated by Auguste Brun's stylistic analysis, has obtained general acceptance: the climactic fifth scene of the second act, in which Perdican utters phrases borrowed from George

---

1. Cf. Lyonnet, Les *"Premières,"* p. 136.
2. "Le Théâtre d'Alfred de Musset—II. Le Théâtre d'Italie," *Conferencia* (October 15, 1920), p. 368.

Sand's 1834 correspondence with Musset, marks the point of cleavage between the earlier and the later texts.[3]

Despite this odd, patchwork creation, *On ne badine pas avec l'amour* does not seem to strike audiences as a flawed piece: its considerable success in that most classical of theaters, the Comédie-Française, bears witness to this. Even the ever-hostile Francisque Sarcey had to give his grudging assent: "Its initial idea does not seem clearly exposited to me; there is preciousness and false wit in the dialogue; the comedy is base and of bad quality; the climax is not at all prepared, and one cannot excuse its violence. All these flaws are swept away, in the theater, by a situation of inexpressible pathos; but they spoil for me that marvelous scene where Camille falls to her knees in prayer, struggling vainly against the love which afflicts her."[4] The play "works." Instead of looking at it as a flawed classic, it would be more fruitful to regard it as possessing a curious thematic and structural unity of its own. From a certain point of view, its very lack of homogeneity may be seen as an integral part of the effect it has exercised on readers and spectators for over a hundred years, both before and after its two-stage creation was brought to light.

Sarcey himself glimpsed an aspect of this unity when he spoke of the character of Camille as a "palimpsest": a superimposed personality composed of the woman created by nature, and the one produced by education.[5] Adolphe de Brisson went even further, when he saw Camille as "prophetic," the first contemporary heroine: "Beneath the wimple of the haughty and flirtatious nun, we descry a long line of complicated, misunderstood, impulsive, heedless, neurasthenic women. Half the heroines of the modern stage are derived from her."[6] Camille is only the more striking example, however, of a psychological phenomenon which affects both of the play's protagonists: the coexistence within a single person of multiple, conflicting personalities. Camille is a pas-

---

3. Gastinel, *Le Romantisme d'Alfred de Musset*, pp. 429–30. Brun, *Deux Proses de théâtre*, p. 93.

4. *Quarante Ans de théâtre*, IV, 266.

5. Ibid., p. 276.

6. Unidentified article of November 25, 1912, Fonds Rondel, Bibliothèque de l'Arsenal.

sionate woman whose thirst for love and genuine tenderness are countered by her ardent idealism and her fear of disappointment: rather than settle for a temporary idyll with a Perdican who will be unfaithful to her as he has been to his mistresses, she will become the "bride of Christ." Perdican is an intelligent but headstrong young man who genuinely loves his cousin, and seeks the calm, durable values that the village and its peasants represent; yet he is too jealous of his freedom, too piqued by Camille's insistence, to be willing to give guarantees or to swear fidelity.

As in *Fantasio*, we are here in the presence of that barrier to understanding which prevents even lovers from achieving real union: individuality, vanity, the insidious claims of the body. For Louis Jouvet, the give-and-take battle between Perdican and Camille is a quasiphysiological misunderstanding, the product of their age: "The two cousins parted when she was thirteen and he fifteen; they were not yet old enough to 'date'; they are reunited five years later; one evening they learn that they are going to meet. The girl has a sudden attack of modesty; she is confronted with a boy who is already a 'male'; she played with dolls in front of him; there is a *bouderie* which grows between these two people for inner reasons, childhood reasons, and everything develops from this *bouderie*."[7] Jouvet's explanation is a director's analysis, with its necessary limitations; but his association of the couple's misunderstanding with the coexistence in them of two mentalities, two ages, is particularly apt. It is one of the roots of conflict in this work, as in all of Musset's major theater. The emotional ambivalence of youth here takes on a special poignancy: Perdican and Camille are capable of knowing love for each other because they are young; but their youthful egoism is the very source of their duel. Camille has some of the child about her still —her despotic idealism is proof of that, as well as her petulance —but she has been given a kind of false experience by Sister Louise which makes her refuse real experience, with its danger, and cling to the absolutes of love and religion. Perdican has returned to the country to seek a kind of simplicity and stability which he lost in Paris—he speaks of a return to childhood—but at the same time he jealously stakes out his future so that no one,

7. *Tragédie classique et théâtre du xixe siècle* (Paris, 1968), p. 188.

not even the woman he loves, can dispute his entire claim to it.

In *On ne badine pas avec l'amour* more than in any other of Musset's comedies, we see the author's obsession with time and its treachery. Nostalgia for the past, even for a painful past; incapability of existing in the fleeting present; fear of the future, with its inevitable deceptions and betrayal of hope: few passages of his writings illustrate Musset's authentic preoccupation with the theme that dominates this play better than an apparently humorous plaint to his friend Alfred Tattet. Referring to his affair with George Sand of a year before, Musset wrote: "Alas! Alas! How I have gotten over it! How my hair has grown back on my head, my courage in my belly, indifference in my heart, on top of everything! On my return, I felt in absolutely fine shape; and suppose I told you that the good time is perhaps when you are bald, disconsolate and weeping!"[8] This is the other side of the coin: if past unhappiness is worth more, in the eyes of memory, than present tranquility, that is because tranquility has been purchased at too high a price—the ransom of youth and love demanded by time. The most painful realization of all is that, despite his lucidity and good will, Musset was condemned like all men to bear within himself the dead and dying remains of past emotions, thus of past selves, and to witness his own impotence to revitalize, to keep alive the stages of his past self, which he realized, nonetheless, were the capital moments of his existence —not only on the level of experience but on that of internal essence. It is this fatality of loss which he expressed through the mouth of the other Octave, the autobiographical hero of his *Confession d'un enfant du siècle*, in 1835: "You began by being good, you are turning weak, and you will end up mean."[9] The three temporal modes seem ineluctably informed by this descending progression.

On ne badine pas avec l'amour, straddling as it does two clearly defined periods of Musset's existence, translates this nagging obsession into striking dramatic terms; and its apparent structural duality should be understood in that frame of reference. But it is important to examine the play's thematic and dramatic structure

8. *Correspondance*, ed. Séché, p. 120; letter of July 21, 1835.
9. *Oeuvres complètes en prose*, p. 276.

in the light of its peculiar literary unity, and not only as an exceptionally moving document of the pathetic circumstances surrounding the "drame de Venise." The intriguing parallels of Perdican-Camille and Musset-Sand have contributed, no doubt, to the disproportionate amount of critical attention paid to the emotional battle engaged in by the protagonists of *On ne badine pas avec l'amour*. The presence of bits of dialogue obviously drawn from life, fragments of correspondence, and the suggestive polemic between hero and heroine shift the focus of interest away from the play's inner structure, toward external points of reference and toward psychological analysis. The work's superficial regularity, which has no doubt facilitated its theatrical success (unlike *Les Caprices de Marianne*, performance variants are limited almost solely to the excision of political and religious references), has further discouraged examination of its construction. As Pierre Gastinel pointed out, *On ne badine pas avec l'amour* is characterized by a curious sort of classical unity, its three acts taking place on successive days around noon.[10] What he did not notice, apparently, is that our awareness of this time setting is dependent on the grotesque Blazius and Bridaine's gastronomic jousts. By examining the connection between the play's external regularity and one of its essential themes—the protagonists' search for self and personal integrity—we may see how the relationships which bind together primary characters and *fantoches*, through the medium of Musset's irony and the multiple points of view he establishes toward his protagonists, are a fundamental element of the play's dramatic structure.

Although Musset uses grotesque characters in *Les Caprices de Marianne* and *Fantasio*, as we have noted, he does not bring us into contact with them so quickly or so strikingly as in this play. The Chorus's half-poetic, half-satirical apostrophes draw wonderfully charged portraits of the pair of tutors which, aesthetically, go far beyond Octave's lightning darts at Claudio in their exchange of insults:

> Swaying gently on his elegant mule, Master Blazius advances through the blooming cornflowers in his new

10. *Le Romantisme*, p. 332.

clothes, his writing-board at his side. Like a baby on its
pillow, he rocks on his well-rounded belly, and with half-
closed eyes, he mumbles *Our Fathers* into his triple chin.
Hail, Master Blazius, you arrive with the harvest-time,
like an ancient amphora.

Joggling harshly on her winded donkey, Dame Pluche
struggles up the hill; her sweating groom swats the poor
animal for all he is worth, and it shakes its head, nibbling
at a thistle. Her long, skinny legs tremble with rage, while
she scratches at her rosary with bony fingers. Good day
to you, Dame Pluche; you arrive like the fever, with the
wind that yellows the woods.   (I, 1)

Furthermore, in the two earlier works we are conscious of a
dialogue, an existential dialectic between grotesques and real
characters. There is more true interaction between the two classes
of being than in this play: Marianne's elderly husband Claudio,
for all his ridiculousness, is the agent of death for Coelio; the
Prince of Mantua is a threat to the happiness of both Elsbeth and
her kingdom. This effective participation of grotesques in the
action is nowhere to be found, however, in *On ne badine pas avec
l'amour*. The Baron, though father and uncle to the protagonists,
is essentially a bewildered, frustrated observer of the course of
events, signifying his impotence by reiterating after each report
that comes in to him, "That is impossible" or "That is unheard
of!" Blazius and Bridaine, far from exerting any effect on the
central dramatic progression, carry out an unrelated action, a
burlesque epic subplot having to do with the gaining or losing
of honors at the Baron's copious table. And Dame Pluche, a dried-
out caricature of Camille's devoutness and prudery, is ironically
limited in her action to the role of unwilling and ineffectual go-
between. Although all of these puppet figures spend their time
discussing and reporting on the extravagant actions of the protagonists, their confusion suggests to us that they live in another
world, totally separate from the emotional and spiritual goings-
on of the real characters.

And yet in this play (unlike *Fantasio*, where strikingly enough the hero and his grotesque "rival" never meet or even share the stage), Musset chooses to have his protagonists and his grotesques appear at the same time in a variety of combinations and circumstances (Act I, scene 2; Act II, scene 1; Act III, scenes 4, 6, and 7), or else to have them divide a scene alternately (Act I, scene 3; Act III, scenes 1 and 2). In the latter case, by making his two sets of characters share, but separately, the place and time of the action, Musset creates a simultaneous sense of division and unity which is in some ways the most typical sign of his theatrical genius. As critics of the author have pointed out, it is his need to dramatize the dialectic of his own personality and of the human soul which lies at the basis of his enduring greatness as a playwright, and the relative decline of his reputation as a poet. Nowhere is this need more manifest than in the double incarnation of Musset in *Marianne*, as Coelio and Octave. But it finds expression as well, if quite differently, in *Fantasio*'s existential dilemma and resolution, where the hero has to defeat the mechanism of destiny by evincing his grotesque double, the Prince.

This dialogue of man with himself (with his other self) is worked out in somewhat more complex terms in *On ne badine pas avec l'amour*. The complication is due to the fact that Musset chooses here to embody his psychological and existential problem—unity and integrity of the personality vs. fragmentation and multiplicity—not only in two central characters, but in two sets of characters: Perdican and Camille (the "real" protagonists), and the grotesques. Furthermore, the problem is stated not only in terms of the dialogue between characters and sets of characters, but also in terms of each one of the main characters themselves, in time: childhood, maturity, and old age. And this time motive is further complicated by the fact that it is distributed as well between Perdican and a third group of characters, existing on yet another plane of literary reality: the Chorus.

It is the Chorus, half caricature and half real character, which makes us aware from the first scene of the play that number—unity vs. duality, and integrity vs. multiplicity—is to be one of the major themes informing the work. Does the Chorus speak as one man or several, at once or separately? Conflicting answers have been supplied in production. At any rate, the Chorus seems to be both humane and anonymous. And it is the Chorus which first reveals to us, through its delightfully artificed introduction of Blazius and Pluche (as well as later on, in its mock epic account of the clerics' duel at table) that all "matched pairs" are inherently ridiculous, whether they are matched by polar opposition or by Tweedledee-Tweedledum similarity.

Placed as it is between grotesques and real characters, the Chorus comments from a middle distance on the progress of affairs between Perdican and Camille (compare, for example, Act I, scene 3, and Act III, scene 4):

> Two formidable eaters are present at this moment in the castle, Master Bridaine and Master Blazius. Have you noticed something? When two men who are more or less similar, equally fat, equally stupid, with the same vices and the same passions, happen to encounter one another, they must of necessity either adore or execrate each other ... I foresee a clandestine struggle between the tutor and the curate. Each one is armed with equal impudence; each has a barrel for a belly; not only are they gluttons, but they are gourmets; both will fight at dinner not only over quantity, but over quality ... Already I see their elbows on the table, their cheeks aflame, their eyes popping, their triple chins trembling with hatred. They gaze at each other from head to toe, they feel each other out by rapid skirmishes; soon war is declared; pedantries of all sorts fly through the air and, to crown the catastrophe, Dame Pluche squirms about between the two drunkards, jostling now one, now the other with her pointed elbows.

> Assuredly something strange is going on at the castle; Camille has refused to marry Perdican; she is to return today to the convent from which she came. But I believe my lord her cousin has consoled himself with Rosette. Alas! the poor girl does not realize what danger she is risking by listening to the words of a young and amorous nobleman.

It thus establishes a sort of parallel between the ridiculous matched pairs of the *fantoches* and the ill-matched pair of protagonists. This parallelism, or ironic echo, is not merely incidental but essential to the structure of the play.

Nowhere else in his dramatic production does Musset make such extensive use of deliberately visible artifice as in this work. His borrowing and adaptation of the Greek chorus is only the first of many palpably "theatrical" and traditional devices in the play. Our entry into the central action—the amorous duel between Perdican and Camille, and its tragic end with the death of Rosette—comes via a series of artificial hurdles which serve as successive frames, creating through the introductory comments of the Chorus, Master Blazius, Dame Pluche, and then the Baron an effect of aesthetic distancing between the spectator/reader and the "real"—internal—action of the protagonists. Despite the intimacy of atmosphere that characterizes this play, one cannot help feeling that the author's irony required this technique of multiple aesthetic frames to reinforce the isolation of his protagonists within their existential framework, and in themselves.

Is this not the real explanation of the fact that much of the action of *On ne badine pas avec l'amour*—of its central plot as well as its subplot—is "narrated" (if we may so term the grotesques' babblings) in a caricature of the classical messenger or chorus, rather than acted? Perdican walking arm in arm with Rosette ("a turkey-keeper!" in the Baron's shocked stereotype) and making incomprehensible ricochets on the duck-pond; Camille giving her note for Perdican to Dame Pluche, who hops up and down in the alfalfa. It is all seen as through a glass, darkly but with a grotesque rather than a tragic darkness of the spirit. That it is Bridaine, in the first case, and Blazius, in the second, who narrates the events in question to the near-apoplectic Baron is of the utmost significance. Both narratives affect the status of the speakers themselves, for better or for worse, in the Baron's myopic eyes. Both also contribute to his sense of confusion and futility in regard to the complex drama that is unfolding under his roof, despite all his plans. The narratives thus contribute to the development of the trivial subplot acted out by the grotesque characters in echo to the real drama. But at the same time, they serve an inverse function of distancing in relation to the protagonists. The audience must look at the latter more objectively, see them not only as they themselves, our hearts, and the author's evident sympathy see them, but also as the indifferent world, the inane, heartless marionnettes (thus our wit), and the author's irony perceive them. This technique of multiple vision fulfills the needs of the deeper theme underlying Camille and Perdican's unrequited love: the problem of human integrity or integration.

Jean Pommier noted one aspect of this theme in speaking of the "duel of the characters" as the central dramatic unity of the play's action. As he wrote, "for Musset the individual is but the mutilated half of the complete being, the couple; and yet it is he [the individual] who thus sets the embattled sexes one against the other."[11] Certainly the joust between the two halves of Aristophanes' primordial jig-saw puzzle is the most evident single manifestation of this theme in the play; as Pommier remarked, it contains within itself the central tragic irony, the struggle between individual integrity and human emotional need. But the problem can be reduced to a lower common denominator: resolution of the conflict between multiplicity and integrity within the individual, what we may call the *duality* of the characters.

Seen in this context, the Baron's heartfelt and inadequate complaint, relayed to Perdican by Master Blazius ("The Baron thinks he has noticed that your natures are not in agreement," II, 1) takes on an ironic double meaning. It is not only that the natures of Perdican and Camille do not "match" properly; there exists within the character of each a profound, irreconcilable split which acts to prevent their match. In the case of Camille, it is the "counterfeit being" or "borrowed character" which Masson astutely sees as her flaw, rather than the traditionally noted pride.[12] Like so many of Musset's young characters, she has a combination of immaturity and precocious disillusionment—in this case, through the vicarious experience of Sister Louise, her initiator into the ways of men. Like Fantasio, she has "the month of May on her cheeks" but "the month of January in her heart."

11. *Variétés sur Alfred de Musset et son théâtre* (Paris, 1944), p. 91.
12. "Le Masque, le double et la personne dans quelques Comédies et Proverbes," p. 569.

It is only in the final scene of the play that the two halves of her character are momentarily reintegrated.

Perdican, too, is a character in quest of his integrity, even more consciously than Camille. He has returned home not so much in search of a bride as in search of his past. Through the comforting "forgetfulness of what one knows" (not merely the material of his studies), he wishes to reintegrate his present, doctoral, and sentimentally experienced self with the innocent joy of his youth. Perdican seeks a harmonization of all the conflicting forces within him, a unity that will reconcile the contradictions of which his experience in time has made him conscious. That is why, in a significant inversion of the Baron's characteristic formula of intellectual rigidity, Musset has him reply "That is possible" to Camille's remark that he has contradicted himself in the climactic scene of the second act (II, 5). Perdican's most ardent desire is to keep for himself the flexibility, the *disponibilité* which will make it possible for all these contradictions to form a unity across time. It is somewhat in the same vein that we have the Chorus' paradox of being both father and child to the returning scholar (I, 4): this is not just an illustration of "the child being father to the man," but a fleeting moment of temporal stasis and integration.

This desire for flexibility as an antidote to fragmentation and as a principle of personal unity is at the basis of Perdican's curious reply to Camille's question concerning an allegoric picture hanging in the castle gallery. Musset here uses the tableau in a characteristic fashion reminiscent of the stirrup-cup in *Fantasio*. The painting, which represents a monk in his cell and a dancing goatherd, suggests that peculiar duality so dear to the author, representing for Camille the dilemma which her pride prevents her from resolving until it is too late: eternity or the present, sacred or profane love. Like Fantasio, she dwells on the source of her perplexity and cherishes the unreconciled duality which the picture expresses. But Perdican rejects the symbol brutally, with a striking affectation of incomprehension: the painting represents for him two "flesh and blood" men, "one who is reading and another who is dancing"—nothing more. With his fourfold doctorate, Perdican ought at least to be capable of perceiving the symbolic significance of the painting to Camille. But he refuses to understand: in part because of his intellectual program ("forgetfulness of what one knows"), in part because he rejects the spiritual dilemma which Camille is attempting to resolve—but also because his principle of self-integration is precisely the opposite of what a symbol stands for. He is seeking human integrity within the life-stream, in time. His attempt to harmonize contradictions is inimical to the rationality of the symbol, which emphasizes duality and choice, Camille's idealistic either-or. To see the two figures as standing for distinct, exclusive types, worthy of more or less esteem according to a hierarchy of values, would be to reject or to censure one of the parts of himself which Perdican is trying to bring into inclusive harmony.

But Perdican's pride, like Camille's, is a self-defeating element in his personality insofar as self-integration is concerned. His response to the Baron's displeasure at the disaccord between Camille's nature and his own has echoes of the grotesques' typical rigidity: "That is unfortunate; I can not remake mine" (II, 1). The hero seems here to be refusing all compromise in his possible adaptation to the emotional needs of the couple; he is also, implicitly and unconsciously, refusing the very principle of flexibility which he will propound to Camille (II, 5). His unwillingness to bend or to yield is the most important element of delay on his part in the series of amorous skirmishes, the "duel" through time, which is the principle of action in this play. Here, indeed, we must take cognizance of the dramatic structure of *On ne badine pas avec l'amour*. Musset's play is not a polemical comparison between two kinds of life, or two manners of looking at life. The drama of Perdican and Camille is that they are indeed, obviously, the mutilated parts of one kind of human integrity: the fragile unity of the human couple, "the union of two of these imperfect, horrible creatures." Their tragedy lies in not being able to realize this integrity *in time*. I mean this latter expression in its ambiguity: the couple's ephemeral moment of knowledge and hope in Act III, scene 8, arrives just before the consequences of their badinage across the time of the action, their game of hide-and-seek with love, are realized in the death of Rosette. It is there, in the sudden cry of recognition ("She is dead. Farewell, Perdican!"), that the real force of Musset's seemingly innocent title strikes us. Not only *must* one not "play with love"; one *does* not play with love: it never turns out to be play.

The profound reason has been established in the work cumulatively throughout its action—in the joust between the protagonists, which has revealed the difficulty of union for a couple composed of powerful (and imperfectly self-integrated) individualities; but also in extensive play with number both among the minor characters and between them and the protagonists. The grotesques' intense consciousness of number recalls Fantasio's temptation to count from one to infinity for the rest of his life, and thereby join their ranks. It is particularly striking in this play, from a thematic point of view, and is typified in the thought and language of the Baron. From the beginning, his highest criterion for recommending Perdican and Camille's union is the "six thousand *écus*" their education has cost him (I, 2). His unhappiness in his solitude at the provincial castle is expressed poignantly by the "three months of winter and three months of summer" he must spend there (ibid.) as royal tax collector. Master Blazius' description of a dispute between Camille and Dame Pluche is transformed by the Baron's obsession, which seizes on and grotesquely magnifies the numbers in the tableau: "What possible reason could Dame Pluche have for crumpling a paper folded in four while jumping up and down in one patch of alfalfa!" (II, 3).[13] The honor of his family, impugned by Blazius' observations on the protagonists' strange behavior, is guaranteed in the Baron's eyes by the sheer number of its members: "Do you realize that we are thirty-seven males and almost as many women, both in Paris and in the provinces?" We must remember also that his severe judgment of Camille's great-aunt, a nun whose portrait the girl admires, is based on her not having contributed to the multiplication of this number (I, 2).

13. The manuscript fragments of *On ne badine pas avec l'amour* published by Jean Richer (Alfred de Musset, *Textes dramatiques inédits*, p. 196) underline Musset's intention in using these numbers: "une luzerne" is a correction for "la luzerne" in the original.

This obsession with numbers, so close to the center of the *fantoches'* nature, is the principle of dehumanization with which Perdican and Camille are struggling. It is thus not accidental that the Baron uses the slightly animalistic genealogical terms "males and women" in the quotation above. The tragedy of *On ne badine pas avec l'amour* is that human time is not to be understood merely in terms of the continuity, the duration, of experience. If that were the case, Camille and Perdican might be expected eventually to achieve union. But time is also, tragically, the accumulation and multiplication of human experiences, which leads to fragmentation of the vital sentimental continuity. We have noted that the grotesques in Musset's theater tend to be old: at least of another generation than that of the protagonists (with the exception of the Prince of Mantua, who represents Fantasio's temptation, thus a kind of premature fossilization). That is not merely circumstance or even, in the accepted sense, a sign of the conflict of generations. The division of nature between younger and older characters is more profound because it is part of the tragic principle of Musset's drama. Old age, grotesqueness, and mechanical rigidity are synonymous in Musset's world, because passing time necessarily brings about that accumulation of sentimental mishaps and failures which eventually leads to fossilization—the hardening of the heart which the author's letters tell us he deeply feared. Is it not symptomatic of Musset's own decline, in this context, to witness the tempering of his *fantoches* which characterizes *Il ne faut jurer de rien* in 1836? That play marks his surrender to the "wisdom" of maturity, and a compromise with the tragic force that gives such poignancy to his youthful dramas (below, page 210).

If, in *On ne badine pas avec l'amour*, we see so much of the central action through the bewildered, distorting eyes of the grotesques, and if Musset constantly jostles our sensibilities by juxtaposing his protagonists' sentimental struggles with the mechanical absurdities of Blazius, Bridaine, Dame Pluche, and the Baron, it is evidently not in order for us to be made more aware of the latter's inanity in comparison with the lovers, which is obvious enough from the first scene. It is true that the grotesques tend to diminish in importance as the play progresses. But their function as aesthetic and spiritual windows—or deforming mirrors—is well established by the middle of the second act; and they remain present in a diminished way right up to the penultimate scene of the play. The reason for this narrative importance is that the *fantoches* are the deformed and deforming voice of Camille's and Perdican's destiny as suffering beings in a hostile universe, where the principal threat is that of fragmentation and destructive accumulation in the lives of those who seek continuity and unity through the endurance of human sentiment. Perdican is condemned at the end of the play to be the banal lover of the series of mistresses Camille has accused him of having—a series to which she both does and does not now belong, since she is one out of many, but not "the one." Camille, too, is left by destiny without having resolved her dilemma: she will be neither a good nun nor a woman loved, she can very well join the ambiguous group of disappointed "brides of Christ" in her convent.

Perdican and Camille thus succumb to their destiny through a double failure. Each fails to achieve a harmony of conflicting forces within his personality: love vs. pride, altruism vs. egotism, youthful passion vs. precocious cynicism. And by this failure they fail to attain that ultimate unity of Musset's romantic vision: the "union of two of these imperfect, horrible creatures" which Perdican, in his celebrated moment of lucidity at the end of Act two, sees transcending the base material reality of the physical world. In both instances the essential fault is rigidity, the triumph of the categorical and the mechanical over the fluid and humane. At the end, the *fantoches'* distorted vision of the protagonists replaces the latter's vision of themselves, for they have been caught in a trap of their own devising. The last-minute realization expressed in Camille's "Farewell, Perdican!" marks the final, total defeat, the end of the couple's brief chance for salvation through love. Its finality is all the more tragic for the implied years of anticlimactic mechanical life which will follow. How far Musset is here from *fin de siècle* optimism, the cyclical historicism with which post-'48, post-Romantic Frenchmen (except the Flaubert of *L'Education sentimentale*) consoled themselves for individual failure! Renan would write in 1885: "Antistius will be eternally reborn, to fail eternally, and, in the final analysis, it will come to pass that the totality of his failures will equal a victory."[14] But for Musset's protagonists, for Perdican, for Lorenzo, the sum of failures is the defeat of the individual, and nothing beyond that is of importance. Only Fantasio escapes that law—through a loophole. For his salvation is based on a perpetual juggling-act: the avoidance of commitment, the espousal of chance, and the acceptance of duality, of ambiguity, as the only defense against tragic realization.

In *Fantasio*, Musset underlines this refusal of final unity by his adoption of an open-ended form, the two-act play. Perhaps we may now also see a deeper significance to the action in Musset's apparent acceptance of classical "unity" and regularity in *On ne badine pas avec l'amour*. The tragedy of Perdican and Camille is symbolized by this reduction of human experience, in all its irregularity, improvisation, and indefinability, to the predictable shape of the traditional comedy. The ironic force of Blazius and Bridaine, that low-comic, mock-epic pair, is that the stroke of noon, echoing in the recesses of their gluttonous stomachs, marking three times the passage of a day in human time, is the death knell of Rosette and of Camille and Perdican's love, hope and youth. The sinisterly burlesque machinery of destiny, acting within the mechanism of the human body, has once again claimed a pair of victims for old age and death.

14. Ernest Renan, *Le Prêtre de Nemi*, in *Oeuvres complètes* (Paris, 1863–1926), XXVII, 261.

Lorenzaccio, Act III, Scene 1. Za Branou Theater of Prague:
Jaromir Janecek, *Scoronconcolo*; Jan Trislea, *Lorenzo*.
Courtesy of Photo Pic, Paris.

Chapter 6 The Strange Destiny

of *Lorenzaccio*

In recent years, more scrutiny has been given by critics to *Lorenzaccio* than to any other work of Musset: none of his plays, indeed no French drama of the nineteenth century, has been the subject of so many monographs.[1] This cannot be due merely to the size and complexity of the work. It is true that *Lorenzaccio* is Musset's only completed five-act drama, thus his sole candidate to the title of tragedy. It is almost twice as long and numbers about three times as many characters and scenes as any of his other plays. But if *Lorenzaccio* were merely an ambitious failure, as it once seemed to be even to Musset's admirers, or another example of that archetypical Romantic form the historical tragedy, its lot today would be that of Hugo's *Burgraves* or *Cromwell*, Dumas' *Henri III et sa cour* and *La Tour de Nesle*, Casimir Delavigne's *Louis XI*, or any of the dozens of specimens of this once-popular but swiftly forgotten genre. Indeed, the story of the first sixty years of the existence of *Lorenzaccio* would lead us to class it among the genre's least fortunate exemplars; for unlike many others it was not performed or even seriously considered for production during this period.

Yet *Lorenzaccio* has found belated success, not only in literary

1. The list includes Paul Dimoff, *La Genèse de Lorenzaccio* (Paris, 1936); Pierre Gauthiez, *Lorenzaccio* (Paris, 1904); Bernard Masson, *Lorenzaccio ou la difficulté d'être* (Paris, 1963); Joachim-Claude Merlant, *Le Moment de "Lorenzaccio" dans le destin de Musset* (Athens, 1955); and considerable portions of Henri Lefebvre's brilliant Marxist study, *Alfred de Musset dramaturge* and of Andre Lebois' *Vues sur le théâtre de Musset* (Avignon, 1966).

histories and studies but on the stage, where its author never really dared hope to see it. Ironically, it may now be termed the one truly stageworthy French historical tragedy of the Romantic era, and that alone would give it a claim to our attention. Its interest goes far beyond this *succès d'estime*, however. For, paradoxical as it may seem, this immense work of historical recreation, inspired directly by the sketch of another writer—George Sand—and elaborated from documentation in Benedetto Varchi's *Storia fiorentina*; this great fresco in five acts and thirty-eight tableaux, involving over thirty characters and set in the streets, marketplaces and palaces of Renaissance Florence is probably Alfred de Musset's most personal dramatic work, the one in which he dealt most intimately and profoundly with his besetting spiritual themes. This sample of an abandoned genre, consciously patterned after Shakespeare's *Hamlet* and his historical tragedies, turns out to be Musset's most original and perhaps his most modern literary creation. Its political and moral themes, which began to find a comprehending audience in France only after the painful experiences of World War II, speak to us now, to the world in which we live, in a terrible way which, save for a few prescient spirits, could not have been imagined in Musset's own time or the century which followed.

It is equally paradoxical that the disquieting facts about *Lorenzaccio*'s origins only came to light after its first public performance in 1896 by the renowned Sarah Bernhardt had inaugurated the play's gradual march to triumph. Throughout the nineteenth century, Paul de Musset's story of the work's creation was the accredited one: during Alfred's ill-fated trip to Italy with his lover, George Sand, he had discovered the subject of the play in "old Florentine manuscripts." Several letters to his family, written during his brief stay in the Tuscan capital and all of which mysteriously disappeared, allegedly told of the poet's plans and his pleasure in visiting the scenes of his future drama.[2] The play was thus supposedly written in its entirety during the couple's stay in Venice and the period following Alfred's return,

2. Cf. Paul de Musset, *Biographie d'Alfred de Musset*, in *Oeuvres complètes*, "l'Intégrale," p. 29.

alone, to Paris. If, like so many of Paul's affirmations, this story smacked of "ideal" literary biography or family legend, its inconsistencies and lacunae only began to trouble Musset scholars toward the turn of the century, when interest in his work was growing.

It was partly coincidental no doubt that the publication of a great deal of private material, both of Musset and of Sand, gradually permitted the truth to appear. In 1899 Madame Wladimir Karénine's biography of Sand referred to her treatment of the same historical material as *Lorenzaccio*. And in 1901, a note in Léon Lafoscade's classic study of Musset's theater revealed the startling information that this still unpublished document (whose contents he outlined) was quite evidently the model for Musset's play, which followed its basic action closely and reproduced some of its scenes in modified form. The document in question was *Une Conspiration en 1537*, a *scène historique* which Sand had written before her affair with Musset, while she was still the mistress of Jules Sandeau, and given to the poet for his use.[3] Two problems were raised: what was Musset's debt to the work of his mistress or, conversely, how original was *Lorenzaccio?*; and when was the work really composed, since Paul's version of its creation had been discredited?

Proper consideration of the first question had to await Paul Dimoff's publication of the Sand text.[4] Subsequent evaluations of Musset's debt seem to depend on the degree of partisanship which scholars and critics devote to the poet or his mistress. André Lebois, for example, criticized Dimoff for exaggerating the importance of Sand's text and Sand's share in the creation of *Lorenzaccio*, but his attitude toward the novelist throughout his study is one of profound disdain.[5] It is objectively certain that *Une Conspiration en 1537* is something between a sketch and a finished literary creation of minor importance. It is a fairly

3. Lafoscade, *Le Théâtre d'Alfred de Musset* (Paris, 1901), p. 129, note 7.

4. First in the *Revue de Paris*, 6 (December 15, 1921), 673–708; then in *La Genèse de Lorenzaccio*, in 1936 (revised edition, 1964).

5. *Vues sur le théâtre de Musset*, pp. 8–10, 43.

typical example of an ephemeral genre which flourished around the time of its writing: the "historical scene."[6] Essentially an off-shoot of the Romantic historical drama, it attempted to carry Stendhal's and Victor Hugo's precepts to their logical conclusion by representing in dramatic guise an actual sequence of historical events, without seeking to organize them into traditional dramatic structures or forms other than their own development. Sand's work is composed of six such episodes in the assassination of Alexander, Duke of Florence, by his cousin, Lorenzo de Medici. Five of her scenes correspond more or less directly to scenes in *Lorenzaccio*, and they provide what Lafoscade termed the "melodramatic portion" of Musset's play: Lorenzo's cowardly refusal to accept a duel, his talk with his mother and his aunt and an ironic discussion with two self-professed republicans, his sword practice with Scoronconcolo, the Duke's rendezvous with Lorenzo, and the assassination scene. Not only the sequence of events, but some of the characterization and even the language of Musset's play can be traced to George Sand's model.

But investigation has proven that Musset went much further than his mistress in examination of Varchi's chronicle; he also corrected several of her misreadings and errors.[7] George Sand's work thus sent him back to the sources, rather than serving as a basic point of departure. Furthermore, the disproportion between the six scenes of *Une Conspiration* and the thirty-eight of *Lorenzaccio*, between George Sand's linear treatment of the central action and Musset's complex tableau of the spiritual life of a city, with three interrelated major plots, makes it evident that the distance separating the two is paramount to that separating "real events" and a work of art. It is not simply a question of dimensions: Sand's hasty psychological and political sketch becomes a powerful, unified whole in Musset's hands, developing through the complex interweaving of its plots and scenes the moral life of the modern political city and its relationship with varieties of

6. For discussion of this genre and its influence on Musset's work, see Dimoff, *La Genèse*, pp. xxv–xxviii; Allem, in *Théâtre complet*, p. 1241; and Hassan El Nouty, "Théâtre et anti-théâtre au 19ᵉ siècle," *PMLA*, 79 (1964), 604–12.

7. See Dimoff, pp. xvii–xx, xxx–xxxiii.

individual conscience. Between its conception and its realization, through a series of intermediary plans and steps, the work became the summum of Alfred de Musset's spiritual and philosophical thought, expressed in a context whose reality and scope go far beyond those of the other works he produced during this time.

As for the second problem, the date of composition can be narrowed down to the years of his four major dramatic pieces, 1833–34, and even to the twelve months between August 1833, when his liaison with George Sand began, and August 1834, when *Lorenzaccio* was published.[8] Normally that would seem a sufficiently precise localization in time for the creation of a literary masterwork. Without going so far as to cite the seven years Flaubert took in writing *Madame Bovary* or comparably lengthy maturations, the establishment of literary chronology is usually a fairly straightforward question of relative dates and points of historical reference. But the case of Musset is exceptional, both for its tremendously accelerated rhythm and for the hectic emotional circumstances surrounding and influencing his work. Thus the second of the two problems raised by discovery of George Sand's historical scene has proven far more thorny than the first, and it has been the object of polemics almost to the present day.

On the one hand, the difficulty lay in assigning relative dates to *Lorenzaccio* and *On ne badine pas avec l'amour*. "Ideal" biography had taken the comedy necessarily to precede the tragedy, given the circumstances of Musset's life. The evidence of a preliminary, rhymed version of the comedy supported it. But as it became increasingly apparent from internal and external evidence that the latter play was actually written in two separate times, the temporal relationship of *Lorenzaccio* to it became more and more confused. In addition, the events of the lovers' unhappy "honeymoon" in Italy were so intricately entwined with

8. In *Un Spectacle dans un fauteuil*, "seconde livraison, prose," volume I, with *Les Caprices de Marianne*. It was the only one of the four plays not to appear first in the *Revue des Deux Mondes*—no doubt because of its length, but also because of its political and religious themes.

the creation of the two works that some effort had to be made to
unravel them, to elucidate the role of fact and fancy in the traditional interpretations of biographical influence on theme and
structure in the plays. For some, like Henry Bidou, *Lorenzaccio*
was more or less completely the product of Musset's stay in
Venice.[9] But the violent circumstances of this stay, marked by
first Sand's and then Musset's illness and the notorious Pagello
affair, made this explanation difficult to justify: when could Musset have found the time and energy to compose such a complex
work? For Pierre Gastinel, and for Paul Dimoff (before the
revised edition of his study), the play was begun before leaving
for Italy and elaborated in Florence and Venice; the question of
exact proportions was left open.[10] More recently, a penetrating,
exceptionally sensitive study of *Lorenzaccio* by Joachim-Claude
Merlant demonstrated in an apparently convincing way that, although the plans and first drafts of the play most likely precede
the poet's voyage to Italy, the terrible scenes in which Lorenzo's
spiritual anguish is exposed (especially in his dialogue with
Philip Strozzi), and the state of mind in which Lorenzo commits his murder had to result from the experience of betrayal by
George Sand and from Musset's own self-disillusionment, and
were therefore added to the play during Musset's convalescence
in Venice and following his return to Paris.[11] Maurice Allem,
who praises Merlant's psychological perception although he does
not share his conclusions, took a conciliatory attitude toward the
various views put forth, seeing the probability of stages in *Lorenzaccio*'s creation before, during, and after the Italian trip.[12]
Maurice Donnay, at another pole, maintained that Musset must
have written the play in its entirety following his return to Paris
from Italy.[13]

But the problem seems finally to have been resolved quite

9. Cf. "Le Théâtre d'Alfred de Musset" (December 1, 1920).
10. Cf. *Le Romantisme d'Alfred de Musset*, p. 448; and *La Genèse de Lorenzaccio*, 1936 edition, p. xliv.
11. See *Le Moment de "Lorenzaccio" dans le destin de Musset*, pp. 82–84, and passim.
12. In *Théâtre complet*, pp. 1243–48.
13. "Les Comédies de Musset" (June 29, 1924), p. 707.

simply by Jean Pommier's discovery of a letter dated from Venice on January 27, 1834, from Musset to Buloz, the director of the *Revue des Deux Mondes*, inquiring about publication plans for *Lorenzaccio*.[14] Pommier's explanation, to which Dimoff adheres in the revised edition of his study, is that Musset left the more or less completed manuscript of the play in Buloz' hands before going off to Italy, and he made only minor changes or additions to it upon his return. The ideal biography's logical interpretation of influence on the play by both Musset's sentimental experience with George Sand and his sightseeing in Italy is thus practically invalidated. The lesson is a sobering one for literary historians and biographers. Musset gives us the rare example of a very young author, with limited worldly and sentimental experience, creating from his readings and his intuition a work which foretells the profound crisis through which he was to live months later in extraordinary circumstances, and drawing the spiritual lesson which reason would tell us could only come from the maturing effects of that very experience. We witness a man writing a powerful historical tragedy, imbued with a deep pessimism, during the first happy months of a love affair which was to mark the emotional climax of his life; then composing the greater part of a comedy (the term, it must be admitted, is not entirely suitable to *On ne badine pas avec l'amour*) after his return from that shattering experience of illness and betrayal in a strange land which was to grow into the celebrated legend of the *drame de Venise*. Thus, in the midst of that astonishing production of four dramatic masterpieces during the brief space of his twenty-third and twenty-fourth years, Musset provides us with an even greater and more disturbing miracle of the creative genius at work.

The action of the play, based on historical events, takes place in Florence in the year 1536,[15] the period immediately following the downfall of the Florentine Republic and the return from

14. Cf. Pommier, *Autour du drame de Venise* (Paris, 1958), p. 100; and Dimoff, *La Genèse*, 1964 edition, p. xli.

15. Notwithstanding the title of George Sand's "historical scene": *Une Conspiration en 1537*.

exile of the Medici family. Alexander, the illegitimate son of Lorenzo II de Medici, has ruled for six years as Duke of Florence thanks to the support of Pope Clement VII and Emperor Charles V. His corruption and exactions at the expense of the common people and the noble houses of Florence are enforced by a body of German soldiers garrisoned in the newly built Citadel, symbol of the once-proud city's shame and subjection. Despite Alexander's tyranny and the disorder of his court, which threatens the honor and safety of every house in Florence, no effective movement of revolt has taken form. The ever-swelling ranks of exiles from the city are the only visible index of the people's resentment.

In this stifling moral and political atmosphere, three characters, members of important Florentine houses, are meditating action against Alexander: Lorenzo de Medici ("Lorenzaccio"), Philip Strozzi, and Marquise Ricciarda Cibo. The evolution of their attitudes and activities provides the three parallel main plots of the play.

The principal action centers about Lorenzaccio. As Alexander's cousin and the legitimate descendant of a collateral line of the Medici, he could have laid prior claim to the throne created in 1530 for Alexander, were it not for Clement's and Charles' machinations. After a studious boyhood in Rome, he has become Alexander's companion in debauchery and purveyor of women (thus earning his nickname: the suffix is pejorative). His mother, Maria Soderini, and his young aunt, Catherine Ginori, have watched Lorenzo's decadence with keen disappointment. Lorenzo's origins and his youthful idealism have maintained contacts for him with some of the republican houses, particularly that of his confidant, Philip Strozzi—but he is suspected of betraying his friends to the Duke. The degradation of Lorenzo's character is illustrated by two scenes early in the play: the opening one, in which we find him managing the abduction of a young girl, and a subsequent scene in which Lorenzo, challenged to a duel following an exchange of insults with Sir Maurice, chancellor of the Council of Eight, faints away at the view of a sword. Our suspicions, with those of the scheming Cardinal Cibo and Alexander's bodyguard, Giomo, are gradually confirmed: Lorenzo has been feigning, wearing a mask of corruption and cowardice in order to gain the intimacy and confidence of his cousin the Duke. He gradually reveals his intentions in a series of scenes culminating in a long dialogue with Philip Strozzi (III, 3). Several years before, in a moment of youthful exaltation, he vowed to rid his country of a tyrant, like the Roman Brutus. Following his exile from Rome for outrage to the Pope (he had struck the heads off statues of emperors in the Coliseum), Lorenzo came to Florence determined to assassinate Alexander and reestablish the Republic. But as he confesses to Philip and as his actions have revealed, the role he assumed has ended up by penetrating his character in insidious ways: he has become imbued with vice and excess, there is no way for him to regain his integrity. More than that, he has lost all his illusions concerning his fellow men, seeing the weakness and complicity with which the Florentines accept his pandering on behalf of Alexander. Lorenzo is determined to go through with the plot to which he has sacrificed his better self, but his act is henceforth devoid of real significance in his eyes: he knows it will be in vain, since the Florentines will not have the courage or the unity to profit by it. Stung to action at last by Alexander's insistence on seducing Catherine, whom Lorenzo idolizes as a model of virtue, he sets an ambush for the Duke in his bedroom, using his aunt as bait. After a vain attempt to rally the Florentine republicans, Lorenzo kills Alexander. His momentary elation at the accomplishment of his plan soon gives way to a profound depression. Lorenzo's forebodings are soon realized: he falls victim to a hired killer in Venice, where he has fled, and his body is kicked into the lagoon by a mob.[16]

The second action is linked to the first, having as its principal point of contact the friendship between Lorenzo and Philip Strozzi. Philip, the patriarch of the Strozzi clan, is represented by Musset as a scholarly idealist, devoted to the principles of justice and liberty. He hopes to bring about a return to the aristocratic republic of the past, convinced that action based on high ideals must eventually prevail. However, when his beloved

16. This is one of the few important historical details which Musset changed: Lorenzo actually was assassinated only in 1548, after twelve years of wandering in Turkey and France.

daughter Louise is insulted by Julian Salviati, one of the Duke's cronies, Philip's hot-tempered son Pierre swears to have Julian's life in revenge. Salviati, whom Pierre and his brother succeed merely in crippling, identifies his assailants and the Duke has them arrested. Outraged at this further insult to his family's pride, Philip convokes the forty Strozzi to a dinner, despite Lorenzo's warnings, to plan action against the Duke. Upon joining in a toast to the Medici's destruction, Louise falls dead, the victim of a poisoner. The Strozzi cry out for vengeance, but Philip, overwhelmed by the fatal consequences of his decision to act, refuses henceforth to take part in any plots. Pierre's attempt to unite the exiles and the leading families of Florence is thwarted by his father's refusal to lend his name and prestige: in a rage, he goes to offer his services to the King of France. Philip retires to Venice, where he receives Lorenzo's confession of futility just prior to the latter's ignoble death.

The protagonist of the third plot, Ricciarda Cibo, never meets either Lorenzo or Philip during the course of the action. Although she is deeply attached to her husband, she accepts a rendezvous with Alexander during the Marquis' absence and becomes his mistress. Her brother-in-law and confessor, the Cardinal Cibo, encourages her mysteriously in the affair. Ricciarda is motivated by an ambiguous mixture of idealism and sensuality. She hopes to use her influence over the Duke to turn him away from tyranny and corruption, to make him free himself from his servitude to the Emperor and the Pope, and by redeeming Florence win himself an enviable place in history. But it is also the Duke's brutish sensuality which draws her, the allure of this "butcher boy" turned prince. It is this side of Alexander which naturally prevails: Ricciarda ends up by tiring him with her highflown phrases, and he turns toward new conquests. But Ricciarda disappoints the Cardinal's plan to use her affair with the Duke to further his own political ambitions: she foils his blackmail attempt by confessing her transgression to her husband. In the end, as we learn by gossip, the husband forgives and the couple is once again as closely united as before.

These various plots (in both senses of the word) are resolved in the final scenes of the play: Cardinal Cibo succeeds in having his candidate, Cosimo de Medici, named Duke of Florence by the pusillanimous and indecisive Council of Eight. *Lorenzaccio* closes with a speech by Cosimo, drawn directly from historical documents, in which he promises to rule in such a manner as to offend no one—particularly the Pope and the Emperor, we understand. On this anticlimactic note the fate of the Florentine Republic and of Florence's glory as a political, intellectual, and artistic center of Europe is sealed forever.

Despite its transcendence of the genre's temporal and aesthetic limitations, there are reasons for taking *Lorenzaccio* as an example of the Romantic *drame historique*. First of all its immediate historical context: the theoreticians of the new literature had been calling fervently for the creation—or rather the fulfillment —of this genre since Népomucène Lemercier's odd melodramatic "spectaculars" in the early part of the century, but especially since Stendhal's call for a historical tragedy (along with a truly modern comedy) in *Racine and Shakespeare* and Victor Hugo's self-proclamation as its prophet in the celebrated Preface to *Cromwell*. Historical drama was the Great White Hope of Romanticism, the high serious genre which would displace neoclassic tragedy in the temples of national culture: in this case, the Comédie-Française, which Hugo's fanatics literally took by storm in 1830 at the triumph of *Hernani*. If, for readers today, the flowering of French Romantic art resides in the renewal of poetic vision and technique effected by Lamartine, Hugo, and Vigny (and Musset himself) which culminated in Baudelaire's *Fleurs du Mal*, for contemporaries and sympathizers the proving ground of Romantic doctrine was the drama. One of its early spokesmen, writing in an "official" journal, said: "Free historical tragedy may not be all of Romanticism; but it is certainly one of its most important branches, the one toward which present currents impell our minds the most irresistibly . . ."[17] The success or failure of the movement was held to turn on the fate of this new genre. It is traditional in France to date the triumph and fall of Roman-

17. Duvergier de Hauranne, in the *Globe* (March 24, 1825), cited by Georges Ascoli, *Le Théâtre romantique*, 5 fascicles, "Les Cours de Sorbonne" (Paris, 1936), p. 81.

ticism by the success of *Hernani* and the fiasco of *Les Burgraves* (1843: both, of course, works of Hugo).

Lorenzaccio thus falls historically in the midst of this genre's turbulent career. It arrived on the scene somewhat late for the initial messianic fervor which imbued the early years—and which success tended to dissipate. But Musset himself was a latecomer to the fold, through no fault of his own: he crashed the ranks of the Cénacle as soon as his precocious genius permitted. And if he was from the start a recalcitrant disciple, soon even a heretic, anathematized for his irreverence toward the cult, he more than paid his obligations in his first published works, which were veritable epitomes (or even caricatures) of the Romantic aesthetic.

In 1833 Musset's break with the Romantics had long been public knowledge. It had been announced as early as July 1830 in his satiric poem, "Les Secrètes Pensées de Rafael, gentilhomme français": "Racine, encountering Shakespeare on my table, / Falls asleep next to Boileau, who has forgiven them both." These strange bedfellows symbolize Musset's incapacity to accept any exclusive dogma. His individualism and his deep-rooted skepticism prevented him from being docile to any school, especially one as fanatical as Romanticism. "Romanticism" was an important and even dominant trait in Musset's nature, and his works present one of the movement's major landmarks. But it was a question of temperament, not a public adherence or a doctrinal allegiance.

Yet for Pierre Gastinel, *Lorenzaccio* represents the abjuration of Musset's literary independence, a gesture of reconciliation toward the Cénacle, its disciples and its dogma.[18] In the evolution of Musset's theater, Gastinel sees it as a return to artistic tenets which *Marianne* and *Fantasio*, indeed all the poet's ideas during the period 1830–33, tend to refute. Its very size, in contrast with the intimacy of the works surrounding it, reminds us of the Romantics' pretentions. Its evocation of a specific era—dear to their hearts—and of a particular sequence of historical events which attracted others in the group; its use of those elements of traditional form which Hugo deigned to accept from the past (the five acts of tragedy; a poetic, if not versified language); its dis-

18. *Le Romantisme d'Alfred de Musset*, pp. 449–50.

play of the required mixture of serious and comic, of "sublime and grotesque," which typified Hugo's revolt against the classical unities, along with the break from unity of time and of place: all these elements place *Lorenzaccio* so near the main stream of Romantic doctrine and practice that we cannot help being some-what surprised. Indeed for many the play remained a model of the type, the ideal Romantic historical drama, with all its ex-cesses and all its weaknesses. Witness, in 1927, Pierre Brisson's review of the work's first Comédie-Française production:

> Nothing is more simple and facile than Musset's philosophy
> [as compared with *Hamlet*]. It is entirely contained in the
> sorrowful, lyrical words that express it. It knows nothing
> of subtleties, innuendos, or dialectics; it is merely an ex-
> plosion of the heart . . . Musset evokes sixteenth-century
> Italy in a helter-skelter sequence of tableaux which seem
> to spring up at the whim of his fancy. The slightest figures
> tempt him to dally because of their picturesqueness. If
> he encounters the young painter Tebaldeo in the shadow of
> a church, he cannot resist the pleasure of writing a scene
> for him and drawing his portrait with a few inspired lines.
> He goes from Marquise Cibo's boudoir to the monastery
> to which old Strozzi retires, he leaves a masquerade for a
> procession, he dawdles along the banks of the Arno, he
> visits the palaces of Florence . . . The characters come to life
> before our eyes, take on Romantic coloration, and mingle
> in the drama.[19]

Brisson, like so many of his compatriots nurtured on the tradi-tion of neoclassicism, took the complexity of *Lorenzaccio* for chaos, its shifts of scene for casual formlessness, its appearance of spontaneity for lack of plan: all sure signs of "Romanticism" at its worst and, above all, most un-French!

Brisson's criticism compares the play—unfavorably—with the "depth" of *Hamlet*. Similarly, Paul Souday was to call Jules Lemaître's comparison of the two plays "taking a molehill for the Caucasus, and bladders for lanterns. The work is on the whole

19. In *Le Temps* (June 6, 1927), Fonds Rondel, Bibliothèque de l'Arsenal.

quite second-rate, one of Musset's worst . . . The comparison with *Hamlet* or *Faust* is simply grotesque. It isn't nearly worthy of *Hernani* or *Ruy Blas* . . . or even the comedies of Musset himself."[20] Here again we find an unflattering assimilation to the Romantics, Shakespeare being their touchstone above all other dramatists. Musset's veneration of the Bard was one of the few enduring loyalties he shared with his youthful companions in literature, although this was a faith which permitted wide divergencies of interpretation among its followers. Whether or not Musset's play is worthy of *Hamlet* is beside the point. The important thing is that Shakespeare's play was manifestly present in the poet's mind: innumerable details in the hero's characterization remind us of it. Pierre Nordon, in one of his excellent articles on Musset and England, clearly defined the "Hamletism" of *Lorenzaccio*: the hero's decadence following student days, his role-playing (with the audience's complicity), his word-play and taste for paradox, his "latent puritanism," his hallucinations.[21] But most of all, Nordon sees this Shakespearian presence in the play's essential dramatic conception, in "the way in which the plot is organized simultaneously on different levels, confronting groups, milieux, as well as individuals, clothed, as it were, in their essence."[22] More than any of the Romantics—notwithstanding Stendhal's and Hugo's manifestos, Vigny's adaptation of *Othello* to French language and taste or Berlioz' great musical setting of *Romeo and Juliet*—Musset was profoundly imbued with Shakespeare's characters and dramatic system, and was determined to transplant them. In that sense he embodies one of the highest ideals of the French Romantic theater, and *Lorenzaccio*, the most Shakespearian of his plays, might very well take its place at the head of the list of Romantic historical tragedies.

But calling *Lorenzaccio* "historical drama" is akin to calling *Hamlet* Elizabethan tragedy: it both is and is not true.[23] Like all

20. *Revue de Paris* (July 1, 1927), p. 201.

21. "Alfred de Musset et l'Angleterre," *Les Lettres Romanes*, 21 (1967), 245–50.

22. Ibid., p. 239.

23. I will not undertake here to determine whether *Lorenzaccio* is real tragedy or not. For an interesting discussion of that question, see

great works of art, as Benedetto Croce pointed out, Musset's is necessarily out of its time, part of another, ahistorical group composed of the masterpieces. André Lebois is perhaps an extreme voice in the evaluation of the play, but he speaks for a considerable number when he says: "It is too little to say that Musset gives us the perfect Romantic drama, the only one, the one which unites Racine and Shakespeare and justifies the reams of theoretical writings which had called for that union."[24] For him, *Lorenzaccio* belongs to the universal company of dramatic Everests: *Hamlet, Julius Caesar, Faust, Mary Stuart, La Vida es sueño, Boris Godunov.*[25] In that sense, if *Lorenzaccio* represents its period and country, it does so alone in its genre, separated from its fellows by the immeasurable distance of genius. Unlike them, it continues to speak to us with an increasingly insistent voice; its characters gain a more indelibly marked life in our minds with the passage of time, rather than grow quainter and more foreign to our preoccupations and our idea of man.

It is not really surprising that *Lorenzaccio* should separate itself so inexorably, with passing time, from the context of the historical drama. Hassan El Nouty has shown, in two penetrating studies, that the work's concept of human history is cyclical and, in the final analysis, antihistorical.[26] The play's circular architecture, which brings us back at the end to the situation from which its action grew; its construction from a "mosaic" of related but disparate pieces; its use of the perspective of daily life to reduce the salience of its protagonist's action, and the sense of profound futility which his desperate act generates—all of these run counter to the historical perspective of the Romantics and their successors, who were deeply convinced of the essential meaningfulness of history, on either poetic or scientific grounds: the myth

---

André Stegmann, "La Remise en cause des valeurs dans le *Lorenzaccio* de Musset," in Centre National de la Recherche Scientifique, *Le Théâtre tragique*, studies assembled and presented by Jean Jacquot (Paris, 1962).

24. *Vues sur le théâtre de Musset*, p. 128.

25. Ibid., p. 12.

26. See "L'Esthétique de *Lorenzaccio*," *Revue des Sciences Humaines*, fascicle 108 (October–December 1962), 589–611; and "Théâtre et anti-théâtre au 19e siècle," pp. 604–12.

of progress and of human perfectibility. The play's echoes of similarly depressing events in contemporary nineteenth-century history—the failure of the 1830 revolution—enhance its internal thematic tenets, making it a terrible rebuttal of the Romantic concept of historical becoming. That alone would make it necessary to reconsider classifying *Lorenzaccio* as typical of its age.

The antihistorical quality of *Lorenzaccio* is not merely one of its elements: it is inseparable from the play's central meaning. This is not a historical drama whose conclusion happens to leave us with a bitter taste, with the feeling that the particular events acted out before us represent a failure and a disappointment. It is rather a drama expressing the meaninglessness of history, of the sum of individual and collective human experience. Henri Lefebvre, in his stimulating Marxist analysis of the play, attempts a similar rehabilitation to the one operated by Georg Lukács on Balzac. Musset's pessimism is for him "critical realism," the inevitable result of the author's situation in history prior to the redeeming message of Marx; therefore it is a healthy contribution to the work of destruction which must sweep away the old bourgeois ideological structures before the socialist order can restore hope to the masses.[27] It is hard to say whether the aristocratic, apolitical Musset would have shared in this view or been consoled by it; in any case that does not really matter. But it is certain that if we leave aside such external historical considerations, *Lorenzaccio* stands as a monument of pessimism, a work built on the theme of universal disillusionment.

The theme, of course, is a persistent one in Musset's work, particularly in his four major dramas. It is especially dominant, under a more intimate guise, in *Les Caprices de Marianne*. Perhaps it is the spiritual kinship of the two works that led Musset to couple them in the first volume of the second series of *Un Spectacle dans un fauteuil*, despite their apparent incongruity. In *Marianne* as in *Lorenzaccio* we have the strange phenomenon of a protagonist who foretells his own failure early in the action. Coelio announces his resignation and his penchant toward suicide in the very first scene. Lorenzo waits until his long dialogue

27. *Alfred de Musset dramaturge*, pp. 123–24.

with Philip Strozzi in the third scene of the third act, but it must be remembered that this is the first moment of the play in which Lorenzo reveals himself to another character, as Coelio has done to Octave. Prior to this there are only hints of Lorenzo's ultimate intention, and no overt statement. Thus Lorenzo's revelation to Philip coincides with his prediction of defeat: "I'll make you a bet. I'm going to kill Alexander; once my work is done, if the republicans do what they have to, it will be easy for them to establish a republic, the finest that ever flourished on earth. Let them get the people behind them and it's as good as done. —I'll bet you that neither they nor the people will do anything." The sardonic matter-of-factness of Lorenzo's tone in this emotional climax of the play bears witness to both his determination to act and his conviction that his action will be fruitless.

Plot Structure: Fragmentation and Alienation

But Musset does not limit himself to recounting the failure of a single protagonist in *Lorenzaccio*: the idea of disillusionment can take on its full power as a dramatic theme only in the complex framework the author constructs around his hero. It would be hard, in fact, to imagine the theme embodied in a linear pattern of action, simply because Lorenzo's disillusionment must become more than a matter of personal effort and defeat. Musset shared with the other Romantics the ambition to represent not just the deeds of a single, elevated hero in the context of history, but the struggle and turmoil of an entire people, the collective movement of history around the focus of a hero and his action. Musset alone, however, seems to have succeeded in synthesizing the individual and the mass in a unified dramatic action: in great part no doubt because his work poses above all the modern question of the individual conscience in its anguished relationship to society.

Thus Lorenzo's disillusionment must be felt in the reinforcing company of the play's two other main plots, which complement and validate it. All three plots are conspiracies to end Alexander's tyranny and restore the Republic. For Philip Strozzi, the noble patriarch who heads one of Florence's most respected houses, it is a question of providing moral leadership. His dialogue with Lorenzo in Act III, scene 3, reveals him as an optimist and an idealist: Lorenzo need only mend his ways and cast off his abominable mask to become an "honest man" again. Philip believes that public action with the support of the masses will suffice to restore freedom and justice: "My intention is to appeal to the people, and to act openly . . . I believe in the honesty of the republicans." He has earlier revealed doubt and hesitation, in the privacy of his study, on learning of Alexander's latest seduction of a merchant's daughter:

> When will the education of the lower classes be strong
> enough to prevent little girls from laughing while their
> parents cry! Is corruption then a law of nature? Is what
> they call virtue just Sunday clothing that they put on
> to go to church? The rest of the week they stay at their
> window, knitting, and watching the young men go by.
> Poor humankind! What name do you bear, that of your
> race, or that of your baptism? And how much of the origi-
> nal stain have we poor dreamers washed from the face of
> man in the four or five thousand years we have been
> yellowing along with the pages of our books?   (II, 1)

But Philip gets hold of himself after this moment of doubt— a moment, it is true, based on knowledge of the history of centuries which have preceded him, one whose weight is unbearably damning for the man who has the courage to look at it squarely. Like Lorenzo, he continues to plan his liberating action. He will, however, abandon hope more suddenly because his hope is based on insecure illusions, as his questions have shown us: illusions about man in general, illusions about himself and his own motives. The death of his daughter brings about the total collapse of his plans and sends him scuttling back to the sanctuary of his meditations.

The Marquise Cibo's plot is independent of the two others, in a physical sense, yet thematically linked to the central idea of disillusionment. In the manner of other Romantic heroines, she believes that she can redeem a villain through the regenerative power of love. Her avowed hope is to win Alexander over by the sacrifice of her virtue. But her image of the tyrant is based on sentimental illusions and is far too grandiose: he turns out to be a bully, a weakling, and a mindless rake. Both her charms and her noble speeches are lost on him once her seduction is accomplished. But she, too, expresses doubt as to the real nature of her motives practically from the beginning, and it is this ambiguity as much as anything which makes her failure seem inevitable:

> Now what will I do? Could it be that I love Alexander?
> No, I don't love him, no, of course not; I said I didn't in
> my confession [to the Cardinal], and I didn't lie. Why
> is Lawrence [her husband] at Massa? Why is the Duke
> pursuing me? Why did I answer that I didn't want to see
> him any more? Why?—Oh, why is there a magnet, an
> inexplicable charm in all this, that draws me on? (*She
> opens her window.*)

> How beautiful you are, Florence, but how sad! There is
> more than one house Alexander has entered at night,
> cloaked in his cape. He is a libertine, I know. —And how
> do you get mixed up in all this, Florence? Who is it I love?
> Is it you? Is it he?   (II, 3)

When the Marquise returns to her forgiving husband at the end, the couple walks through the streets of Florence as if nothing had happened to sully their union. But they know, and others do too, that all is not the same. Better than anyone, the Marquise knows that her "sacrifice" was not really a sacrifice, that her return to virtue is the result of Alexander's indifference, and that the patriotic ideal which supposedly motivated the entire episode strangely resembles an ordinary adultery when one looks at it squarely. Her husband ends up oddly reminiscent of Claudio seen in a less comical light, from another perspective. As one passing gentleman warns another: "I wouldn't advise you to mention it to him; he's a master of all weapons, and jokers *fear the air of his garden*" (V, 3; italics mine). For Marianne-Ricciarda to return complacently to the arms of her husband is a disheartening evolution of a woman's aspirations, all the more so when we consider the grandeur of the Marquise' illusions.

The central characters determine the general movement, but they are not alone in this pattern of failure and disillusionment. From the earliest scenes of the play, Musset puts us in contact with minor characters whose lesser aspirations are also doomed to frustration. Philip's headstrong son Pierre, who seems for a time to personify a kind of reckless courage in the name of pride that even Lorenzo is moved to respect (II, 5), ends by losing control of the exiles. He goes sulking off to France, abandoning his honor along with his vengeance and the liberation of Florence. His last words in the play reflect his disillusionment: "The king of France protecting liberty in Italy is exactly like a robber protecting a pretty woman against another robber on a voyage. He defends her until the moment he rapes her. Whatever may be, a road is open before me where there's more good grain than dust. A curse on that Lorenzaccio, for having the idea of becoming something! My vengeance has slipped through my fingers like a frightened bird; I can imagine nothing more that is worthy of me" (V, 4). In less developed ways the pattern is repeated at all levels of society, from the merchant's erring daughter (and his angry son) to the burghers, artisans, students, and teachers who wander in and out of the action, commenting on their own debasement or unaware of it and charting the rise and fall of the principal characters. The final, bitter statement comes in a grotesquely elevated discussion on art and liberty in which two pedantic tutors engage while their young charges, a Strozzi and a Salviati, exchange kicks and insults (V, 5).

Time and the City

In *Lorenzaccio* as in *Marianne* everything moves inexorably, even predictably, toward failure. In both plays, time's passing is equated with decay and loss. Here we rejoin the larger Musset theme, time as the enemy of human internal experience. It is because we *are* only in and through time that our lives are predestined to failure. *Lorenzaccio* represents this on two levels: that of its hero, and the collective level of the city in its moral and political history. Like Dante, the great fugitive whose words are echoed by Musset's exiles, Musset thinks of glory and integrity as the lost perquisite of Florence's past. Several of his characters express this idea: the goldsmith's voice rings with the indignation of a passing, virtuous generation, a kind of popular chorus lamenting the end of virtue in the city: "Florence was still not long ago a sound, well-built house; all those great palaces, which are the lodgings of our great families, were its columns. There wasn't one among those columns an inch higher than any of the others; they all supported an old but solidly cemented vault, and we walked around under it without fear of a stone falling on our heads" (I, 2). For a burgher (I, 5), the present state of affairs is the result of bad government. For the exiles, the Florence of the present is the "hideous spectre" of the ancient city (I, 6). For the painter Tebaldeo, Florence's corruption is the result of a "bloody wound" spreading gangrene through a once-sound body (II, 2).

To these minor characters, as to Lorenzo, Philip Strozzi, and Ricciarda Cibo, Florence is a symbol of the world of men. They may despise or love it (generally both at once), but they are part of it whether they want to be or not. Even the exiles are bound to the city by their hatred and their thirst for vengeance. Thus they participate inevitably in the process of its decadence: even more, they *are* its decadence, since their failure to achieve the political action which almost all the characters supposedly desire is the cause of the city's decline. This peculiarly reversible subject-object relationship, which is reflected in the play's shifting perspectives, makes Florence a wonderfully apt image of Musset's conception of time the corruptor: the city is a complex superposition of past deeds, present activity, and future aspirations embodied in its streets and houses, structured in its laws and institutions, fostered by its growth and the rhythm of its collective life, which drives its inhabitants inexorably toward slavery even when they think they are masters of their destiny. Ricciarda's confusion between the city and the man, her aspirations and her desire, illustrates the ambivalence of the symbol on both the moral and the poetic plane. It is no wonder that some of the critics of *Lorenzaccio* have seen Florence as its real protagonist.[28] It is above all a work that represents the subtle interplay of man and society, which form and compose each other mutually through the passage of time. In this context, society (Florence) is history, inseparable from it by the very definition of a civilization; just as man is time, inconceivable outside of its frame of reference. The growth and development of the city in Musset's world are inevitably a matter of aging and decomposition. In the case of Florence, a series of irrevocable acts—the return of the Medici, the naming of Alexander as Duke, the installation of the German garrison, and, in the end, the succession of Cosimo de Medici as the puppet of the Emperor and the Pope—has been prepared and seconded along the way by a series of irreversible moral surrenders: the acceptance of corruption, sedition, and tyranny by the people of the city on all levels. Men are the accomplices of the city's decay, just as they are the accomplices of "l'ennemi vigilant et funeste— / Le Temps" (in Baudelaire's phrase), the terrible force within them that changes them into spectres of themselves.

This idea of unwitting complicity or willing complaisance which we have seen typified by Marquis Cibo thus becomes, when applied to a city and a civilization, one of the play's dominant temporal themes, inextricably linked with the moral center of Musset's world. This is a world where it is always, inherently, too late for action. As Hamlet's need to know and to prove prevents him from striking well and betimes, so Lorenzo, too, is the victim of delay and of knowledge. But Musset's prosecution of the temporal enemy goes beyond Shakespeare's by its absoluteness. In the Elizabethan tragedy a final reordering of the world takes place beyond Hamlet's tomb, as fortune rights the wrongs perpetrated through a series of usurpations. If in *Lorenzaccio* there is a return to order, it is to an essentially meaningless, anti-human one, the absurd order of tyranny and surrender. Something was temporarily "rotten" in Denmark, and has been purged by the tragedy's resolution; Florence is in a permanent and progressive state of rot, suspended briefly by the action of the play.

28. Cf. El Nouty, "L'Esthétique de Lorenzaccio," and Eugene H. Falk, "Musset's 'Lorenzaccio,'" *Tulane Drama Review*, 2 (1958), 32–37.

Thus Lorenzo's complicity with time is not so much a question of hesitation or delay as one of necessity: his plan requires him by its very nature to *use* time, since he must gain the confidence and the intimacy of his cousin, despite the latter's suspicions and those of his associates. Once he has taken time as his instrument or accomplice, Lorenzo is doomed to be its victim.

It has been traditional since Bernhardt's premiere of the play to speak of Lorenzo's moral dilemma in terms of his mask, just as modern criticism has evoked the notion for writers like Stendhal and Baudelaire, showing that it is essential to the Romantic concept of personality and the ethic of the dandy.[29] In this view, the disguise adopted by Lorenzo, his debauchee's face which conceals the virtuous one beneath it, at length grows inseparable from his real person—*becomes* his face, displacing the original one. Lorenzo himself uses the term in his scene with Philip Strozzi, along with several other images representing the appearance of a man in opposition to his internal reality:

> A statue descending from its pedestal to walk among men
> in the public square would perhaps resemble what I became,
> the day I began to live with the idea that I must be a Brutus.

> No, I won't blush; plaster masks can't redden in the service
> of shame.

> Vice was like a garment to me; now it is glued to my skin.
> (III, 3)

The common denominator in analyses of Lorenzo has been the idea that a borrowed face—the mask—has at length been substituted for an original one, the face of Lorenzo's youthful virtue. Bernard Masson, in his remarkable study of *Lorenzaccio*, was the first to point out that this is a misconstruction or a simplification of what Musset actually suggests.[30] Does Lorenzo himself not say:

> When I began to play my part as the modern Brutus, I
> walked in my new uniform of the great brotherhood of vice,

29. Cf. the quotation from J. Cantel cited below, p. 175. Julien Sorel and Rastignac are, of course, Lorenzo's immediate literary contemporaries.

30. See *Lorenzaccio ou la difficulté d'être*, p. 22; cf. "Le Masque, le double et la personne dans quelques Comédies et Proverbes," p. 565.

like a ten-year-old in the armor of a fairy-tale giant. I believed that corruption was a stigma, and that only monsters
bore it on their brows. I had begun to say aloud that *my
twenty years of virtue were a stifling mask*—Oh, Philip! I
entered life then, and I saw that at my approach everyone
did the same as I; all the masks fell before my eyes; Humanity lifted her robe and showed me, as a disciple worthy
of her, her monstrous nakedness.   (III, 3; italics mine)

Thus there is no essential qualitative differentiation between
the mask and the face: rather there is a superposed series of
masks, like the boxes in a Chinese puzzle—the innermost one
perhaps too small to be perceptible. Lorenzo's identity is really
a series of identities, none of them more "real" than the others.
As Masson points out, we see Lorenzo as at least five successive
personalities: the innocent child at Cafaggiuolo to whom he
harks back nostalgically just prior to Alexander's murder (IV,
9; the Duke, with unconscious irony, suggests in IV, 10 that
Lorenzo's suspicious escape arrangements, reported by Cardinal
Cibo, are just preparations for a trip to Cafaggiuolo. Indeed, his
murder is an attempt to recapture innocence); the scholarly
adolescent to whom his mother refers with equal nostalgia in her
conversations with Catherine Ginori (I, 6), and who appears to
her as a spectre in a dream (II, 4); the "adolescent in crisis" who
meditates one night in the Coliseum, and is "struck by the thun-
derbolt of action" (III, 3); the borrowed, ambiguous mask of
Brutus—Tarquin's and Caesar's Brutus are mingled confusedly
in Lorenzo's confession, and thus his act is mythically identified
with both the founding and the fall of the Republic (III, 3; V,
2); the debauched companion of Alexander, behind whose mask
lurks the entire series of Lorenzos, emerging each in turn from
time to time in a Pirandellian play of interpersonal relationships.
    None of these is more "real" than the others, nor is there an
original, pure, ideal Lorenzo which the masks successively hide.
For such a Platonic or Goethian *noumenon* to exist, man would
have to be capable of existing outside the reference of time; he
would have to possess an eternal model (one for each individual)
which time would progressively alter or embellish. At what age

would the real personality exist? Which part of life would be its formation, and which its modification or deterioration? Once we accept the concept of the mask, of the series of multiple super-posed personalities, we are forced to admit they are endless and indistinguishable in quality. Lorenzaccio's masks are, each in turn, his face. We are reminded of Sartre's "Hell is others": we are defined, whether we will it or not, by our encounter with objective reality and the subjective appraisal of our fellows, by the role we play through action in the world of men. But Mus-set's hell is also the self, in its incapacity to remain constant and congruous to a self-image. The series of masks is the inevitable result of existence in time, as becoming; for man like the city is time, nor can he *be* in any other mode.[31]

The reference to spectres illustrates this concept in Musset's thought. No doubt they are a legacy of Shakespeare's theater, and of a general Romantic theme like the "double" we find in *Marianne* (and who appears briefly in III, 3 of *Lorenzaccio*: "I walked the streets of Florence, with my phantom beside me"). But the ghost here is not a supernatural apparition intended to inspire primitive fear or add an element of irrational spice to the emotional brew as in Gothic tales and their French imitations. Musset's phantoms are familiar spirits who haunt his characters through memory. They are the survival into the present of past selves come to mock Lorenzo and his fellows. To the idealist, or to the alienated, they seem more real than present reality. Witness the exiles' reference to the modern decadent Florence as a "hideous spectre" of the former city: their helplessness is really a function of this curious optical illusion, which prevents them from acting effectively in and for the present, real city (I, 6). Lorenzo's ghost, which appears to his mother in a dream, is the mocking survival of an identity that she, like Lorenzo himself, would like to believe was the true one, one to which he may one day return.[32] But Lorenzo is more aware than his mother of the

31. This is the anguished theme which Musset, like Lamartine in *Le Lac* and Hugo in *Tristesse d'Olympio*, attempted to resolve lyrically in his *Souvenir*: the latter's resolution is foreshadowed in *On ne badine pas avec l'amour*, II, 5. See above, p. 92.

32. There is a striking resemblance between Maria Soderini's despair-

imperatives of temporal existence. He half-flippantly asks her to tell his ghost, next time she sees it, to expect a surprise. For Lorenzo to need a third party, even his mother, as spokesman to his own phantom, he must be convinced of his separation from the personality, the old mask, which the ghost recalls. Comparison with *Hamlet* emphasizes this fact: the gap between father and son in the latter, the idea of an unfulfilled external obligation passed on as an inheritance, is replaced in *Lorenzaccio* by an internal gap, the one between successive metamorphoses of a given individual self in search of its reintegration through action.

This sense of alienation *within* the self, this fragmentation of the soul in time, thus provides a further dimension to the persistent theme of isolation in Musset's work. Lorenzo's inability to reconcile the successive avatars of his personality renders his anguish more poignant, just as it contributes to the internal justification of his failure. How, indeed, could Musset's hero hope to accomplish an act of spiritual resolution or reintegration (the Duke's murder), when the man who commits the act—symbolically enough an act of destruction, albeit in the name of something positive—is no longer the one who conceived it, whose presence intact, unsullied, could alone give it validation? Even more: we know that the former Lorenzo—whether the idealistic youth or the emulator of Brutus—could not, physically, carry out his plan, since he had not sufficient access to his proposed victim. Could he have done so morally either? Nothing proves that the virtuous youth did not have to become the debauchee in order to attain, more than the opportunity, the terrible drunken brutality which characterizes him in the climactic fourth act. By then Alexander's murder has become a pure act of revenge: on Alexander, for making Lorenzo what he is; on Lorenzo himself, for allowing himself to become alienated from his former purity; on the world, for disillusioning him and making his act objectively meaningless.

Alienation from the world, also, becomes heightened by the

---

ing attempt to keep Lorenzo alive as she remembers him and Donna Anna's post-mortem fantasies concerning her son in *The Life I Gave You* of Pirandello, which lead her to reject his death and to proclaim his true, enduring life in her memory.

dimensions of the play. Lorenzo himself is subject to more numerous forms of isolation in this context of the city than any of Musset's other protagonists, all of whom (with the possible exception of Andrea del Sarto) exist in a timeless, stylized, and rarefied environment. We have seen this already with his masks, which must be varied to some degree to meet his interlocutors. Thus the full, public mask of vice which we see in Lorenzo's encounters with a large number of "indifferent" figures (Sir Maurice, Cardinal Cibo, Valori, etc.) takes on varying degrees of transparency and different colorations according to circumstances. With the Duke, his intimate (his "minion," as they repeatedly avow), by his very relationship, Lorenzo must let some appearance of internal personality shine through. We have glimpses (in I, 1; II, 4; and IV, 1) of an inner Lorenzo, revealed by irony and double-meanings. With characters for whom he feels some degree of sympathy, he is forced by turns to tighten and to loosen the bonds of secrecy. Thus Tebaldeo Freccia, the young painter—in some ways an image of Lorenzo's former self—elicits first a heightened irony, as if in self-defense and mistrust (a hesitation to acknowledge what he sees), then a relative relaxation of Lorenzo's defenses. With Catherine Ginori, the young aunt who represents to him an ideal of feminine purity, or with his mother, the mask of cynicism is liberally pierced by shafts of genuine tenderness, and a pressing if momentary desire to reassure and console (II, 4, first half; IV, 5). Philip Strozzi is granted the greatest degree of unmasking: in III, 3, and the subsequent scenes which confront the two characters, Lorenzo pays him the honor of revealing the story of his spiritual anguish. Philip thus becomes the privileged instrument by which we, the audience, finally pierce the shell of this strange hero, who previously has seemed impenetrably ambiguous when viewed from the perspective of his actions before Alexander, Sir Maurice, Valori, and the Cardinal, and their analysis of him.

But Philip is the sole exception to the general rule of impenetrability and isolation; and he is thus privileged only to discover the further mystery of Lorenzo's emptiness and absurdity. Like those masks of others which Lorenzo's disguise has permitted him to see through, Lorenzo's self-unmasking opens the door to disillusionment—even for Philip himself, since Lorenzo's revelations mark the first step toward the old idealist's retreat from the world. Apart from this exception, Lorenzo is cut off from all those around him, even (or especially) those he loves. Partly this is a question of pride, as he reveals to Philip (III, 3): the desire to act alone, to "be Brutus" (thus a "star actor"). But more than that, it is a question of necessity. Lorenzo, in order to act, cannot afford to jeopardize his mask, to risk discovery before the time is ripe. Even his apparent slips are part of his disguise: he needs to reveal "hidden" republican sympathies in order to maintain some degree of contact with their camp—if only to be able to betray them and secure Alexander's confidence. Of course, the need to win Alexander then automatically guarantees Lorenzo's failure to inspire republican support, to make his act fruitful. This is part of his fatality, and what makes it impossible for Lorenzo to communicate any of his intent or his inner anguish to those around him. Furthermore, it ensures his disillusionment as to the republicans' capacity for action in support of their creed. An illustration of this complex interplay of conflicting desires can be seen in Lorenzo's wonderful scene with Bindo and Venturi, the Rosencrantz and Guildenstern of the play. Lorenzo's need to keep his mask intact before these staunch and voluble republicans, coupled with his hardened skepticism, forces him to alienate them by his mockery when they invite him to join their ranks: "I'm with you, uncle. Can't you see by my haircut that I'm a republican to the soul? See how my beard is trimmed! Don't doubt it a single moment; love of country breathes in my most intimate garments" (II, 4). (The theme of the mask is here joined with the satirical form it takes in *Fantasio*, for example, where the idea of clothing replacing internal essence is treated with great comic verve in the person of the Duke of Mantua and his changes of costume.)

At the same time, the self-knowledge given by his mask makes him penetrate Bindo's and Venturi's pompous rhetoric: not only does he answer them with biting sarcasm, but he must also expose their emptiness by trapping them into accepting political favors from the Duke. The irony of the scene, which points up Lorenzo's isolation, is that his mask is not only a cognitive instrument associated with his plan of action; it is equally instrumental, also, in the frustration of his intended aim, since it turns those for and with whom he would act into the very hypocrites his growing cynicism suspects them of being. Isolation is not merely a passive state, it becomes an active force in the fulfillment of Lorenzo's destiny.

This isolation can be seen as a symbolic structural element in the play. As in *Marianne*, the fragmentation of consciences is reflected in the discontinuity of *Lorenzaccio*'s action, of its scenic distribution. On the level of overall plot movement—what we can call the horizontal strata or counterpoint of the principal actions—we find one plot which, although it is similar in aim to the other two, never enters into direct contact with them: Ricciarda Cibo's attempt to reform the Duke. It is remarkable with what tenacity Musset refuses to allow Ricciarda's path at any time to cross Lorenzo's or Philip's. Only the omnipresent, sinister Cardinal Cibo and Alexander himself provide liaison of a sort; and that has little to do with the idea of conspiracy. The Duke confides the progress of his conquest to his minion and panderer; the Cardinal presses Ricciarda to profit from her adultery—for his own purposes—and watches Lorenzo's actions with growing suspicion. All of Ricciarda's scenes after the first take place in the privacy of her bedroom or her boudoir, creating an insulated compartment in which her ostensibly altruistic action for Florence is buried and dispersed into lust, then abandonment. Ricciarda thus becomes, like the hero, a victim of the inevitable isolation which dogs all the characters.

Similarly, if Lorenzo's and Philip's plots touch, unlike Ricciarda's, they do so in a nonreinforcing way. There is never really any question of these two actions' being mutually auxiliary: the lengthy dialogue in III, 3, makes that clear. Lorenzo can act only as an individual until the moment of his crime—those are the sole terms in which his plan could be conceived. Indeed, the immediate reason for his terrible revelation to Philip, in whom he has not previously confided, is his wish to prevent the latter from yielding to the temptation to act. Lorenzo knows the consequences which await his friend if he leaves his ivory tower: Louise' death comes as no surprise to him (cf. IV, 1). But beyond practical questions, he knows from experience the price paid for the folly of translating ideas into action, and his confession is intended as an exemplary warning to Philip. Although Philip chooses to ignore it and go ahead with his attempt to foment a revolt of the notables against Alexander, the brief contact between his action and Lorenzo's has played only a negative role. One positive effect alone can be attributed to this scene and the later ones in which Lorenzo completes his revelations to Philip after the murder: they hold up to Philip's eyes a mirror of futility which does, indeed, foretell the truth about his project. But that is a function which cannot be called reinforcement of action. The three plots, in spite of their similarity, remain totally isolated from each other on the level of action, even mutually exclusive in a positive way (Ricciarda's regeneration of Alexander would naturally be frustrated by his murder at Lorenzo's hands). So, as we have seen, do the minor conspiracies interwoven with them. Lorenzo's act of murder frustrates Pierre's designs; Philip's retreat destroys any hope for Pierre to rally the exiles against Florence. It is not accidental that the most secretive, self-contained character in the play, Cardinal Cibo—who has wandered in and out of the various actions, now speculating as to Lorenzo's plans or trying to thwart them at the last minute (IV, 10), now attempting to use Ricciarda's adultery and apparently being foiled by her return to conjugal "virtue" (IV, 4)—is despite all expectations the principal winner in the play's outcome. It is as if the very fragmentation of this character fitted him for survival and victory in a universe such as Musset's, whose chief attribute is discontinuity. Not that the Cardinal's character lacks a unifying principle: through all his obscure machinations there runs the thread of his opportunism and his naked ambition. But the Cardinal is not troubled by any guiding ideal. Unlike Lorenzo, Philip, and Ricciarda, he has not gambled his hopes on the victory of the Republic, or Liberty, or Humanity. He is free to adapt himself to any turn of fortune, to attach his ambitions to whatever protector or instrument emerges from the shifting chaos of events.

The Cardinal's protean appearance in a variety of contexts

and postures is congruent with another structural aspect of the play which expresses the theme of human isolation: the vertical or scenic fragmentation that characterizes its plot movement. This is, of course, the technical element which explains the long delay in producing *Lorenzaccio* and its spotty history since (although its hero's ambiguous character and the play's political and moral pessimism must be held equally accountable). Not only does the scene shift recklessly back and forth, in and out, from bedroom to public square to palace hall to open country: the three major actions and the several minor ones are constantly interrupted and suspended. It would have been possible for Musset to give plot-continuity of a relative sort, even with the changes of decor, by continuing the same general action through two or more scenes in succession. But if we examine the sequence of scenes throughout the play, we find that the author chooses to do so in only three places among its thirty-eight tableaux. Such disproportion is remarkable, and can only be considered an aesthetic device knowingly practiced by Musset, for purposes we can infer.[33] When we look at the three exceptions to this rule of discontinuity, however, it is apparent that they also were made for a specific dramatic purpose.

Analyzing the distribution of scenes among the principal actions, we find that those in which Lorenzo's plot is the dominant concern number seventeen; Philip's short-lived plan of political action dominates ten scenes; and Marquise Cibo's dream of regenerating the Duke, six. The remaining five scenes of the play reflect elements of these central actions but are primarily given over to Pierre Strozzi's plot, the comments of the Florentines, or the problem of Alexander's succession and the Cardinal's machinations. These numbers cannot, of course, be taken as a firm index to the relative importance of the various actions within the play's structure. Several scenes contain elements of more than

33. Several critics have noted this disruptive principle, which tends to reduce the structural significance of the play's division into five acts, making the latter seem arbitrary or simply tradition-dictated, as compared to the unit of the tableau. Cf. especially Hassan El Nouty, "L'Esthétique de Lorenzaccio."

one plot (III, 3, is the most striking example); furthermore, the degree of variation in length and complexity which characterizes Musset's construction of scenes, here as in *Marianne*, makes it impossible to judge the dramatic presence or density of these actions merely on the basis of numbers (in *Lorenzaccio* they range, in Dimoff's edition, from one page—V, 3—to thirty-three pages—III, 3). But even taking account of these variables, the above figures correspond fairly well to the relative importance of the three plots and confirm our impressions concerning the central preoccupations of the play. Lorenzo's assassination of Alexander is indeed the heart of the matter, with Strozzi and Ricciarda providing significant but secondary counterpoint. As to the claim that Florence is the real protagonist of *Lorenzaccio*, it is somewhat weakened, I think, by the strong dominance of Lorenzo's action, which is far from buried under the weight of subplots and mass scenes. Indeed, it might be said that the impression of large scale given by the play is an optical illusion: most of its scenes are relatively intimate. The sense of number and mass is given by a quasicinematic effect of rapid change and succession, a kind of "persistence of vision."

Lorenzo's plot is distributed quite regularly through the play from beginning to end. Only once do more than two intervening scenes interrupt its progress: at the close of Act III, when Ricciarda's plot, reaching its climax, holds the stage for two successive scenes and is followed by the banquet at the Strozzi's palace. Otherwise the principal action returns in regular alernation now with one, now with another of the secondary plots; occasionally one scene of each of them intervenes (I, 1–3; III, 1–3). The Marquise' plot, in addition to being the least important, is also the shortest lived: after its premature climax in III, 5–6, it returns only briefly, for the reconciliation (IV, 4) and an ironic external retrospect (V, 3).

The exception to this generally regular alternation—the continuance of a given plot line through more than one successive scene—occurs once for each of the play's three protagonists at a crucial moment of his action. For Philip Strozzi it is the moment when his sons Pierre and Thomas, having gone out to foment an uprising of the noble houses against Alexander, are arrested in the street for their ambush of Salviati; this leads into Philip's anguished scene with Lorenzo in which he reaffirms his decision to take action (III, 2–3). In the cases of Ricciarda and of Lorenzo, the moment is still more climactic. Ricciarda's nervous exchange with Cardinal Cibo is followed by her desperate attempt to reform Alexander and the couple's "chance" discovery by the Cardinal (III, 5–6). Lorenzo's sequence is the climax of the play: his fantasies and divagations at nightfall on a public square are followed by Cardinal Cibo's and Sir Maurice's warnings to the Duke, then by the murder scene (IV, 9–11). Thus Musset chooses to grant an exceptional continuity to the action of his play only at those points where his protagonists' plans are being converted into action, where the dramatic tension of the play is at its greatest. He thereby creates a momentary feeling of achievement or realization that emerges out of the chaos of conflicting intentions which dominates the rest of the action.

These sequences are all the more striking for their contrast with Musset's general practice. There can be no doubt that they represent effective dramaturgy; but they are nonetheless exceptions. Throughout the rest of the play, the spectator or reader is consistently kept off balance by the discontinuity between its scenes, insofar as pure "plot" development is concerned. This is especially true of some of the shorter, staccato tableaux which emerge from time to time, more frequently as the play progresses (II, 7; III, 4; IV, 3, 7, 8; V, 3, 4). That all the plots are thematically related does not really lessen this disorientation. On the contrary, the sense of discontinuity is enhanced by the links of action which *ought* to be established and which are not. The Cardinal's presence in a variety of differing contexts (the Duke's and Ricciarda's, primarily) exemplifies this phenomenon: there seems to be little in his language and actions to bind together the various contexts for him, in terms of a temporal continuity from one scene to another. His final triumph with the nomination of Cosimo is not visibly prepared by what has come before, and is validated only by the Cardinal's well-established personality. Temporal discontinuity or confusion is also active in Marquise

Cibo's plot: between the scene in which she ponders her altruistic adultery (II, 3) and the climactic scene in which we find her trying in vain to realize her intentions (III, 6), we have one in which the Duke is already initiating the planned seduction of Catherine which will lead to his murder (II, 4: end). Here we find not only discontinuity but interference, which obscures the lines of development—like lines connecting asymptotes on a graph—that might otherwise aid the spectator in imagining the movement between scenes of a given plot. When there is not interference, there is often at least a deliberate opacity of which Musset's plans and reworking give us proof. For example, to consider Ricciarda's plot once again, the Comédie-Française manuscript of *Lorenzaccio* which Paul Dimoff published includes a continuation of IV, 4, which Musset evidently decided to cut from the published text. In it Ricciarda, who has fainted after blurting out to her husband the news of her infidelity, discovers upon her revival that he insists on taking her confession as delirious ranting.[34] The effect of this text is to bridge the gap between Ricciarda's avowal and the brief later scene in which her reconciliation with the Marquis is ironically noted by two "gentlemen" (V, 3). It cannot be construed as changing the meaning of the play in any significant way, and its deletion does not materially alter the progression of Ricciarda's action. Lafoscade, who first mentioned this fragment, suggested that Musset eliminated it because he was "dissatisfied with the attitude given to the Marquis."[35] But this "attitude," or one similar, is the only explanation possible to link IV, 4, with V, 3. We are forced to interpret the couple's reconciliation as resulting from some such gesture of complaisance on the husband's part after his wife's awkward burst of truthfulness! If Musset deleted the scene, it must have been from dramatic motives: he wanted IV, 4, to end abruptly with the Marquise' confession and fainting spell, like the original version of Act I, scene 2, of *Marianne* and for similar reasons. Not only does this render the scene more "dramatic": it also creates a stark hiatus between it and the following one

34. *La Genèse de Lorenzaccio* (1964), p. 402 note.
35. *Le Théâtre d'Alfred de Musset*, p. 300, note 3.

(Lorenzo's conversation with Catherine and his preparations for Alexander's rendezvous with death) which underlines the total lack of coordination between the various conspiracies; and it further augments the discontinuity in the progression of Ricciarda's plot in such a way as to emphasize symbolically the dark places of human motivation and action. What Musset was seeking was suggestion, not discursive logic, and a complex kind of musical organization in which thematic resolution is delayed while other themes, in other tonalities, are being developed and resolved. His concept of structure again foreshadows the Symbolist aesthetic, which values obscurity in obtaining the reader's active participation in the work of art. The "dark places" and discontinuities in the structural organization of *Lorenzaccio* give free rein to the imagination, to the instinctive sentiment we have about the inner life of its characters. They contribute to our impression that the work is larger, more complex than the words of any of its actors can make it. This is an antilinear structure, in contrast with the ideal of "well-made plays" in vogue during Musset's later years. Its elements of discontinuity were not a simple question of dramatic suspense, as the complicated knitting-together of threads in a Scribe drama might be, but rather a need to render symbolically through the play's dramatic construction the isolation which characterizes his protagonists' inner lives and which stifles their spasmodic attempts at action. It is true that in *Lorenzaccio* this also contributes to the sense of collective existence which some of the play's admirers have spoken of. We feel, through this quasipointillist or impressionist technique, the necessity of viewing the play's action beyond the frame of reference of any one protagonist, extraindividually, in the context of Florence—and by extension, of society and the world. But that is only part of its effect. Musset's use of plot alternation, shift of decor, and discontinuity in action and characterization also gives his reader or spectator a strong sense of the moral quality of the city: not its collective life so much as its fragmentation, its incorporation within walls and laws of a multiplicity of surrenders, compromises, cowardices, and martyrdoms parading under the guise of men.

The Impossibility of Action

The impossibility of meaningful action in such a world is self-evident: more than anything else, that is what *Lorenzaccio* is "about." All the major characters of the play draw this lesson in their own individual terms through the frustration of their attempts to act. That is the primary message of Lorenzo's long dialogue with Philip Strozzi: any attempt to translate a political or moral ideal into physical action is predestined to failure:

> It is because I see you as I was, on the point of doing what I did, that I'm speaking this way to you. I don't despise mankind; the mistake of books and historians is to show it to us other than it is. Life is like a city,—you can stay there fifty or sixty years without seeing anything but boulevards and palaces;—but don't go into the gambling dens, or stop to look into the windows in bad neighborhoods on your way home. That is my advice, Philip. If you're thinking of saving your children, I advise you to stay calm; that's the best way to get them sent back to you with just a warning.—If you're thinking of attempting something for mankind, I advise you to cut off your arms, for it won't take long for you to see that you're the only one who has any . . .
>
> All I ask of you is not to meddle; speak if you want, but watch your words, and watch your actions even more. Let me do my job;—your hands are clean, and I have nothing to lose. (III, 3)

The conflict between ideal and action which characterized *Marianne* in the personality split between Coelio and Octave here becomes both more complex and more concrete, because it is translated into terms of numerous characters and of a political reality. On one level, the conflict between political ideal and political action is symbolized by Ricciarda's confusion as to her motives and the distressingly banal outcome of her sacrifice. (This will be discussed in more detail under the topic of love: below, page 151.) It is important to note her unsureness concerning the object of her emotions: the city or the man. From the vantage point of her bedroom the city is distant and abstract compared with her insistently physical lover. When she finally does talk (III, 6), her words fall on deaf ears and seem pointless, even hysterical, in the context of the reality of her adultery. She knows it. That is why she answers, "Yes, thank God!" when the Cardinal taunts her with having been another of Alexander's many mistresses. Whatever the "sacrifice" involved in her ideal motivation, the physical reality was pleasureable enough to evoke this tribute. Somewhere between the conception of this act and its execution, it ceased to have its original meaning. This was not so much through a fault of Ricciarda in particular as through something perhaps inherent in this "act" above all acts, but which it nonetheless symbolizes for the rest: the prostitution of an ideal by its realization.

Philip Strozzi's experience is parallel to Ricciarda's, although its terms are quite different. Philip is a scholar and a dreamer in Musset's transformation of Varchi's material. He has managed to preserve into middle age the purity, the virtuousness which Lorenzo has lost so young. For Philip, the words that express his ideal have a value that endures in the face of the disappointments of everyday reality, of history:

> That the happiness of mankind may be only a dream is hard
> to bear; that evil is irrevocable, eternal, impossible to
> change—no! Why should the philosopher who is working
> for all look about him? That is his mistake. The tiniest
> insect passing before his eyes hides the sun from him. Let
> us go on then more boldly! The republic—that is a word
> we need. And even if it be only a word, it is still some-
> thing, since the people rise up when it rings through the
> air . . .   (II, 1)

Lorenzo's terrible confession to him in III, 3—the revelation of his moral disintegration in the service of liberty—is more than Philip can bear to face. Having once decided that it is time to leave his intellectual sanctuary and put his ideals into action, he cannot believe the necessary corruption of those ideals through contact with the world. On the contrary, if Philip has previously chided his son Pierre for rushing into action, it is only because that action will not be the ripening of a preexisting ideological principle:

> You haven't decided anything—no plan, no measures taken? Oh children, children, playing with life and death! Questions that have moved the earth! Ideas that have whitened thousands of heads and made them roll like grains of sand over the executioners' feet! projects that Heaven itself looks on in silence and terror, and lets man accomplish, not daring to touch them! . . . Do you know what a republic is, the craftsman in his workshop, the plowman in his field, the citizen in the public square, the entire life of a kingdom? the happiness of mankind.— God of justice! (III, 2)

He is convinced despite Lorenzo's skepticism that his own maturity, his long meditation on mankind's history, will guarantee the action undertaken in haste by Pierre, with whom he has associated himself (after their argument) in a burst of generous passion (III, 2). Philip will not accept what Lorenzo proves by his own example. In answer to the latter's revelations, he cries: "Stop! don't break the staff of my old age as if it were a reed. I believe in what you call dreams; I believe in honesty, in virtue and in liberty . . . It is possible that you have taken a dangerous route; why may I not take a different one leading to the same point? My intention is to appeal to the people, and to act openly" (III, 3).

In the end Philip acknowledges that he has been forced to act: his sons are in prison, his anger has risen, and his reason has yielded to his emotions: "My vitals are too keenly moved: you may be right, but I have to act." Here we glimpse briefly the idealist's recognition of an ambivalence in the motivations, or at least the circumstances, of his action. When Philip decides to go into the street with his ideas, it is not because the time is objectively ripe—on the contrary, his earlier meditation has shown how unprepared he feels Florence to be. It is his viscera that provoke his rash gesture, not his head. Family pride, paternal outrage, the spirit of emulation with his son's boldness, fear of further insult if he does not take a strong stand—none of these has much to do with the ideas he expressed in his first scenes. Indeed, they represent the contrary of Philip's ideological phrases and undermine the purity of his motives at the point where action begins. It may thus be seen that Musset wanted Ricciarda and Philip to represent two modes of compromise in the transfer from idea to action: two points at which the decision to act encounters contamination and distortion. In Ricciarda it is the very base of the transaction—the confusion between intellect and sense which transforms sacrifice into adultery. In Philip, it is the emotional chemistry that catalyzes thought into action, leaving him incapable of self-domination at the moment in which his decision is made. Once he has set foot on that treadmill, forces within and beyond him, all out of his control, determine a series of events leading to his daughter's death and the collapse of his personal will to action. The final stage of Philip's life is a meditation on death which has lost the last vestiges of will, a retreat no longer colored by utopian idealism. Only his vicarious pride in the achievement of Lorenzo will remain, to be destroyed by the dismal, anticlimatic events of the fifth act.

In Lorenzo's case the contamination is a lengthy process of decay that is identified with his very life. He may share the faults that undermine Philip's and Ricciarda's inchoate designs, but his determination has carried him beyond initial disgust and deception, through long patience, toward the accomplishment of his plan. Nothing henceforth can stop him from assassinating Alexander: neither his disillusionment concerning the propensity for action of his fellowmen, for whom the deed was to be performed and who would give it both moral justification and active fulfillment; nor the distaste which the cowardly complaisance of his willing victims has engendered in him; nor his horror at the depths of vice and depravity which he has discovered in himself through his life with Alexander. But he goes toward this consummation of his will with dreadful lucidity, recognizing that the act once done will not be the one he intended at the outset. It will have lost its significance both to the world and to himself, and become a gesture of self-vindication, of desperate revenge. Not a Gidean "gratuitous act," as it has been suggested, since the gesture has a terrible, pressing personal meaning and fulfills a deep need in Lorenzo:

> You ask me why I'm going to kill Alexander? Would you have me poison myself then, or jump in the Arno? Would you have me be a ghost, and when I strike this skeleton (*he beats his chest*) no sound come forth? If I am the shadow of myself, would you have me break the only thread that still connects my heart to a few fibers of my former heart? Do you realize that this murder is all that remains to me of my virtue? Do you realize that I have been sliding down a steep rock for the past two years, and that this murder is the only blade of grass I can clutch at? Do you think I have no more pride, because I have no shame, and do you want me to let the enigma of my life die in silence? And yet it is certain, if I could return to virtue, perhaps I would spare that ox-driver,—but I love wine, gambling, and tarts, do you understand that? If you honor anything in me, you who are speaking here to me, it's this murder you honor, perhaps merely because you wouldn't do it . . . I'm sick at hearing humanity bawling in the wind; the world has got to know who *I* am and who *it* is . . . Whether men understand me or not, whether they act or not, I'll have said all that I have to say . . . My whole life is on the tip of my dagger, and whether or not Providence turns its head, hearing me strike, I'll toss human nature heads or tails on Alexander's grave; in two days mankind will stand before the tribunal of my will. (III, 3)

This cry of determination and despair represents the funeral oration of Lorenzo's plans. Once his act is reduced to a pure gesture of hatred and self-vindication, there is no possible connection with the reasons of its inception. Lorenzo himself admits that the murder is meaningless, since he would not commit it if he did not have to justify his self-vilification. The act has become independent, it has taken on a life of its own unconnected with the idea that generated it. Lorenzo's experience, for all its strange originality, is paradigmatic of the process of realization: in this world of Musset's, any transfer from ideal to action necessarily involves contamination and divorce. This is the ultimate ideological dimension which Musset's theme of alienation achieves in the context of *Lorenzaccio*.

Musset sardonically celebrates throughout the play the surrender of reason to reality, the intellectual defeat of the humanistic spirit. All his minor characters participate willingly in the debacle. The Council of Eight finds good reason to welcome the choice of Cosimo de Medici which has been rammed down its throat (V, 1). The silk merchant whom we heard talking politics with his goldsmith neighbor toward the opening of the play finds esoteric justification for all the depressing events which surround this further blow to his liberty and dignity: "We can deduce that six Sixes concurred in Alexander's death" (V, 5). And the goldsmith, for all his disdain, cannot muster any more effective reaction than to go and see what is happening: his skepticism remains passive and unconstructive. The pedants turn their erudition toward the composition of sonnets in celebration of a new, "bitter" liberty which strikingly resembles that of the Greek colonels. Marquis Cibo finds good reason to think that his wife had spoken in delirium and to act out the comedy of conjugal trust.

The Duke and Cardinal Cibo represent, each in his own way, the reverse face of this counterfeit coin: the travesty of the ideal. Alexander, the target of all the conspiracies, triumphs over them until the very moment of his death. He is brute action personified, devoid of any guiding principle. The voice that dictates his seductions, his exactions, and his corrupting of those around him is that of pure sensuality. He is incapable of even seeing what the Marquise has in mind (beyond fornication) when she speaks to him of honor and of posterity (III, 6). Ricciarda might as well be talking to a wall or to a dumb animal: Alexander is constantly referred to as "ox-driver," "butcher boy," or "wild ox." As Ricciarda implies, his entire political philosophy is summed up in the coat of mail which he counts on to protect his body from revenge. Beyond that, he has no concern except the provision of fodder for his constantly renewed appetites. Even the bloody carnage of his death represents a symbolic triumph of his materialism over the once-pure thought of Lorenzo.

The Cardinal represents the victory of another sort of thought, "Machiavellian" and free from the bonds of principle. His triumphant ruse is a mechanical parody of the intellect's moral guise, just as his cardinal's robes are a caricature of the Church, a travesty of the spiritual principles they symbolize. Here again we see the ideal corrupted by the real, by action: the original church turned by contact with the world into an evil political power, an organization dedicated to the spiritual and physical enslavement of man. Of all the ideals which have succumbed to the corruption of the flesh, this is the most tragic and exemplary one, and Cibo dominates the play through it.

Love: a Pervasive Absence

It has been said that Lorenzaccio is a play in which the idea of love is notable for its absence.[36] That is all the more remarkable in that Musset's theater as a whole is so generally defined as a theater of love: in André Maurois' eyes, "there is only one subject for Musset: it is love."[37] The fact remains that, unlike the great majority of Musset's works of all genres, this most ambitious of his plays seems to relegate the theme of amorous love to secondary status. Certainly prime importance is given in Lorenzaccio to political and moral themes of a very different sort, and the sentimental considerations that tend to dominate the action of his other plays—courtship, marriage, fidelity—are subordinated here to the life and death of the city.

Yet the play is full of references to love in all its forms; and much of its action turns on differing varieties of both sexual and platonic love. I think it can be stated, paradoxically, that nowhere did Musset examine the manifestations of human love so exhaustively as in Lorenzaccio, and nowhere in his work does

36. E.g. Maurice Allem, Alfred de Musset, p. 110: "A striking trait of Lorenzaccio is the absence of love."

37. "Alfred de Musset: Les Comédies," Revue des Sciences Humaines, fascicle 101 (January–March 1958), 22.

the theme appear so pervasively, in such manifold guises and implications. It is true that there is no equivalent here of what usually passes for a "love story," as we find in *Marianne, On ne badine pas avec l'amour, Il ne faut jurer de rien,* and most of his other plays, where it is the principal action and theme. If there is Love with a capital *L* in *Lorenzaccio,* it is Mallarmé's "Absent of all Roses," the ideal which is implied by the complex of imperfect manifestations that are represented in it. But it is nonetheless omnipresent, intimately connected with the predominant political and moral themes of the play.

Ricciarda Cibo's affair with Alexander in the principal example—at least the most readily apparent on the level of dramatic action—of this linking of the idea of love with political and moral questions. Musset takes pains from the beginning to establish her as a passionate, "loving" woman. When we first see her (I, 3), she is saying goodby to the Marquis, who is leaving for a week or two to inspect their property at Massa. Ricciarda's tears and request to accompany him seem ample testimony to her devotion to her husband; unless, as we later suspect, they are the result of her anxiety at the Duke's love notes. Cardinal Cibo, her brother-in-law (another traditional bond broken, that of the family), who intercepts her correspondence, teases Ricciarda about the excess of her reaction, given the brevity of the absence: he already knows the ambivalence of her emotion and the use to which it may be put. But it is not until her next appearance (II, 3) in the confession scene that we penetrate the real cause of her anxiety: first in the Cardinal's monologue, then in Ricciarda's reflections on the strange language he has used during their abortive attempt at confession. The Cardinal, unhampered by any temptation to sin through excess of love, has seen through the mask of conjugal fidelity that Ricciarda herself does not realize she is wearing. He also penetrates the unconscious hypocrisy of a sensuality masquerading as love of country, and he will use it for his own political ends. "Who knows how far the influence of an exalted woman may go, even over that coarse man, over that living suit of armor? Such a sweet sin for so lofty a cause—it's tempting, isn't it Ricciarda? To press that lion's heart against your tender breast, pierced through and through by bloody arrows like Saint Sebastian's; to speak with tears in your eyes of the country's misfortunes while the beloved tyrant passes his rough hands through your disheveled hair; to make the holy spark spring forth from a rock—that's worth the sacrifice of conjugal honor, and a few other trifles." Ricciarda herself, shaken by the Cardinal's disquieting questions during their confession, begins to wonder what her real fascination is: "Why do you mingle in all this, Florence? Who is it I love? Is it you? Is it he? . . . It is strange, that Malaspina has left me all trembling" (II, 3).

When finally the Marquise brings up the political questions which supposedly motivated her adultery with Alexander (III, 6), it is already too late: the Duke is tired of her, as he has tired of dozens of other women. She has lost time in sensual pleasure —at least from the ideological viewpoint—and her political discourse falls unheeded. Alexander is satisfied, he needs nothing further from her. But his brutal indifference to the questions she asks—about his subjects, his loyalties, his posterity—makes it evident that he would never have understood or been moved by them. Ricciarda has sacrificed her fidelity to a kind of sensual machine, a stallion in man's shape. Mythically, her love is reminiscent of Pasiphae's: only she has clothed herself, hypocritically, in patriotic ardor rather than in bronze. The mythical tenor is nonetheless similar: the fascination of woman by pure brute virility. Her love retrieves its original pretext only at the moment of separation, when Ricciarda is overwhelmed at the enormity of her failure, in terms of both the patriotic ideal and personal honor. She flings her last, desperate appeal, as if against an inhuman statue: "I beg of you, don't let me be lost beyond recall; don't let my name, my poor love for you be set down in an ignoble list. I am a woman, it is true, and if beauty is everything for women, many others are more worthy than I. But don't you have anything, tell me—please tell me, for God's sake, don't you have anything there? (*She beats against his heart.*)" (III, 6). In the end, her idealistic, selfless love is transformed into hysteria, the cry of a woman's irrationality. But this final burst of visceral sincerity is far less depressing than the mendacious arrangement which succeeds it, the lie of conjugal reconciliation which masks the lie of conjugal sacrifice. Two forms of love have here been exposed as vile hypocrisies, and a golden ideal has been transformed into base metal.

The varieties of love—in a catalogue reminiscent of a less didactic *Ship of Fools*—are illustrated at several levels of action and language. The corruption of Florence is represented by the seduction of its daughters: Alexander has "entered more than one of its houses at night," in Ricciarda's *litotes*. Musset initiates the play's action with one of these seductions, which Lorenzo describes in glowingly complaisant terms: "I'll answer for the little wench. Two great, languid eyes, you can't be misled. What is more intriguing for a rake than perversion at the mother's breast? To see the future bawd in a fifteen-year-old child; to study, to plant, to insinuate with fatherly care the mysterious vein of vice with a friendly counsel, a stroke on the chin . . . gently accustom the developing imagination to give bodies to its phantoms, to touch what frightens it, to scorn what protects it" (I, 1). The description might characterize the entire process of decomposition which *Lorenzaccio* finds in the moral life of the city. We see it illustrated as well in the fascination exercised by the nobles' dancing and festivities on the silk merchant's young wife (I, 2), in a noble woman's boast of her German officer lover's male stupidity (I, 5): the latter, especially, provides a telling detail of the link between sexual laxity and the political surrender of the city. For Musset to introduce us to his hero under his panderer's mask gives a special symbolic value to the act and sentiment of love in the thematic structure of his play.

Of all Lorenzo's activities in pursuit of his aim, that of the panderer seems to be the most symptomatic of his own personal sense of moral degradation. He comes back to it frequently in his speeches, both in those which form part of his public role and in his meditations on himself. Thus his insult to Sir Maurice, which leads to the threatened duel, is that of a pimp: "Cousin [Alexander], when you're tired of one of your middle-class conquests, send her to Sir Maurice. It's unhealthy for a man like him, with such a short neck and hairy hands, to live without a woman" (I, 4). Later, in his great scene with Philip, the image of himself as a debased monster, fit to be slain by the citizens of Florence (and despising them for not daring to), is a sexual one: "Their daughters' beds are still warm with my sweat, and yet the fathers when I pass by don't take up their knives and sticks to slaughter me? . . . Oh, Philip, poor women shamefully lift up their daughters' veils when I stop on their door-step . . . I would have wept with the first girl I seduced, if she hadn't started to laugh" (III, 3).[38] And his divagations on the night of Alexander's murder turn upon images of lost sexual purity represented by Catherine, by the poisoned Louise Strozzi, and by the peasant girl, Jeannette, whom he remembers washing linen at Cafaggiuolo during his childhood (IV, 9).

Such is Lorenzo's nostalgia for sexual purity that his final impulsion to act is closely linked with the threat of Catherine's seduction by Alexander and his own complicity in it. It is the Duke's insistence on having him do his job as panderer on his pretty, young aunt that forces Lorenzo's hand. Throughout the play Catherine represents an ideal of virtue going beyond the limits of sexual innocence: her love of letters is a link between her and the former Lorenzo, and she, like Tebaldeo, might be a symbolic representation of what he has lost. It is all the more horrifying for him, therefore, to surprise himself in the act of encouraging her curiosity about the Duke just as he described himself doing to the girl in the first scene: "What does that innocent little heart think . . . Weren't you flattered by it? A love that so many women would envy! such a fine title to conquer, the mistress of . . . Go away, Catherine, tell my mother I'll be right there . . ." And he meditates alone, "I believe I would corrupt my mother, if my brain took it on itself . . . Poor Catherine! you would die like Louise Strozzi, or you would fall like so many others into the eternal abyss, if I weren't around" (IV, 5). Lorenzo's one glimpse of a possible redemption is offered by the thought that his deed may preserve Catherine's purity for an

38. The latter remark does not seem sufficient justification to me for Masson's "Adlerian" interpretation of it as a confession of sexual impotence: cf. *Lorenzaccio ou la difficulté d'être*, p. 5. Nothing in the context really supports such a view.

honest love.[39] The idea of moral innocence, the purer self that Lorenzo's plot has caused him to destroy, is thus repeatedly associated with sexual purity, as corruption is represented by sexual depravity. Although love as such is thus not the apparent subject of the play, it provides a symbolic paradigm for the general problem of moral and political integrity.

Another aspect of Lorenzo's perversity is represented by the sexual ambiguity of his role. A discarded scene involving a visit of Benevenuto Cellini to the Duke was to open on Lorenzo and Alexander asleep together.[40] The compromising nature of this circumstance does not seem to be responsible for Musset's abandonment of the scene (which I will discuss further under the topic of art): there are too many other evidences of homosexuality in the complex relationship of Lorenzo and Alexander. Their reference to each other as "minion" gives it a precise historical resonance, with echoes of the roughly contemporary court of Henri III. So does the Duke's reference to him as "Lorenzetta" for his apparent cowardice, but with evident sexual overtones. Lorenzo speaks disgustedly of himself to Philip in terms which cannot be taken as purely figurative: "To become his friend and secure his confidence, I had to kiss the remnants of his orgies on his thick lips. I was pure as a lily, and yet I didn't recoil from that task. Let's not speak of what I became because of it . . ." (III, 3). This aspect of Musset's hero must certainly account for the long hesitation to bestow the role on a male actor—or the latter's reluctance to play it—once a saving precedent had been established in 1896 by Sarah Bernhardt. But homosexuality is only one facet of Lorenzo's vice, which has probed all the dark corners of depravity. Musset was perceptive enough to realize the relativity of all sexuality, and the frequent coexistence of homo- and heterosexual behavior in man. He would no doubt have been

39. This aspect of his deed must not, however, be exaggerated, as Paul de Musset was ready to do. His proposed revisions of *Lorenzaccio*, offered in vain to the Comédie-Française, included a more immediate linking of Alexander's murder with the preservation of Catherine's virtue, for the sake of attenuating the premeditated brutality of Lorenzo's deed. Cf. *Théâtre complet*, ed. Allem, pp. 1252–53.

40. See Dimoff, *La Genèse*, p. 169.

amused at the Victorian prudery which dictated his hero's emasculation, transforming him into a mere transvestite instead of a complex male character.

More than any single element, it is the image of Florence as a corrupt woman which expresses the theme of sexuality as the representation of all moral experience. This apocalyptic or Dantean symbol appears at several points in the play (I, 6; II, 3, 5; III, 3, 6) but is developed most extensively in Lorenzo's sarcastic exchange with the painter, Tebaldeo, in II, 2. Deriding the youth's enthusiasm for art and religion, Lorenzo offers him a commision to paint a naked prostitute. When Tebaldeo refuses, Lorenzo suggests he paint a view of Florence for him. This offer accepted, he teases the young painter for his inconsistency: he would paint a bordello, but not a courtisan? Tebaldeo is offended: Florence is his mother. But then, says Lorenzo, Tebaldeo is a bastard, for his mother is a whore. The aura of sexuality which is attached to the city throughout the play is here defined precisely: Florence has been raped by Alexander, and through him by the political powers which control him, the Emperor and the Pope. The once-virtuous woman, mother of her citizens, has been transformed into a bawd, her "wound" degenerated into a gangrene corrupting the entire body. There is an unspoken parallel between Florence's state and Alexander's, for he is a bastard, the son of Lorenzo II de Medici and a "country woman," and he has usurped the throne. The city's accession to whoredom is thus a reflection, distorted in its details but recognizable nonetheless, of Alexander's role. His prostitution of her daughters is but an image of the moral rape to which he has subjected her.

It is too facile to say that Lorenzo's plan is to make an honest woman of her. But the language in which he expresses his aim repeatedly refers to its consummation as a "wedding." He first uses the expression, it is significant, in his scene with Tebaldeo when, having assured himself of the young artist's honesty and courage, Lorenzo invites him to do a picture for "my wedding day" (II, 2). The picture, we later learn, is the half-nude portrait of the Duke whose sittings give Lorenzo the opportunity to steal Alexander's ever-present coat of mail, which protects him from attack. If we have any doubt as to the nature of Lorenzo's "wedding day," it is dispelled in subsequent scenes. In his violent exercise with Scoronconcolo, during which Lorenzo, preparing himself and his neighbors for the murder, loses control of himself and, falling to the floor, cries out irrationally, the theme returns again: "Oh, day of blood, my wedding day! . . . Coward, coward—panderer—the skinny little man, the fathers, the daughters—farewells, endless farewells,—the banks of the Arno swollen with farewells! . . ." (III, 1). The initial conception of his plan to murder a tyrant is described in terms of love—the closest thing to a profession of love Lorenzo utters during the play: "I reached my dew-soaked arms toward heaven, and I swore that one of my country's tyrants would die by my hand. I was a peaceful student and I only cared for arts and sciences; it is impossible for me to say how that strange oath arose within me. Perhaps that is what you feel when you fall in love" (III, 3). His period of preparation for the act and of contact with its intended beneficiaries, the people, he characterizes similarly: "I observed . . . as a lover observes his fiancée while awaiting the wedding-day! . . ." (ibid.). In the fourth act, when the accomplishment of Lorenzo's plan is identified with the rendezvous he is supposedly preparing for the Duke with Catherine, the theme of wedding-consummation takes on further density and reality in its connection with the murder, and gives rise to ghastly plays on words. Lorenzo: "Say when you want to receive her, and at what time it will be convenient for her to sacrifice what little virtue she has to you." Alexander: "Are you serious?" Lorenzo: "Dead serious. I'd like to see an aunt of mine who wouldn't sleep with you." Then, in his reflections on the depth of his depravity, after his arch scene with Catherine, Lorenzo visualizes his redemption by the act of murder in the "honest children" Catherine may one day be able to bear as a result of it: as if they were the spiritual children of his "marriage" (IV, 5). Lorenzo's divagations in the dark town square shortly before his murder of Alexander mingle images of Catherine as a virginal bride coming to her wedding bed with references to the act of murder itself as the wedding consummation:

I'll tell him that it's a question of modesty, and I'll
take away the lamp;—it's done every day:—a young
bride, for example, requires that of her husband, to enter
the nuptial chamber, and Catherine is supposed to be very
virtuous . . . "Take away the torch, if you will; the first
time a woman gives herself, it's only natural." . . . Ah,
minion, ah, minion! put on your new gloves, a finer suit
than that, tra la la! deck yourself out, the bride is beautiful.
But let me whisper in your ear, watch out for her little
knife.   (IV, 9)

When at last Lorenzo stabs Alexander, Musset takes a detail
from Varchi's chronicle and elaborates it into a final element of
this metaphorical sequence. The *Storia fiorentina* notes that, in
the struggle, Alexander bit Lorenzo's finger and did not loose his
grip on it until he fell back dead.[41] In the climactic scene of the
fourth act of the play, this becomes the symbol of Lorenzo's
"wedding": "See, he bit me on the finger. Until my death I'll
keep this bloody ring, this priceless diamond" (IV, 11). The
metaphor derives its power from the mingling of the two levels
of meaning which have become attached to the idea of Lorenzo's
wedding: the symbolic redemption of his sexual corruption at
the hands of Alexander, and the ritual blood sacrifice that the
act of murder represents. The element of confusion in the assign-
ment of roles for this wedding is suggestive: we cannot say if
Lorenzo or Alexander is the bride, the former for his references
to himself as "mariée" and his sexual ambiguity, the latter for
his bloody "defloration" under Lorenzo's knife.

It can be seen from these illustrations that carnal and ideal
love, although they are not central to the work on the plane of
action, play a major role in its structure on the symbolic and
thematic level. The act of love is taken as a richly suggestive
metaphor for all human moral activity, and particularly the
theme of the ideal versus its realization in worldly terms. The
varieties of love, its spectrum of manifestations from platonic

41. Dimoff, p. 54.

through worldly to carnal prostitution, with its echoes of religious symbolism opposing the spirit and the flesh, provide a powerfully evocative metaphorical texture for Musset's tapestry representing the political and moral life of the city, with its opposition between credos and practices, documents and deeds, past hopes and present deceptions. Musset does not use his symbols didactically or allegorically: they are integrated into the scenic reality and the action of his play. Rather the corruption of love, echoed in its varied guises at every level of composition, becomes an obsessive theme, a moral thread interwoven through the work's entire fabric. When we take stock of the conception of love that pervades the play, we see its similarities to the idea Musset expresses in most of his work: the simultaneous necessity and impossibility of love in the lives of men.

Musset shares, in much of his poetry, the Romantic elegiac theme of love's conquest, and man's tragic defeat, by time. Like those of other poets, Musset's lyrics proclaim a symbolic redemption on the level of sentiment or of art through memory. The love that flares momentarily then is swallowed in the darkness of time endures through the creation of metaphor, combining the earthly with the spiritual to give it lasting poetic form and through the formulation of linguistic vehicles that will keep it alive in the memories of men. Love and art are thus identified with each other and with the theme of memory, of "souvenir," which is man's sole victory over time. In his "Nights" and particularly in "Souvenir," Musset proclaims this redemption. "I can only tell myself: 'At that time, in that place, / One day, I was loved, I loved, she was beautiful. / I bury this treasure in my immortal soul, / And carry it off to God!" Or, in the famous speech from *On ne badine pas avec l'amour* whose paternity Musset apparently shared with George Sand, "You are often deceived in love, often wounded and often unhappy; but you love, and when you are on the edge of the grave, you turn around to look back and you tell yourself:—'I have often suffered, I've been mistaken sometimes, but I have loved. It is I who have lived, and not a false being created by my vanity and boredom' " (II, 5). Musset thus gives memory a value transcending its origin in reality, seeming thereby to provide, with a sort of aesthetic symmetry, a corresponding and counterbalancing resolution to the conflict between the ideal and the real: real love, despite the imperfect, corrupt translation of its spiritual intent, is repurified and given enduring life by the magical properties of memory. The spirit thus takes its revenge on the flesh.

This sort of redemptive memory is notably absent, however, from the text of *Lorenzaccio*. There is no elegiac funeral oration for the lover, as in *Marianne*, to consecrate Coelio's immortal accession to his ideal; nor do we find a character even momentarily celebrating the triumph of love over the crude realities of human nature, as does Perdican before he plunges to his perversely self-inflicted defeat. There is a final oration in *Lorenzaccio*, but it serves a very different purpose from Octave's: it consecrates the burial of all the play's ideals under the stifling mediocrity of political reality. Or, in the case of the two noblemen's distinctly nonlyrical remarks, it ironically celebrates the triumph of conjugal hypocrisy over loyalty and sentiment. Thus love remains almost totally bound to frustration and futility throughout the play. With the possible exception of Lorenzo's hypothesis of a future from whose perspective his sacrifice will have borne fruit, through Catherine's preservation from taint and her virtuous marriage—a very brief respite in the play's integral pessimism—there is no transcendency of love, no redemption through time, but rather the consecration of its surrender and defeat at every level. It is a striking illustration of Musset's personally lived theme: that destruction of a deep psychological need by psychological reality that was to characterize all the notable love affairs that became part of his legend (George Sand, Aimée d'Alton, Madame Allan-Despréaux). The nature of Musset's love, in his work as in his life, seems to be the antithesis of Stendhal's doctrine of crystallization. Instead of the Stendhalian process of accumulation and elaboration which constructs the enduring image of the beloved in the lover's mind, we find in *Lorenzaccio* a disposition to love, on all levels of the word—carnal, ideal, patriotic, humanitarian—which contact with its object serves only to decompose and dissolve.

Art: surrender of an ideal

What, then, of the idea of art as a sublimating redemption, the fixing of the ideal and of experience in enduring integration as a victory over time? The numerous references to art in *Lorenzaccio*, as well as the presence of several artists or dilettantes among its characters, prove that Musset was conscious of this question and gave a significant place to it in the elaboration of his thematic structure. Furthermore the evidence of his plans, particularly of the scenes which he deleted from the published text of the play, indicates that he originally intended the theme of art to have a more positive place in his work.

As it happens, both of the scenes published by Paul Dimoff in his *Genèse de Lorenzaccio*, which figure in the Comédie-Française manuscript but were dropped from the published version, involve art and artists as their central concern. It is therefore provocative that Musset should have abandoned them. The first, labeled cryptically "Sc[ene] I. At the Duke's," is difficult to place in the sequence of the drama's final form. Elements of it appear in I, 5, II, 4, and IV, 1; but they are accessory elements, and the central topic, Benevenuto Cellini's visit to Alexander's apartment, appears nowhere.[42] If it was intended as an opening scene, it would have to be in either Act III or Act IV, since its references to Catherine place it after II, 4. Lorenzo's thinly veiled allusions to his assassination plans make the fourth act, following his scene with Philip Strozzi, seem the more likely place in the play's development.

Cellini comes to visit the Duke and finds him and Lorenzo asleep. The goldsmith has brought a model of the medallion Alexander has commissioned for himself, and he asks for advice on the design of its reverse side. This gives Lorenzo the opportunity to promise a suitable reverse for the Duke's medal, "one such as the world has never seen . . ." But the main point of the scene is Cellini's announcement of his departure for Rome and Alexander's inability to make him stay, either by fiat or by gifts.

42. Cf. Dimoff, pp. 169–75. Cellini is mentioned briefly in I, 5, the scene of the San Miniato fair where Salviati insults Leon Strozzi.

If the great artist thus was added to the list of historical figures in the play, it was evidently to illustrate the thesis that art is not subject to political or social laws: this scene would then have formed part of a sequence representing the theme of artistic transcendence and liberty to counterbalance the ideological failures of the play.

The second unpublished scene, marked "Sc[ene] IV, a small bedroom," is harder to place than the preceding one; but evidently it is a continuation or elaboration of Lorenzo's conversation with Tebaldeo Freccia in II, 2, to which it specifically refers at one point.[43] It would therefore have to be placed between that scene and III, 2, where we find Tebaldeo painting Alexander's portrait. Since it is, at least in principle, a part of that sequence, it is more convenient to discuss it in its context as an element of concept of art developed around the young painter's personality.

When we first encounter Tebaldeo in the second scene of Act II, he interrupts a discussion on the subject of art and religion between Lorenzo and Cardinal Baccio Valori, a papal emissary to Alexander's court. The latter has expressed an aesthete's view of religious ceremony which recalls Chateaubriand's *Spirit of Christianity*:

> Ah, dear sir, what satisfaction there is for a Christian in
> this magnificent pomp of the Roman church! What man
> can remain insensible to it? Doesn't the artist find in it his
> heart's delight? Don't the warrior, the priest and the mer-
> chant discover in it all that they love? The admirable
> harmony of the organ, the splendid velvet hangings and
> tapestries, the pictures of the great masters, the warm, sweet
> perfumes swung by the censers, and the delightful singing
> of silvery voices, all of that may shock the severe and
> puritanical monk by its worldliness; but for me, nothing
> is more beautiful than a religion which endears itself by
> such means.   (II, 2)

The aestheticism of Valori's speech reminds us also that Musset took a jaundiced view of Chateaubriand, whose *Memoirs from*

43. See Dimoff, p. 178.

Beyond the Tomb he later parodied, in 1849.[44] Lorenzo's terse irony cuts him off sharply: "No doubt; what you say is perfectly true, and perfectly false, like everything in the world." But Tebaldeo, the young artist, is carried away by enthusiasm at Valori's encouraging words, and cannot help expressing his warm agreement—nor does he neglect the opportunity to display a view of the Campo Santo which he happens to be carrying with him. In counterpoint to Lorenzo's sarcastic comments concerning art and life (including his reference to Florence as a whore), Freccia expounds an optimistic thesis. The artist is essentially a religious figure whose work finds its natural place in the church. His creation reaches its highest level when it rises toward God, like prayer. The artist's role is that of "realizer of dreams": the term is strikingly relevant to the moral themes of the play. He would thus accomplish the task which we have seen as Lorenzo's tragic failure. When the latter tells him that the city which he loves and paints in expressing his ideal is a bordello, a corrupt and depraved body, Tebaldeo replies that art is an aromatic healing herb, a flower, which like Baudelaire's *Flowers of Evil*, thrives on corruption:

> Art, that divine flower, sometimes needs dung to fertilize
> the ground and make it fecund . . . Peaceful and happy
> nations have sometimes shone with a pure but feeble light.
> There are several cords to the angels' harp; the zephyr
> may murmur in the most delicate ones, and draw a sweet,
> delightful harmony from their accord; but the silver string
> vibrates only in the north wind. It is the most beautiful
> and the noblest; and yet the touch of a rough hand favors
> it. Enthusiasm is the brother of suffering.

Lorenzo retorts that it is quite fine for his sensibilities to be titillated by the people's sufferings, but his piety loses some of its credibility in the process. Tebaldeo answers that his pity is not alleviated by his aesthetic satisfactions; in response to Lorenzo's taunts, he pronounces a credo of freedom, independence, and

44. "Mémoires d'Outre-Cuidance," in *Oeuvres complètes*, "l'Intégrale," pp. 918–19.

creativity which sets the artist apart in the world of men, implying a possible resolution on the plane of art for the moral dilemma of the play. It is of course a noncommitted one: to Lorenzo's
question "Are you a republican? Do you love princes?" Tebaldeo replies, "I am an artist: I love my mother and my mistress." Yet Tebaldeo's courage and independence make him, at
this point in the play, one of its few really sympathetic characters, and seem to promise further development of this optimistic
theme.

Musset's unpublished sequel to this scene appears, indeed, to
have been intended as a kind of resolution of *Lorenzaccio*'s moral
problem, the impossibility of realizing the ideal in the world,
through an artistic sublimation outside the frame of reference of
political or social reality. In this transfer of an insoluble spiritual
problem to another sphere, where it can be symbolically resolved,
the projected scene is remarkably reminiscent of *Fantasio*. There
we have a hero who takes on the guise of a court jester and finds
a retreat from his harassment by material cares in the private
world of a princess' garden, where he is free to come and go as
he pleases, indulging in healing word-play to chase away the
spectres of obligations and boredom.[45] In the scene from *Lorenzaccio*, Lorenzo tempts young Freccia with promises of a brilliant
career as a "society" painter, if he will only swallow his pride
enough to flatter and cajole, or of intervention on his behalf with
the Duke. All of this Tebaldeo refuses, saying his only ambition
is to be given a small chapel in Santa Maria to decorate with
frescoes and statues. Lorenzo finally offers him a kind of "paradise of choice," artist's style: he will be permitted to use Lorenzo's
excellent personal library, play on his harmonium and paint
whatever he desires. Food will be brought to him as he wishes,
he may work at whatever time he finds suitable, and he will have
a key to come and go as he wants. It will be, in other words, a
painter's private Eden, a microcosm of freedom, pleasure and
creative joy sheltered from the sufferings and compromise of the
world.

It is difficult to say how this theme would be further developed

45. See above, pp. 87–88.

and resolved in the context of the play. As it stands, the artist's dream come true would perhaps be so isolated, so dependent on Lorenzo's whim (and subject to his fall) as to provide no satisfactory equilibrium for the ideological failures that dominate the play. It may be that Musset was meditating further scenes with Freccia to give him greater importance in the play's central action. But the published text returns him to the stage only once, in the scene where he is painting Alexander's portrait. He thus becomes merely an accessory to Lorenzo's plot—a pretext for the theft of Alexander's body armor—and is reduced to a somewhat truncated aspect as a character. It is clear that Musset changed his mind about Freccia and what he represents when it came to shaping the final version of the play. Freccia, like Cellini, is one of the untied strings of *Lorenzaccio*. It must have been a fairly late decision on Musset's part to drop the element of optimism which these two figures lent: the revindication of human history by the enduring creations of art and by the exceptional personal liberty which great artists alone can attain. Like *Andrea del Sarto*, the play echoes the names of Cellini, Michelangelo, and Raphael: Tebaldeo Freccia, one of the few fictitious characters in *Lorenzaccio*, was to represent a hope of future glory, the young artist who might achieve in a succeeding generation the work of integrating dream and reality which great art represents.

Instead, we last see Tebaldeo trembling somewhat comically as he listens to Alexander's gristly jests with his bodyguard Giomo, and answering the Duke with cowed obsequiousness. The dream of art evaporates with him, halfway through the play (II, 6). When Musset returns to the theme, it is in different terms with far less optimistic implications. Lorenzo's exalted ravings in the scene preceding his murder of Alexander contain one last reference to Freccia's idea of the religious nature of art. Seeing workmen still busy late at night in the nearby church, Lorenzo exclaims:

What's that light under the church portico? They're cutting and moving stones. These men seem to have courage when it comes to stones. How they cut! How they dig! They're

> making a crucifix; how courageously they're nailing it! I'd
> like to see their marble corpse suddenly take them by the
> throat. (IV, 9)

Lorenzo's savage irony about the artistic "courage" of men, their willingness to repeat in symbolic form the crucifixion of Christ although they dare not turn their knives against their oppressors, is a violent rebuttal of the religioaesthetic argument announced by Valori and developed by Freccia. This is perhaps where Musset comes closest in his intentions to the Marxist ideas imputed to him by Lefebvre.[46] Musset's Christ resuscitated in anger and vengeance, tired of serving as a symbol of submissiveness and resignation to injustice in the world, is in the line of the Christ which Nerval and Vigny were later to formulate.[47] For a brief moment, through Lorenzo's impassioned vision, we see prefigured the terrible proletarian Christ of Orozco's murals, risen from a Cross which he has chopped down, to bring justice and liberation by the ax and by the sword. The idea of aesthetic consolation in conjunction with religion is violently rejected by Lorenzo at the moment when his sanguinary deed is about to be performed. The apology for art which Musset seems to have entertained until an advanced stage of his work finally receives its definitive negation in this passage and in a scene which celebrates the surrender of art to reality in the fifth act.

There, as we have already mentioned, two pedants complete the silk merchant's and goldsmith's futile commentary on the play's events by their unintentional parody of the artistic doctrine enunciated earlier. Instead of the work of art emerging compassionate but triumphant from the sufferings of the people, the tragic circumstances and the struggles of human existence, we see the two pedants elaborately lauding each other's moral and intellectual stature, singing the praises of the odious new political order to which their city has surrendered. Out of the turmoil, the disappointment, and the ruthless suppression of those few mis-

46. Cf. Werner Bahner, *Alfred de Mussets Werk*, p. 68.
47. See Nerval's sonnet sequence *Le Christ aux Oliviers* in *Les Chimères*, and Vigny's poem *Le Mont des Oliviers*.

guided students who naïvely attempt to carry through Lorenzo's intentions, the learned doctors find material for a sonnet in praise of liberty:

First Preceptor: Sapientissime doctor, how is your Lordship
    feeling? Is the treasure of your precious health
    in its regular disposition, and does your equilibrium
    remain suitable amid the tempests in which we
    find ourselves?
Second Preceptor: So erudite and florid an encounter as yours,
    Lord Doctor, is a weighty thing, upon this care-
    worn and crazed earth. Suffer me to press that
    gigantic hand from which the masterworks of our
    language have flowed. You must admit it, you
    have recently written a sonnet . . .
First Preceptor: Can this poor frolic of our muse have reached
    so far as you, who are so conscientious, so grand
    and austere a man of art? . . . You will perhaps be
    astonished that I, who began to sing as it were
    in praise of monarchy, seem this time to be singing
    of the republic: "Let us praise liberty, which
    reflowers more bitterly, Under more mature suns
    and more vermillion skies."   (V, 5)

Not only are the pedants busily shifting gears to accommodate their inspiration to new circumstances without actually showing the break; but the placement of this scene make it evident that their calculations are false. The republic is already snuffed out, as the goldsmith has just told the silk merchant. If the pedants had some grasp of the reality they are desperately trying to hitch themselves to, they would be singing of monarchy once again. They thus succeed in being both servile and ineffectual. It is obvious that they and their art will survive only because of their lack of importance to the world—for all the flattery they bestow on each other's "gigantic" genius. *Lorenzaccio* thus having suggested a vision of the artist as redeemer, as an island of integrity and permanence in the flux of a deceiving world, closes with a glimpse of the artist's surrender, his voluntary and cowardly adaptation to a world he is powerless either to influence or to comprehend.

The Triumph of Reality

In this context of artistic failure we may see a new symbolic value in the last scene of the play, which has troubled both critics and producers.[48] It must be admitted that the scene with which Musset closes his drama is a strange and unsettling one: in the central square of Florence, where tribunes have been erected for the coronation ceremony and the people have flocked in great numbers, Cosimo de Medici privately swears an oath of allegiance to the Emperor, before Cardinal Cibo. He promises, ironically, both to carry out "justice" without restriction and to avenge Alexander's death.[49] Then, turning away from the play's audience and speaking "into the distance," he pronounces a speech which Musset translated directly from the document in Varchi's chronicle. The play ends upon this note, anticlimactic and antidramatic in the highest degree, foreshadowing the documentary novel or *cinéma vérité* by its incorporation of reality into the context of a work of art.

For Musset, however, this ending forms the final link in the chain of disappointments and frustrations which marks the last act of *Lorenzaccio*. Cosimo de Medici's speech, the expression of a middle-of-the-road monarch concerned above all with the conservation of the politicosocial status quo and the avoidance of offense to the powers that be (the real meaning of his phrase "to offend no one"), is in its very banality the perfect representation of what *Lorenzaccio* is about: the triumph of everyday reality over the dreams of men. It is fitting that, in a play which has shown the inability of art and the artist either to effect meaning-

48. Paul de Musset wanted to replace it with something more "dramatic" and politically relevant, as we have seen.

49. It is an interesting aspect of the play's "discontinuity" that Lorenzo is already at this point the victim of a mercenary killer.

ful change or to preserve man's moral integrity, the final curtain should be rung down on a bureaucratic document delivered undramatically away from the audience, as if in cold disdain of theatrical effect, leaving the stage empty at the end of its protagonists' bloody, futile struggle. Musset thus raises nonart to a high symbolic level, and ends his play with a nonclimax of daring originality. His procedure, it is true, has evident sources both in reality and in literature: Cosimo's speech must have borne unmistakable echoes for its contemporaries of the *révolution ratée* of 1830, which resulted in a triumphantly bourgeois monarch whose motto could very well have been Cosimo's "To offend no one"; it seems clear also that Fortinbras' speech at the end of *Hamlet* and Malcolm's in *Macbeth* provide the dramatic model from which Cosimo's takes its point of departure. But it is Musset's achievement to have integrated this Shakespearean procedure into the thematic structure of his play, through the profound artistic irony that underlies this "return to order," this reestablishment of the status quo ante which marks the real defeat of all that his protagonists have attempted.

This refusal of facile heroism or tears, this world that ends "not with a bang but a whimper," is part of what makes *Lorenzaccio* so startlingly modern. At a time when the French theater was glorifying individualism in all its forms, celebrating its triumph over conformity and malevolent destiny, Musset's terrible lucidity showed him the real drama of contemporary man: the ignominious defeat of the individual in the face of an anonymous, mediocre collectivity. Lorenzo does not share in the exaltation of Hernani's poison, of Antony's knife-stab—the Romantic self-immolations that culminate in Sidney Carton's "far, far better thing" and Brunhilde's funeral pyre. He steps out of the door of Philip Strozzi's study in Venice, saying only "I'm going to take a walk around the Rialto," and is swiftly dispatched by a hired killer's knife. His body is kicked with ignoble alacrity by a faceless mob into the canal, to join the rest of the debris of human activity that floats there and to disappear without a monument. He remains the symbol of modern man's struggle against the forces that threaten him: not an inimical destiny whose very malice and will to destroy him give man a tragic or heroic stature, but an overwhelming, engulfing indifference that swallows up the would-be hero without leaving a trace on the smooth surface of time.

A political commentator writing in a weekly news review gave recent expression to the contemporary relevancy of *Lorenzaccio* in the world of housing developments and shopping centers which we call the consumers' society: "Tomorrow, in no time at all, a home-grown Fidel Castro would be torn to bits by the fury of the housewives, and indeed of their out-of-work proletarian mates. *Lorenzaccio* for the era of the supermarkets!"[50]

The Destiny of *Lorenzaccio*

The destiny of Musset's drama is almost as strange and symbolic a story as that of its hero. Like Lorenzo, the play for long years might have boasted: "When I'm dead the good Lord won't fail to post my eternal condemnation at all the crossroads of eternity." Despite the efforts of admirers, *Lorenzaccio* was not produced until 1896, more than sixty years after its composition, almost thirty years after Musset's death. Furthermore, the circumstances and conditions of its productions until very recent years were such as to prolong the injustice already perpetrated on the work. This series of misguided or unfortunate efforts on the play's behalf is absurd enough to merit a brief recounting.

Musset himself seems to have been convinced of the unsuitableness of *Lorenzaccio* for production in its original form. From 1847, following the unexpected triumph of *Un Caprice*, to 1852, he adapted several of his earlier plays and arranged their production, but there is no evidence of any such effort for *Lorenzaccio*. We have no stage version or revised text for it as we do for *Marianne*, and no sign of steps being taken toward an eventual production for which Musset might have undertaken a revision. Given the play's inordinate length compared with those generally produced, and especially the enormous production difficulties for

50. Maurice Clavel, "La Grande Société anonyme," *Le Nouvel observateur*, 265 (December 8–14, 1969), 47.

the theater of his time posed by its thirty-eight transformation scenes, it is easy to understand why the dramatist turned to more realizable projects.

His reluctance is imputable as well, no doubt, to the fact that two other playwrights had meanwhile based dramas on the events in *Lorenzaccio* produced by the Comédie-Française, without success. One was *Laurent de Médicis* by Léon Bertrand (1839), the other a more noteworthy case, Alexandre Dumas père's *Lorenzino*, performed in March 1842. Neither of these plays would be of interest to us today on the basis of literary or dramatic value, but the latter work, minor though it may be, is the product of one of the most successful Romantic dramatists. It is interesting to see what he made of this material first treated by Musset.

It seems likely that Dumas' motives were opportunistic, judging by his character and by the internal evidence of the play itself. The redoubtable literary businessman, sensing the possibility of a good deal missed by Musset through lack of theater acumen, decided to correct his errors and miscalculations, both of dramatic structure and of character-plot development (at the expense of historical truth, it should be said). His Lorenzo is deeply in love with Philip's daughter Luisa Strozzi, endangering her honor because of his bad reputation but unable to marry her until he accomplishes his mysterious, unknown design. Only the republican Michele, who has attempted to assassinate Lorenzo disguised as an actor playing Brutus(!), has been initiated into Lorenzo's plan to kill the Duke. Untroubled by the metaphysical problems of his model, Lorenzo casts aside his mask of vice at the end, and the play closes on the suggestion that he will become a righteous Duke of Florence. A pathetic note is furnished by the death of his beloved Luisa: fearing that Lorenzo has sacrificed her to the Duke —since he has used her as bait for his trap—she takes poison and dies, consoled somewhat by the revelation of her lover's honesty.

The simplification of the plot, thematic development, cast, and dramatic structure of the play make it a fine example of second-rate Romantic drama. All of its elements are familiar to readers of works of the period: the love of a pure young woman for an outcast, the final dramatic revelation of the hero's goodness, the highflown political and moral sentiment with which the play abounds, the linear plot development in which a number of temporary obstacles are vanquished, a setting that changes only between acts: it is *Hernani* repeated for the fiftieth time, minus the brilliance of Hugo's verse. The rapid exchange which concludes the play will suffice as a sample of Dumas' caricatural mastery of Romantic dramaturgy:

> *The Duke* (uttering a cry in the next room): Ah!
> (Michele reappears).
> *Lorenzino:* Well?
> *Luisa:* My father!
> *Lorenzino:* Saved.
> *Luisa:* Florence?
> *Lorenzino:* Free.
> *Luisa* (falling back into Lorenzino's arms): Then I can die.
> *Lorenzino:* My God, my God! Why am I then condemned to live?
> *Michele* (coming out of the next room and wiping his sword under his arm): No matter, it's easier to live when you're avenged!

FINIS

The prevailing bad taste did not prevent Dumas' play from getting a very cold reception and falling rapidly into oblivion: so we are informed by the ever-loyal Gautier, who used the production of Bertrand's and Dumas' works as a pretext for his oft-repeated cry for production of Musset at the Comédie-Française. In 1839 he had evoked the complexity and depth of Musset's Lorenzo, to the detriment of Bertrand's, calling Musset's hero a "mixture of Brutus and buffoon [whose] mask of corruption has become attached to his face." Gautier praised the "superior manner in which this character is rendered; it is a magnificent philosophical study, with a terrible, painful comical quality. The Florence of the Middle Ages [*sic*] breathes fully in it; its details have a truly Shakespearean reality and fantasy."[51] Gautier was more interested in voicing his enthusiasm than in keeping strict account of the truth; the same may be said of his claim in 1842 that

51. *Histoire*, series 1, p. 298.

Dumas' *Lorenzino* "follows quite precisely the material of Alfred de Musset's [play]." Gautier was trying to right a wrong—Musset's absence from the French stage—and to improve the quality of French theater life thereby. We have seen his mixed satisfaction at the production of *Marianne* as well as several of Musset's other works during his lifetime. Although he was to reiterate his particular desire to see *Lorenzaccio* produced, it remained the one major play of Musset which was not performed during Gautier's lifetime.[52] But that was probably for the better: the series of transformations through which the work passed before it finally reached the stage would have upset him even more than the changes to *Marianne*, *Fantasio*, and *On ne badine pas avec l'amour*.

Alfred's brother Paul proved willing to go to almost any lengths in order to render *Lorenzaccio* dramatically and morally acceptable. Maurice Allem has revealed in his notes the series of negotiations through which Paul went with two directors of the Comédie-Française and one director of the Odéon in hopes of seeing the play produced.[53] As with *Fantasio*, he alleged conversations with his brother as justification for his proposed changes. The most important of the latter are outlined in an unpublished document of 1874 in the Archives of the Comédie-Française, entitled "Observations on production of *Lorenzaccio*." They included reducing the sets to one per act, shifting scenes around "for greater effect," making Lorenzo's delay in executing his design a practical question by emphasizing Giomo's constant menacing presence, inserting allusions at the end to the political situation of nineteenth-century Italy, and adding a scene to make the murder more palatable by having Lorenzo do it to protect Catherine Ginori from imminent dishonor. Paul de Musset's revised text has disappeared, through a series of perhaps well-deserved misfortunes; it is evident, however, that he did not hesitate to delete, manipulate, and add to his brother's work for the sake of rendering it acceptable. But theatrical and political considerations were militating against it, as well as what Edouard Thierry, director of the Comédie-Française in 1863, termed the

52. Ibid., series 5, p. 295.
53. See *Théâtre complet*, pp. 1249–54.

"priapism" of the Duke and Lorenzo's ambiguous employment as purveyor to his needs. Even more than *Marianne*, the play was too shocking for the contemporary public, and Paul de Musset, like Gautier, did not live to see it produced in any form.

But an even harsher fate awaited *Lorenzaccio* when it finally reached the stage. In 1895, Lugné-Poë abandoned plans to produce the play with future playwright Henry Bataille in the title role, when he found that "the divine Sarah" Bernhardt was planning to add it to her roster of transvestite parts: obviously the Théâtre de l'Oeuvre could not compete with Sarah's gilded circus. Paul's modifications proved insufficient for the actress, and it was in a drastically reworked version by Armand d'Artois (who had the virtue, in his own eyes, of looking like Musset) that the play was finally produced at the Théâtre de la Renaissance on December 3, 1896.[54]

Aside from this curious sex inversion, which Sarah practiced with equal success on Hamlet, the play was modified to bring each act into a single set.[55] It ended with Lorenzo's assassination of the Duke, followed by an epilogue in Venice to play down the anticlimactic quality of Musset's unprofessional fifth act. The subplots were attenuated or deleted in order to focus interest on Sarah's role as well as reduce the play to manageable proportions. Several scenes were shifted, even though that produced evident inconsistencies in the plot. And Armand d'Artois did not hesitate to match his own prose with Musset's in scenes where the original text seemed insufficient.

This production, which can justifiably be called a travesty as well as an act of literary piracy, nonetheless provided Bernhardt with one of her important successes. Her performance was

54. Cf. Lyonnet, *Les "Premières,"* pp. 179–80. D'Artois' revised text was published by Ollendorf in 1898. The production had costumes by Alfons Mucha and music by Paul Puget: its poster by Mucha, showing Madame Bernhardt in her richly bejewelled, ample robes, is one of the classics of *art nouveau*.

55. Act I: A square in Florence, at night; Act II: Lorenzo's apartment in the Soderini palace; Act III: A great hall in the Strozzi palace; Act IV: A room in the Duke's palace; Act V: Lorenzo's room.—at the back, a bed enclosed with curtains; Epilogue: Philip Strozzi's study in Venice.

greeted with almost unanimous praise. The critics were in equal agreement that Musset's work required the scrubbing it had received in order to be made stageworthy. One of the rare exceptions was J. Cantel, writing in the *Revue hebdomadaire*, whose review showed a subtle appreciation of Musset's original work:

> The drama's admirers will regret ... that the adaptor, disturbing the order of scenes, transporting the words of one character into the mouth of another, suppressing many of the bold expressions of thought, and introducing into Musset's supple and robust prose passages of his own invention, has in sum distorted not only the Shakespearean aspect of its composition, which was inevitable, but the very character of Lorenzo, and in part made the moral interest and the philosophical significance of the whole disappear ... This hero buried voluntarily under the mask of a coward, who when he wishes to tear off his mask at the end finds it sealed to his face and can no longer remove it, is a particularly moving and original type.[56]

These intelligent strictures did not prevent Bernhardt from reviving the play several times in the coming years—as late as May 1912 at the theater that now bore her name. More curiously still, her precedent had a lasting effect on future productions: for the next fifty years the role of Lorenzo was to be taken by female players! After another star-vehicle production with Réjane in the title role at the Odéon, *Lorenzaccio* finally reached the stage of the Comédie-Française in June 1927, with Marie-Thérèse Piérat in the role of Lorenzo.[57] The text was more or less the original, but with cuts that brought the number of scenes to twenty-eight. (Among the most important of these was the meeting of the timorous Council of Eight to choose a successor to Alexander.) Although this was one of the most ambitious and spectacular productions undertaken in recent times by the Comédie, it was greeted with only moderate enthusiasm: its use of the proscenium for transformation scenes was termed a makeshift,

56. December 12, 1896, pp. 262–63.
57. She had already played three scenes of the play at a war benefit performance in May 1918.

in the absence of suitable stage machinery, and Mlle. Piérat's noble effort was judged to be necessarily ill-fated.[58] Several critics called for a male performer—Pierre Fresnay, Le Roy, or Max Weber. But in 1934 it was Marie Ventura who succeeded Mademoiselle Piérat in the role.

Meanwhile Falconetti (Karl Dreyer's Joan of Arc) succumbed to the same temptation as Sarah Bernhardt: to prove her power and versatility in a male role. She appeared in limited engagements at the Casino of Monte Carlo and the Théâtre de la Madeleine in Paris, in December 1926 and December 1927 respectively. The production was once again a considerable personal triumph and had a revival at the Odéon in January 1932. But productions like these did nothing to establish the play as an enduring part of the repertory. Rather, they confirmed the judgment of critics like Paul Reboux: "Alfred de Musset, who had a great deal of tact and foresight, did not write his plays to be produced"; and they served to maintain the play as a sort of monster to be used only in unnatural circumstances.[59]

If we look at the brief history of the productions of *Lorenzaccio* with male heroes, we find an equally curious sequence of events. It is not completely surprising to learn that the first man to take the part of Lorenzo, as far as I have been able to discover, sang the role in an operatic version with music by Ernest Moret produced at the Opéra-Comique in 1920. The singer was the celebrated Vanni-Marcoux, who, like his female predecessors, scored a personal success in a work whose music was judged unmemorable, and whose text was a rhymed four-act version by the composer.

Three years later Musset's own text had the honor of being interpreted at the Théâtre des Champs-Elysées, by a male actor, without music but in Italian translation, the hero being played by Ermete Zacconi, a noted Italian tragedian! It can only be sup-

58. Claude Berton, *Les Nouvelles littéraires*, June 11, 1927, Fonds Rondel, Bibliothèque de l'Arsenal.

59. *Paris-Soir*, December 4, 1927, Fonds Rondel. A film version of the play, produced by Lux Artis in 1922, of course had its title role interpreted by a woman: a certain Saffo-Momo.

posed that the French were making every possible effort to prevent the normal performance of Musset's great drama. Paris maintained its defense to the bitter end: the first regular production of the original text with a male interpreter of the title role seems to have taken place in January 1933 at the Grand-Théâtre of Bordeaux, with Jean Marchat of the Comédie-Française as Lorenzo. Marchat evidently undertook the voyage south in despair of seeing a man play the role at the national theater, and his despair has proved justified: the play was dropped from the Comédie's repertory, evidently because of technical difficulties, without ever having a male Lorenzo.

Two post-World War Two productions finally revealed the power and viability of *Lorenzaccio*. The first was an adaptation of the play in 1945 by Gaston Baty, an indefatigable promoter of Musset's work during the 1830's and '40's. His Lorenzo, at the Théâtre Montparnasse, was Marguerite Jamois—still, alas, a male impersonator. But the qualities of Baty's production and the play's reference to German occupation and the problems of liberty and compromise made it extremely relevant to the moral climate of the postwar years: suddenly *Lorenzaccio* seemed to have found its context and its public after more than a century of neglect and abuse.

But the real triumph came seven years later, in 1952, when Musset's masterpiece found a theater, a director, and a star. The theater was the Théâtre National Populaire, with its vast stage, its ultramodern facilities and machinery, and its revolutionary principles of production. The director was Jean Vilar, who made imaginative use of modern stage lighting to bring about the rapid change of scene and sets required. And the hero was Gérard Philipe, in one of his greatest roles, who brought to the part of Lorenzo all the subtle play of forces in tension of which he was capable. At last the conflicting tendencies of Lorenzaccio, the paradoxical heroism and weakness he incarnates—and the moral dilemma faced by an idealist in the world of action—had been fully realized in a performance that made its predecessors seem two-dimensional. Since Gérard Philipe's death, the TNP has dropped *Lorenzaccio* from its repertory, but it is to be hoped that it will be reinstated to its deserved place: it would be depressing to think that the play had thus once again fallen victim to the star system.[60]

60. I was privileged to attend Otomar Krejca's production in Czech of *Lorenzaccio* by the Za Branou Theater of Prague at the Odéon-Théâtre des Nations in May 1970. Krejca's technique of keeping all his characters on stage at all times, masked and miming when not "*en scène*," furnished a brilliant solution to the problem of scene-changing: the actors participated in shifting the semi-abstract decor, as well as performing choral and individual mimetic movements to effectuate aesthetic transitions. The relevance of the play's moral and political themes to post-1968 Czechoslovakia provided a further degree of emotional power to a production whose insight and imaginativeness succeeded in surmounting the language barrier. It is curious (and moving) to note that by subtle shifts in interpretation, Tebaldeo Freccia was given a more positive moral stance than that suggested by the text: thus symbolizing, perhaps, these dramatic artists' spiritual victory over the forces of oppression.

Chapter 7 The Epigoni I:

Le Chandelier

Of the theater works Musset wrote after his extraordinary two-year spasm of creative genius, four are deserving of continued interest and have been so confirmed by readers and theater-goers: *Le Chandelier* (1835), *Il ne faut jurer de rien* (1836), *Un Caprice* (1837), and *Il faut qu'une porte soit ouverte ou fermée* (1845). The latter two are one-act plays, delightful in their marriage of wit and sentiment, and more closely tied to the parlor origins of the proverb genre than are Musset's great comedies. Although they provide testimony to the poet's undiminished intelligence, his mastery of language, and his psychological insight, they are too light in weight to be subjected to comparison with their predecessors. It is no doubt significant that Musset owed his first successful theatrical productions in 1847 and 1848 to these two plays, which put their author's talents at a level accessible to the public taste of his time. They eventually opened the theater to *Marianne* (1851), *On ne badine pas avec l'amour* (1861), and *Fantasio* (1866). But their attractiveness and their success should not create any illusions as to their relationship to Musset's first-rate works. They are pale echoes: the last reverberations of their author's diminished gift before the disappointing works of what should have been his maturity, if his character had not cheated him of it.

Le Chandelier and *Il ne faut jurer de rien* are more substantial. If Musset had written nothing else for the theater, he might still have acquired a reputation on the basis of these quite different and yet typical comedies. They form an intermediate stage between the great quartet which precedes them and the gradually diminishing train of subsequent works: a brief plateau on which Musset's precocious gifts, already bereft of that poignant vision which had given moral power to his linguistic fantasy and his psychological penetration, continued to produce works reminiscent of the past. By their evocation of the pains and joys of youth, of the spirit of freedom and desire which goads Musset's heroes to the brink of death, these plays seem to be a logical continuation of their predecessors. By the subtle change in spiritual perspective which characterizes their protagonists and action, they testify unmistakably to the process of dissolution taking place in their author.

Le Chandelier (The Candle-Bearer) was Musset's first play, aside from a distinctly minor opus, Barberine, to follow the four great ones. Little more than a year separates it from Fantasio and On ne badine pas avec l'amour. Yet despite superficial resemblances between them, we are in a different moral world. As for Lorenzaccio, all that links the two plays is a peculiarly cynical atmosphere and the fact that their male leads were first played by women.[1] The former connection is a serious one, it must be admitted. But associated as it is with a comic rather than a tragic dramatic form, its literary significance is considerably altered. What prevented Lorenzaccio from reaching production (aside from its technical difficulties)—its moral ambiguities, the political and social skepticism it exuded—posed a less formidable obstacle in the context of the comic tradition, always granted a certain license. Yet even in that context Le Chandelier was shocking to the critics and censors of its time. If it was first produced at all, the relaxation of censorship during the 1848 Revolution

1. Madame R. Debrou, at the Théâtre-Historique, August 10, 1848. The reason in Le Chandelier was not the hero's sexual ambiguity, but merely his youth. At the play's premiere at the Comédie-Francaise, the actor Delaunay played a long-remembered Fortunio. The work had an on-and-off career at the Comédie-Française during the Second Empire, thanks to censorship troubles. In 1916 Mlle. Piérat, who was later to be the Comédie's first Lorenzaccio, revived the tradition of the female Fortunio. Meanwhile a proposed revival at the Vaudeville, with the actress Réjane in the role, was evidently inspired by Bernhardt's recent success as Lorenzo.

was evidently a crucial factor, and the precedent established by the Théâtre-Historique, a boulevard theater, paved the way for Comédie-Française production just as the censorship was being reestablished. Arsène Houssaye, the director of the national theater and Musset's great admirer, fought a difficult and ultimately losing battle for the play under Napoleon III's quasi-Victorian reign. It was only with the Third Republic that it finally gained a secure place. Musset, who, as with *Marianne*, provided a simplified stage version of *Le Chandelier* for the Comédie, had gone so far as to write two more "moral" endings for his play, in the hope of placating the Imperial censors—to no avail.

Even the play's supporters have tried to defend or to mitigate the peculiar moral values of the work. Gautier, writing with his usual enthusiasm about the premiere, took up the cause in casuistic terms: "Although strict morality may suffer a bit by it, isn't Fortunio Jacqueline's true husband? Aren't the proprieties of youth, beauty, wit and sentiment united in this charming couple?" As for Jacqueline, the adulterous heroine, "we see, in all her relations with the captain [Clavaroche], that she has let herself be taken, and has not given herself!"[2] All these strictures and as-it-were's in defense of a play whose basic situation is not terribly different from that of *Marianne*, insofar as it deals with adultery and the deceiving of an elderly husband by a young wife; yet *Le Chandelier* seems to elicit far more indignation. For Francisque Sarcey, writing at the time of the play's post-Empire revival, "This comedy is terribly sad. The sentiments which permeate it are all quite scabrous; however admirable the style in which the author has clothed them, they nonetheless have something repellent about them. This woman is a trollop; unconscious or perverse, it doesn't matter, she is abominable . . . Fortunio is the only frankly likeable character of this drama."[3]

Leaving aside the hypocrisy of both official censorship and journalistic criticism in nineteenth-century France, there can be no doubt that even when compared with the sensuality of *Marianne*, *Le Chandelier* makes a rather shocking impression on the

2. Gautier, *Histoire*, series 5, p. 304.
3. Unidentified clipping from 1871 in the Fonds Rondel, Bibliothèque de l'Arsenal.

reader, one that with further acquaintance grows rather than lessens. The impression seems to come from the play's fundamental ambivalence: the coexistence within it of two seemingly inimical ethics which makes it difficult to assign it to a single moral world. There can be no doubt that this reflects the state of bitterness, doubt, and cynicism in which Musset found himself during the year following his adventure with George Sand. But it also seems to betoken the premature loss of youth and enthusiasm which characterized his artistic and psychological existence: a precocious senility which *Fantasio* and his other plays had foretold as an ominous threat to youth, but which here permeates the fabric of the play in a more sinister, disquieting manner—with complaisance and surrender.

The plot of *Le Chandelier* is a simple one. The play opens with one of Musset's freshest and most delightful scenes. Master Andrew, a middle-aged notary, bursts into his wife Jacqueline's bedroom early in the morning, to accuse her of infidelity. One of his clerks has seen a man climb into her window during the night. Jacqueline replies, at first with sleepy astonishment, then with increasing indignation, and manages to make her husband beg forgiveness and to send him off about his business by the end of the discussion. Upon which her lover, Captain Clavaroche, climbs with relief out of the clothes closet in which he has been cramped all this time.[4] To prevent further disturbances Clavaroche, who has considerable experience in affairs of this sort, recommends a Standard Operational Procedure: Jacqueline must provide herself and her lover with a "candle-bearer," a young, enthusiastic swain who will settle for small attentions in public and distract the husband's jealousy, while Clavaroche enjoys the

4. One of the play's most successful revivals, directed by Gaston Baty at the Comédie-Française in 1936 with Madeleine Renaud, Julien Bertheau, and Maurice Escande, was justly criticized for a pantomime scene at the beginning which showed Clavaroche entering Jacqueline's room, making love to her, then hiding as the husband appeared. The sense of delightful contrast produced by Jacqueline's convincing display of outraged innocence, followed by her lover's appearance, was obviously spoiled by this addition.

lady's full favors in private.[5] Although Jacqueline is dismayed by the plan's callousness, she chooses a young clerk, Fortunio, for the role. The latter, who is already under her spell, is only too glad to be offered the opportunity to serve his lady—ostensibly as go-between for her secret jewelry expenses—and vows to give his life if she needs it. While Clavaroche is delighted by her success, Jacqueline is more and more troubled by it, intrigued and vexed by Fortunio's sincere eloquence. At a dinner during which Clava-roche sardonically prompts the youth in his new functions, and even Master Andrew is touched by Fortunio's eagerness to serve Jacqueline, the young clerk sings a love song he has written in honor of his lady.[6] Fortunio profits by an interview which Jacqueline grants him to plead the sincerity and seriousness of his love, and to elicit a hasty, involuntary "I love you" from her before being sent about his business. But his illusions are shattered when he overhears Clavaroche, joking about his ruse with Jacqueline, suggest that it is time for Fortunio to be dismissed from his functions. Realizing that Clavaroche is Jacqueline's lover, Fortunio nonetheless gallantly offers himself for an ambush which Master Andrew, suspicious again, has set. Stirred by this mark of his devotion, Jacqueline confesses her love for the young clerk. The play ends with a repetition of the dinner scene, with Master Andrew once more appeased, and this time with Clavaroche in the unwilling role of unrequited lover.

Le Chandelier has several structural resemblances to its pre-

5. The term, which literally means "candlestick," is of uncertain origin in this usage. Most commentators refer to Littré's definition: "In the language of gallantry, the candle-holder is the name given to those more aptly called screens, and who are made the object of the husband's jealousy, when it is another who is courting the wife." But this definition appears to be derived from Musset's play, since Littré indicates no other source. There seems to be little internal or external connection with Giordano Bruno's comedy of the same name (Il Candelaio); there the term is applied to the cuckolded husband, and seems to have more scabrous connotations.

6. This celebrated text has been set to music by several composers, including Jacques Offenbach: "Si vous croyez que je vais dire / Qui j'ose aimer, / Je ne saurais pour un empire / Vous la nommer..."

decessors, and is organized along similar dramatic lines. There are three acts, as in *On ne badine pas avec l'amour*, divided into ten transformation scenes (in seven different sets: as with *Marianne*, Musset in 1848 arranged a version with only three sets for Comédie-Française production). The characters are roughly divided between "real" people and caricatures, as in Musset's great comedies: Fortunio and Jacqueline versus Clavaroche and Master Andrew. The language employed by the protagonists—especially Fortunio—is a mixture of poetry, wit, and eloquence that recalls the speech of Perdican, Octave, and Fantasio. There are elements of symmetry and repetition as in *Marianne* and *On ne badine pas avec l'amour*: particularly the two dinner scenes with their refrain, "Sing, Fortunio"—"Sing, Master Clavaroche." The exchanges between Fortunio and his fellow clerks are reminiscent of the dialogue between Fantasio and his friends. Certain details of the plot, like Master Andrew's ambush and the young hero's willingness to let himself be sacrificed, inevitably remind us of the first of Musset's great plays, *Marianne*. Indeed, several critics have remarked on the parallels between the two "quartets" of protagonists in *Le Chandelier* and *Marianne*: the idealistic lover (Coelio-Fortunio), the married woman (Marianne-Jacqueline), the blasé rake (Octave-Clavaroche), the elderly husband (Claudio-Master Andrew—both men of law).[7] It would seem as if Musset, having explored the possibilities of his dramatic talent in its various guises, returned once again to his point of departure for new inspiration and energy.

We cannot forget, however, that 1835 was also the year of the *Confession d'un enfant du siècle*, whose composition was interrupted by *Le Chandelier*. The man who wrote that depressing pseudo-novel, a thinly disguised account of his affair with George Sand, and consented to have it published, was no longer the ironic antiromantic of 1830 to 1833. The earlier Musset would never have signed his name to such a pathetically personal, confessional work. Something had happened to him, not only in the purely psychological sense which has fascinated his biographers but in the roots of his literary personality, the idea of art which

7. See in particular Gastinel, *Le Romantisme d'Alfred de Musset*, p. 504.

his works embody. This is proven by the *Confession* but also by the intensely subjective lyric poetry of his "Nights," and by the painful, lachrymose literary quality of his letters to his mistress during this period. It is therefore not surprising to find that even a comedy, emerging from this background, reflects a very different artistic and moral world from that of his earlier work.

But it is not exactly in the way which we might expect. There is certainly nothing lachrymose—or even very personal—about *Le Chandelier*. It is true that for Henry Bidou the triangle of the play reflects the Musset-Sand-Pagello triangle of Venice in 1834, with the "happy ending" as an "ideal revenge which the poet gives himself."[8] But his opinion has found no approval among more recent critics. If the situation and characters of *Le Chandelier* have a connection with Musset's sentimental life, it seems to be with an earlier experience involving a woman identified variously as the Marquise de la Carte or Madame Beaulieu. Whatever its relationship to Musset's experience, the play is too far from the highly charged emotional atmosphere of the post-Sand period to offer us any useful ground for biographical investigation. Rather, it is in the peculiar shift of moral values that Musset's new literary personality must be sought, and in the subtle yet unmistakable evidence of retreat from the structural originality of his earlier dramatic works.

For if in its original version *Le Chandelier* features multiple settings and a changing decor within each act, the procedure is used much more timorously, less imaginatively than in his earlier plays. Instead of ranging over a city—or beyond—the set goes no farther than the garden of Master Andrew's house, and it is quite easy to imagine a unitary set such as the one used in Baty's 1936 production (even a hundred years later, that seems to have remained a shibboleth at the Comédie-Française). The individual scenes form a less basic unit of construction than in *Lorenzaccio* or even in such an externally regular play as *On ne badine pas avec l'amour*, and the division into acts becomes proportionally more significant. Thus Act I ends on Jacqueline's offer to accept Fortunio as her gallant, with a highly effective departure speech

8. "Le Théâtre d'Alfred de Musset," *Conferencia* (November 1, 1920), p. 411.

by her providing a theatrical climax; Act II closes on Fortunio's astonished discovery that Clavaroche is Jacqueline's lover: two striking curtains that cannot help reminding us of the popular "well-made play," as does the final curtain line: "Sing, Master Clavaroche." The latter, a happy end that strikes a new note in Musset's theater after the bitter, flat or ambiguous endings of his earlier plays, is the first (after *Barberine*) in a long series stretching to the end of the author's dramatic career with *Carmosine*: for paradoxically Musset's plays following the period of his greatness end happily, without exception. In other words, *Le Chandelier* is far more easily classifiable as a sentimental comedy than his earlier works, and thus helps set the pattern of regularization for the plays of his decline.

When we examine Musset's use of caricature in the *fantoches*, we find a significant transformation as well. At first glance Master Andrew may remind us of Claudio, and Clavaroche of the Duke of Mantua, Elsbeth's princely lover. The two former characters are both husbands "designed on purpose" (in Octave's words) for cuckolding and men of law; the two latter, pretentious lovers whose claim on the heroine cries out for thwarting by a young, imaginative hero. But Master Andrew *is* deceived by his wife right from the beginning, unlike Claudio; and he only threatens a revenge which never remotely promises the sinister reality of the close of *Marianne*. Clavaroche is Jacqueline's flesh and blood lover, not just a wooden suitor: he thus brings the role of the *fantoche* into a contact with emotional reality that neither the Duke nor Musset's other grotesques could have, by the very definition of the term. Thus we may see that the function and utilization of these characters is modified in *Le Chandelier* in a way that is related to the shifting moral perspective of their creator.

Their internal nature is also quite markedly altered from Musset's earlier practice. It is not even certain that the term *fantoches* can justifiably be applied to them. Master Andrew is an elderly husband and he is a cuckold. He is ridiculous in his scenes with his wife—particularly the opening scene, the two dinners, and his alternate accusation and retraction which reminds us of Claudio's unreasoning, mechanical changes of mind concerning Marianne's virtue. But he is not really grotesque, he never seems inhuman: on the contrary he is a highly human if ineffectual personality, who engages our sympathy even as we laugh at him and participate in the hero's good fortune. Master Andrew's desire to believe in his wife's innocence, his pitiful backtracking before her counterattack, the self-abasement to which his adoration of Jacqueline leads him, all impart a somewhat bitter taste to our laughter when Clavaroche appears from the clothes closet, and cause a twinge of pain at Fortunio's eventual triumph. Master Andrew is old—that is his invincible fault, which makes Jacqueline's infidelity inevitable—but he is neither odious nor mechanical, as Musset's elderly characters once had to be by the nature of his poetic universe.

Clavaroche, too, is more human being than puppet. It is true that, like the Duke, he is concerned more with his uniform than with his heart when he steps out of the closet: that is why Musset made him a soldier, after all. His boasting, his lack of insight into his mistress' mind and emotions, and a certain patent, formulistic approach to affairs of the heart and other human concerns put him into a traditional category not far from the marionettes of Musset's earlier comedies: that of the *miles gloriosus*, or the braggart. Doesn't one of Fortunio's fellow clerks, commenting on the garrison of soldiers in town and their good luck with the ladies, say:

> All soldiers are alike; if a woman loves one, she loves a hundred of them. It's only the lapels of the jacket which change, from yellow to green or white. For the rest, doesn't she find a mustache curled the same way, the same regimental air, the same language and the same pleasure?
> They are all cut from one pattern; in fact, she might easily mix them up.

Clavaroche is thus categorized from early in the play, both by his own actions and by being a military officer, as a stock, stereotyped figure.

Yet Clavaroche, like Master Andrew, escapes rigid classification as a *fantoche*. He may be callous, sensual, and opportunistic, but he is neither stupid nor mechanical. Once he has put his uni-

form in order, he even manages to be witty: "I was in a bad position when you closed the door, so I felt like a biological speci-
men in a jar of alcohol." "Only grand-parents and judges say that
'the truth will out.' They have a good reason to: what doesn't
come out isn't known, and consequently doesn't exist." "What a
cruel closet you have! I wouldn't like to be one of your dresses."
His portrait of the "candle-bearer" is trenchant enough to make
Jacqueline laugh in spite of her anxiety, and to reconcile her to
his plan:

> If her armchair lacks a cushion, he's the one who dashes
> off to get it, for he knows the house and its layout, he's
> part of the furniture, he can find his way through hallways
> without a light. He plays bridge and whist with her aunts
> ... He is like one of those great nobles who have an
> honorary charge and are invited to gala balls; but the
> cabinet is closed to them: that isn't their business. In a
> word, his favor ends where the real ones begin; he has
> everything one sees in women, and none of what one de-
> sires. Behind this convenient dummy the sweet mystery
> lies hidden; he serves as a screen for the flame burning
> under the mantelpiece ...   (I, 1)

It is noteworthy in this speech that the "puppet" Clavaroche, far
from being unconscious of what a puppet is (as are Claudio, the
Duke, and the Baron), applies the term to the unidentified young
man who is unwittingly going to be of service to him. He uses
the expressions "candlestick," "furniture," and "screen"—inani-
mate objects, furnishings which serve a useful purpose for the
human inhabitants of the house, the "real" people; in this case
Jacqueline and himself. This sort of lucidity did not characterize
Musset's previous *fantoches*. Indeed, the word *mannequin*, "dummy," is most apt, and Clavaroche's intention is to make it apply
to Fortunio, not himself, by keeping the young man in an entirely formalistic, ceremonial role, playing the externals of love
while he is enjoying its intimacies and fruits. This is a new situation in Musset's theater, for the line of demarcation between
protagonists and puppets had always previously been clear, fixed,
and irreversible. The threat of the mechanical was there for his

heroes: Fantasio's temptation to surrender, Perdican's game of hide-and-seek—but none of them actually played the part of a marionette, even momentarily.

Clavaroche's monologue at the beginning of the second act (in the 1835 version; II, 2, in the 1848 text) completes the impression that this is as much a real person as a caricature. In it he analyzes with humor and lucidity his role as lover, the annoyances and inconveniences it subjects him to, and the inanity of running after married women (and outwitting their jealous husbands) as compared to the comforts of the barracks and the café. Of course there is a strong element of the grotesques' dominant vanity in this declaration, which faintly echoes the lucubrations of the Duke and Bridaine. But there the comparison ends, for Clavaroche's monologue like all his speeches is infinitely more intelligent and objective than any of theirs, and his humor is not unconscious.

Thus we can see that, as far as the category of the *fantoches* is concerned, the existential and psychological barrier that separated them from the real characters is seriously breached in *Le Chandelier*, creating a new relationship between puppets and heroes, as well as between puppets and audience. Whatever the play may gain in humanity or in realism from this procedure, it loses a good deal of the thematic significance which Musset derived from the implacable opposition between life and its sterile imitation in his great works.

When we turn to the protagonists, we see that an analogous process has beclouded the definition of their character. Fortunio's unwitting role-playing, his involuntary casting in the part of a screen or dummy, is but one aspect of his troubling ambiguity. Superficially, this is the same young, impassioned lover we have found in all of Musset's comedies, torn between idealism and desire, between the dream and the real world—perhaps even a more perfected version of him. For Pierre Gastinel, "There is, in . . . *Le Chandelier*, an ardor which we may seek in vain in *Marianne*, a richness of resonance which Andrea [del Sarto's] harangue lacks . . . Listening to [Fortunio], we feel ourselves half-way between Perdican's grandiloquence and the somewhat overimaginary sufferings of the *Spectacle*; but closer to the latter, for

Fortunio's distress avoids exaggeration. . . . Musset's psychology stays more constantly close to real life."[9] The last statement is unquestionably true: the psychological realism which character-izes Musset's later theater is inaugurated here. But it is a realism in the philosophical sense as well—a rejection of idealism—and it comes at the expense of Musset's imaginativeness and fantasy. As Gastinel admits, that is why the delightful *fantoches* soon disappear from his plays. As to his first point, certainly Fortunio is eloquent: unlike Coelio, he has no difficulty whatever in ex-pressing his emotions to his mistress once the opportunity has been offered to him, and he obviously makes a verbally more ap-pealing lover than Clavaroche, for all the attraction the latter's colorful uniform exercises. Jacqueline finds his eloquence indeed almost too impressive. She doubts that Fortunio's actions can be in harmony with his words, until his offer of sacrifice convinces her of his sincerity:

> *Fortunio:* "Ah! Jacqueline, have pity on me; it's not just
> yesterday that my suffering began. For two years
> I have been following your footsteps through these
> bowers. For two years, without perhaps your even
> knowing of my existence, your faint, trembling
> shadow has not appeared behind your curtain, you
> have not opened your window, you haven't stirred
> the air, without my seeing you; I could not approach
> you, but your beauty, thank heaven, belonged to
> me as the sun belongs to everyone . . . My Lord, I
> have nothing but my tears. Do tears prove that one
> loves? What, here I am on my knees before you; at
> every beat my heart wants to fly up to your lips; I
> am cast down at your feet by a pain which crushes
> me, that I have been fighting for two years, that
> I can no longer restrain, and you can remain cold
> and incredulous?" (II, 4)

Given the hero's youth, beauty, and verbal facility, the central sentimental action of *Le Chandelier* becomes not a question of struggle between the protagonist and the world, but one of suc-

9. *Le Romantisme d'Alfred de Musset*, p. 508.

cess in overcoming a woman's hesitancy and her habit of a titular lover. Fortunio's name is no doubt symptomatic: it reminds us of the ambivalence associated in French with the word "fortune" when it is applied to affairs of the heart. "Une bonne fortune" is a brief amorous adventure, a flirt which succeeds beyond expectations. "Un homme à bonnes fortunes" is the French equivalent of a "ladies' man," carrying with it the pejorative sense of amorous opportunism, shallowness, and fickleness. Fortunio is not yet that (although Jacqueline's maid hints at his success with the *grisettes*), but we can well imagine him becoming one, with Jacqueline as the first step in his "progress."

When we first encounter Fortunio (I, 2), he is questioning Landry, his fellow clerk, about the nocturnal intruder whom the latter has reported seeing to Master Andrew. Fortunio's curiosity is stronger than might perhaps seem normal, even for one who evidently has been peering at his mistress for two years. He wants to know every detail of Landry's observations, and his questions have a sensual precision to them that creates a slight impression of vicarious voyeurism which Landry is happy to satisfy. Fortunio, unlike Coelio, makes no secret of his infatuation to those around him (all the household seems to know about it except the masters), and the form which it takes, though it must be taken in a historical context of regarding such activities more innocently, is from the first less elevated than that which we find in Musset's earlier plays. What can we make of his statement that he would like to have been there, to have watched all night, to be the morning bird who warns the lovers of danger? It makes Fortunio's later shock at the discovery that Clavaroche is Jacqueline's lover less credible, or at least less significant: instead of crying out "Christ, he's her *lover!*" he must merely be saying "Christ, *he's* her lover!"

Fortunio's pursuit of Jacqueline and his final triumph at Clavaroche's expense thus becomes a dual, parallel movement of victory and defeat. Victory, in the sense of reality (winning a beautiful, elegant mistress); defeat in the sense of the ideal, since Fortunio's progress is a kind of *éducation sentimentale* which revises his views on love and women. From the very beginning, Fortunio not only is used by Clavaroche and Jacqueline, he leads

himself willingly to his role as the latter's accomplice in a sub-
terfuge against her husband, Fortunio's master, against whom he
has no justifying complaints or rancor. The initial ruse of her
secret jewelry-shopping, with Fortunio as go-between, is not yet
adultery, but it is a first step in deceit. The role of cavalier-servant
which he subsequently plays at Master Andrew's dinner is not a
particularly glorious one, either; the fact that the latter treats
him with jovial acceptance makes it all the more ignoble, especially if we compare Master Andrew's complaisance with
Claudio's murderous punctilio. Only Fortunio's extreme youth
provides an excuse for such a lack of conscience, such egocen-
tricity—and that will not remain valid for long.

When Fortunio learns that he has been played for a fool, he
has to make drastic adjustment to his idea of woman and of love.
The shock opens his eyes to the world:

> Deceiving, lying, lying from the bottom of her heart; using
> her body as bait, playing with all that's sacred under the
> heavens, like a thief with loaded dice; that's what makes a
> woman smile! . . . This is your first step in learning the
> ways of the world, Fortunio. Think, reflect, compare,
> examine, don't judge hastily. That woman has a lover
> she adores; she's suspected, tormented, threatened; she's
> afraid she is going to lose the man who gives meaning to
> her life, who is worth more to her than the world . . . She
> must save the sole object of her anxieties, her worries, and
> her sorrows at any price; she must love in order to keep
> on living, and deceive in order to love. She looks out her
> window, she sees a young man down there; who is it? . . .
> She doesn't know; she needs him, she calls him, she beckons
> to him, she puts a flower in her hair, she speaks, she has
> put her life's happiness down on a card, and she bets it on
> the red or the black . . .   (III, 2)

It is only by ill chance that she elected him, Fortunio, and that he
happened to be in love with her. Or is it? Pursuing his reflections
to their conclusion, Fortunio sees the probability that Jacqueline
chose him (as was indeed the case) because he was infatuated
with her, and would therefore lend himself more willingly and

devotedly to her plans. He is forced to conclude that she is a scheming, cold Jezebel: "God of justice [Fortunio seems to take the Lord's name more easily and frequently than any of his fellow heroes], if that is true, what kind of monster am I dealing with, into what abyss have I fallen?"

The flash of insight proves too much for him to sustain, and he immediately retreats from it. But the revelation remains once it has crossed his mind, and henceforth Fortunio's pursuit of Jacqueline (which becomes more passive, it is true) involves at least an unconscious resignation, a tacit admission that the fascinating, seductive woman he loves and will possess is a strange mixture of angel and devil, of ingénue and tramp:

> No, so much horror isn't possible! No, a woman can't be
> a malevolent statue, both alive and frozen. No, even if I
> saw it with my own eyes, if I heard it from her own mouth,
> I would not believe she can play such a game . . . No,
> Jacqueline isn't evil; this isn't scheming or callousness.
> She lies, she deceives, she's a woman; she's a coquette, she
> teases, she's gay, bold, but not vile, not unfeeling. Ah!
> you fool, you love her! You love her! You pray, you weep,
> and she laughs at you!   (III, 2)

All of which does not prevent Fortunio from returning to the lure, from offering himself as a victim for Master Andrew's trap in order to save his mistress and her lover. Certainly there is something generous and noble in his sacrifice, but it is not on the same moral plane as Coelio's, it doesn't have the redeeming elevation attached to the preservation of love's purity as an ideal, Perdican's "muck" turned into "dream." Rather, it seems to be an act of desperation at the death of his illusions. The same may be said concerning Coelio, but the context is very different. Fortunio has plunged much further into a world which Coelio only brushes against, before his quasisuicide: he is more contaminated by it, by the role he has been willing to play in it. And especially, he is the winner at the end, and that changes everything.

For at the final curtain Fortunio has replaced Clavaroche as Jacqueline's lover. We may say all we want about the advantageous difference for her: that Clavaroche was a rake, and Fortunio is a boy; that Jacqueline was seduced by Clavaroche, she is the victim of her mismarriage and of an unscrupulous Don Juan, whereas her love for Fortunio is real and based upon esteem as well as attraction; that Fortunio merits his good luck because of his persistence and his willingness to serve, just as in courtly romances. But we see too clearly the other side of this romance, through the hero's eyes and our own, and we know that it is really adultery, that Master Andrew is its victim, that Jacqueline is an older woman initiating a young man into the mysteries— and disillusionments—of love; that she has now had two lovers, and will evidently have more before she is finished. Fortunio's turning of the tables on Clavaroche at the end, underlined by the exchange of roles in the repeated dinner scene and its varied refrain—"Sing, Master Clavaroche"—is an ironic commentary on the young man's introduction to love and life. It is painful and disquieting to see this acceptance of a dubious role associated here with the idea of a "happy ending" when precisely the same material would earlier have provided Musset with one of his bitter, ambivalent curtains.

As for Jacqueline, Musset makes it difficult if not impossible to think of her as a schemer, as a Jezebel: his talent for delineating seductive feminine portraits was quite undiminished in *Le Chandelier.* If anything, she seems richer and more human than Marianne or Camille—certainly warmer, because she is more mature, more experienced than either the young wife or the fiancée. If she, too, is a product of convent education, she is farther away from it, less dogmatic in her virtue (having in any case already lost it). Musset brings us closer to her thoughts and feelings, making her emotional development more accessible to his audience through the use of monologues and exchanges. Where Camille and Marianne both appear to be capricious, somewhat inscrutable representatives of the "feminine mystique"—all the more fascinating for it—Jacqueline lays her cards frankly on the table (for us if not necessarily for Fortunio) without guile or malice.

But part of what makes Jacqueline so troubling, so disquieting, is precisely her candor and sweetness, the feeling she gives us that she is a good, ordinary, if exceptionally beautiful woman who is blandly playing a vile game. Jacqueline is Musset's first bourgeoise heroine and his first contemporary woman. Camille, Elsbeth, and Marianne all come from imprecisely identified past eras, from mythical countries or idealized provinces: Naples, Munich, the Baron's manor house. They are noble or even royal, if only, like Marianne, of the "nobility of the robe." *Le Chandelier* takes place in a garrison town, in a time close to Musset's present: Master Andrew speaks of bringing a sugar Napoleon to Jacqueline as a placating gift (II, 1). That is part of Musset's new realism: most of his subsequent comedies were to reflect this familiar, contemporary world peopled by ordinary, if verbally distinguished characters.

Thus when Jacqueline is involved in somewhat unsavory maneuvers, she is not protected by distance or mystery; she is not, like Marianne or Camille, the necessary victim of human misunderstanding and isolation. She has taken a lover—not the ideal one, but neither a brute nor a monster—and she gradually sees the possibility of a fresher, more attractive one. All ends well, since she manages to effectuate a trade for the better without incurring the wrath of her husband. Indeed, she even turns the tables on her first lover through a ruse of his own devising, and we can admire her part in realizing that age-old comic resolution, dear to our hearts, of the trickster tricked. But our admiration is not at all of the same quality that we feel, with mixed pity and sorrow, for Camille and Marianne. Jacqueline's triumph, unlike their defeat, has only brief, rather trivial reverberations in time and emotion. What Jacqueline has become, she will no doubt become repeatedly and more easily, while her beauty lasts; what Marianne and Camille—even Elsbeth—have become, they will remain forever.

But there can be no doubt as to Jacqueline's dramatic interest. Her complexity is a challenge to the talents of a worthy actress. In the words of Louis Jouvet, "There is something of the ingénue in Jacqueline, otherwise she would be a bitch . . . If there isn't a great purity in her, she becomes one of those *bourgeoises* whom I find rather shabby, as when she was played by mature actresses who copied the tone of *La Parisienne* or *Le Demi-monde* to play Musset."[10] From a theater man's perspective, this statement defines Jacqueline's ambivalence quite well, and might even be used to characterize what distinguishes *Le Chandelier* from Musset's earlier comedies: the peculiar blending of incongruous elements which pervades it. Jacqueline is not the ingénue-turning-woman of those former works: but she must be played, and appreciated, *as if* she were. If she does not convince us that there is something innocent, something still intact, behind the appearances of her role, then she does indeed resemble the tarnished matrons of boulevard comedy, the sentimental tarts and warm-hearted adulteresses of Dumas fils and the nineteenth-century realists. Certainly Musset provides the dramatic wherewithal for avoiding such interpretation: Jacqueline does not turn facilely from Clavaroche to Fortunio as if she were changing dresses. Instead, her development as a character is closely associated with the awakening of her sentiment for Fortunio, so that she seems to be born to him, and what she felt for his predecessor seems psychologically of a different nature and level. Thus it is Clavaroche who does most of the talking in their early scenes together, and Jacqueline appears to us to be a fairly passive mistress, one who has, as Gautier said, been taken more than she herself has taken. She is more expansive—more voluble and resourceful—with Fortunio, although in the beginning it is only to deceive him. With Clavaroche, her character begins to define itself only as her resistance to him takes form: in her laconic, preoccupied "yes" and "no" answers to his questions concerning the success of their ruse (II, 1); in the way she begins to disagree with him as to the continuing usefulness of the "candle-bearer" (II, 4); in her gradually increasing resistance to carrying out the callous orders which he gives her (III, 1); and finally in the ironic triumph with which she answers Clavaroche's bewildered complaints: "I am only doing as you told me" (III, 4). Her great scene of self-revelation is one she shares with Fortunio just before the finale. There she shows her courage and a kind of honesty, when she acknowledges her perfidy and tries to make amends, even going so far as to offer never to see Clavaroche again. It is

10. *Tragédie classique et théâtre du XIXe siècle*, p. 185.

only with the realization that Fortunio is indeed different, and better than the men she has previously known, that her distrust and resistance finally melt. We thus feel that at least for the moment this is something new, this is really a first time for her as for him—even if it is not the last—and that therefore what had happened with Clavaroche did not really matter, since it happened to a different woman. Her last, blurted admission of guilt and remorse, coming at the climax of this painful emergence of her real character, thus takes on some of the spiritual nature of a confession, of a catharsis which purifies her passion of its scabrous elements, and permits us to look on Jacqueline and Fortunio as if they were fresh, untarnished, and destined to enduring love:

Jacqueline: You knew that I lie, that I deceive, that I mock you and hurt you? You knew that I love Clavaroche and that he makes me do whatever he wants? that I'm acting a part? that here, yesterday, I played you for a fool? that I'm cowardly and despicable? that I'm exposing you to death for my pleasure? You knew all that, you were sure of it? So, then, what do you know now?

Fortunio: Why, Jacqueline, I believe . . . I know . . .

Jacqueline: Do you know that I love you, child that you are? that you have to forgive me or I'll die; and that I ask it of you on bended knee? (III, 3)

For a moment, Musset's eloquence makes these two dubious characters and their guilty affair seem like Romeo and Juliet— we forget both the adulterous context and the bourgeois setting. But the use to which the author's talent has been put is of a diminished order, its results less moving and less noble than what has gone before. Whatever may be the origins of this change, his moral exhaustion after the Sand affair or the premature constitutional decay which illness and excess had initiated, the Musset of *Le Chandelier* is a markedly lesser creator than the one of two years before. Bitterness and a passion for the ideal have been replaced by cynicism and complaisance with "the ways of the world." In the struggle within him between the Romantic ethic of love and suffering and the Voltairean irony which always threatened to surge up and engulf it in doubt, the latter had continually been rejected: Rolla's sentimental death song is a monument to the conflict, as is Perdican's and Octave's nostalgic praise of love and innocence. Here, instead, we see the victory of the eighteenth-century spirit over the Romantic, the skeptic over the believer, the disillusioned man of the world over the dreamer. Fortunio's travesty and betrayal of the Romantic hero mark the real end of a privileged moment in dramatic literature, the death of an ideal in its painful struggle with the world, and the birth of a new, diminished, and domesticated theater of moral realism.

Chapter 8 The Epigoni II:

Il ne faut jurer de rien

Il ne faut jurer de rien is Alfred de Musset's most successful comedy, in several senses of the word.[1] Successful in the theater from its suspense-charged first night on the eve of the 1848 Revolution, which interrupted further performances; successful in its unbroken favor with audiences and readers (it is Musset's most frequently performed play at the Comédie-Française); successful in the marriage of wit and sentiment, of language and rhythm, of content and structure, which makes it seem a perfect work of art from beginning to end, a play which could not be improved by adding, moving, or excising a single line. Reading it, one cannot help being struck by the absolute mastery of its twenty-six-year-old author, his sure sense of language, character, and scene. On the stage it lends itself to the subtlest of comic talent, the most imaginative direction, provided they have a sense of style, elegance, and character. Of all Musset's plays, this is the one which best corresponds to the idea of comedy, which offers through both laughter and happy resolution the feeling of catharsis that it should produce. It is a work without bitterness and without regret, a joyful paean to reconciliation with the world. And yet it is the work which, more than any other, closes the door on Musset's brief period of theatrical greatness.

After *Un Caprice* (1847) had given Musset his entry into the

1. The title, which literally means "Never swear to anything," would best be translated by some equally proverbial expression in English such as "You can never tell," "Don't bet on it," or "Never say never."

Paris theater, *Il ne faut jurer de rien* was the third of his four comedies performed and acclaimed within less than a year. The author once again made extensive changes to bring the play into conformity with Comédie-Française practice, as he did with all his earlier works that were produced during the last ten years of his life. The 1836 text's eight scenes, involving six different sets, were reduced to three sets, one for each act, by some ill-advised reshuffling. As in *Marianne*, transitions were inserted to make the play's logic clearer, at the expense of the elliptical organization and shifting perspective which contribute so much to the poetry of Musset's earlier stage works. The play in its original form is thus a last reaffirmation of the original stagecraft of Musset's "armchair theater" before the series of regular plays marking the final decade of his life. The author's reworking seems less damaging, however, to the basic quality of this play than was the case with *Marianne*; not only because it is less extensive, but because of the nature of *Il ne faut jurer de rien* itself. Commenting on the play's return to the stage after two months' interruption by the 1848 Revolution, Théophile Gautier allowed himself a moment's irony at the expense of the temporarily renamed Comédie-Française: "The Theater of the Republic ought to show itself a little more revolutionary." But he found that the play's exquisite appeal survived its regularization more or less intact: "How charming, when one is sentenced for life as we are to vaudeville and melodrama, to hear a work in human language, in pure French dialect, and to be rid once and for all of that horrible, vulgar jargon which is spoken and written today! How incisive, lively and alert his lines are! How his wit sparkles in the clash of dialogue! . . . The love scene under the trees has a freshness, a pure and decent passion, which are delightful."[2] The words "pure and decent" have more than passing significance in the context: coincidentally, Gautier's review of the premiere of *Le Chandelier* at the Théâtre-Historique was to appear in print the following day. There was certainly no cause for moral offense in the case of *Il ne faut jurer de rien*. On the contrary, the play seems almost a reply to its companion, the vindication of that decency which

2. *Histoire*, series 6, p. 295.

Le Chandelier so badly shocked and was to continue to offend for many years. After Musset's hymns to adultery and passion in *Marianne* and its successors, the Comédie-Française finally had a comedy to which young ladies might be taken with full confidence ...

The moral softening of Musset's vision in *Il ne faut jurer de rien* is not merely a question of language, although the latter is certainly far chaster than in *Marianne, On ne badine pas avec l'amour*, or *Lorenzaccio*. It reaches the heart of the play's ethic, the world-view which gives it form and meaning. Unlike *Le Chandelier*, however, this altered vision is not particularly to be found in the work's dramatic structure: that is doubtless why Musset felt it necessary to revise it for performance more thoroughly than its shocking predecessor. The construction of *Il ne faut jurer de rien* is still the apparently free-wheeling, spontaneous organization of the great comedies. Its action ranges from Valentine's fashionable Paris *garçonnière* to the Baroness of Mantes' provincial chateau, from her salon to the park, a neighboring inn, and the surrounding woods. The scene shifts blithely from one set to another: the first act is divided between Paris and Mantes (Musset decided to end the act after its initial scene, in the performance version, to avoid transformation scenes); the second act moves from park to salon; and the third act's four scenes span one indoor and three outdoor settings. The alternating movement characteristic of *Marianne* and *Lorenzaccio* is prevalent here as well: particularly in the contrasting decors and character-groupings of the first act and in the indoor-outdoor movement of the final act. As much as any of its predecessors, *Il ne faut jurer de rien* can be called "Shakespearean" because of this mobility and freedom which *Le Chandelier* lacked. Its stylization and poetic quality contribute further to this impression. And the open-air scenes, particularly the final one in the woods, are redolent of *A Midsummer Night's Dream, The Merry Wives of Windsor*, or *As You Like It*. The battle of the sexes, with the final domestication of one of the parties, cannot help calling to mind *The Taming of the Shrew*. But here the title would have to be changed to *The Taming of the Dandy*: that is why French source criticism has thought to find a model in Marivaux's minor comedy, *Le Petit Maître corrigé*.[3]

This stylization, it is true, is somewhat different from what we find in Musset's earlier comedies. While here too there are grotesques, the play continues *Le Chandelier*'s redefinition of their nature, function, and relationship to the real characters. The repetition and symmetry, used with Musset's accustomed verve, seem to be designed for more purely comical aims than, say, in *Marianne*: the dandy Valentine repeats the rhetorical formulas employed by his stolid uncle, Van Buck, in order to make fun of his middle-class values; Van Buck's repeated and undignified game of hide-and-seek in the Baroness' park contributes further to this effect—but is ironically counterpointed by Valentine's own pendulum-swing of changing sentiment concerning his intended, Cecile. The non sequiturs or haphazard associations of the Baroness' simultaneous conversations with her bumbling curate and her niece, Cecile, remind us of both Claudio's and Fantasio's speech, without, however, either the sinister social implications of the former or the latter's iconoclastic fireworks; the Baroness is merely a charmingly absent-minded and eccentric *grande dame*, carried to the point of caricature. In the final analysis, the formal symmetry of *Il ne faut jurer de rien* is a principle of regularity, of order; it is thus sensibly opposed to its implications in the earlier comedies, where it counterpointed and underlined the profound spiritual disorder of Musset's protagonists.

Here is the plot: Valentine's wealthy uncle, Van Buck, irrupts into the young man's fashionable digs with a well-rehearsed sermon which gradually splutters into wrath before his nephew's elegant if affectionate irony. He is tired of paying the debts Valentine incurs through his expensive taste in food, drink, and clothing. Van Buck can see but one way out of his nephew's financial problems, short of his own premature death (and testament): marriage. And he has a highly suitable match to propose: the daughter of the Baroness of Mantes. Valentine is as confirmed a bachelor as he is a dandy; a precocious experience in adultery gave him the firm conviction that he would never willingly put

3. Cf. Bernard Masson's edition of *Il ne faut jurer de rien* (Paris, 1966), p. 31.

himself in the unlucky husband's place. He and Van Buck finally
hit on a compromise: if Valentine succeeds in seducing Mlle. de
Mantes within the week, his uncle will admit that his chances of
eventually being cuckolded are what he claims. Otherwise he will
marry the girl. Valentine proposes a variant on a stock comic
plot: his coachman will have an accident in front of the Baroness' chateau; Valentine, incognito, will feign injury, and he will
profit by the Baroness' hospitality to seduce Cecile: Van Buck is
shocked, but ends up agreeing.

As Van Buck is making excuses to the Baroness for his nephew's failure to accompany him to the chateau—a delightful scene
in which Cecile is taking a dancing lesson, the Baroness is looking
about for her embroidery wool, and the curate is talking literature, all at the same time,—the proposed accident takes place.
But Valentine's coachman is so zealous that the accident is real:
we find Valentine walking in the park with a sprained arm in
a sling, discussing strategy with his remorseful, worried uncle.
Cecile wanders in several times, and each time Van Buck hides
precipitately in the bushes, since he is not supposed to know
Valentine. Once Cecile inquires about Valentine's "sprain" and
offers him a cup of fortifying "broth" (Valentine finds the words
crude and unbecoming), then she returns to convey her mother's
invitation for dinner and cards. Van Buck is delighted by the girl's
simple decency and good manners; but Valentine, piqued by her
apparent aloofness, professing to find her unattractive and yet
growing gradually more curious, decides to resort to drastic mea-
sures: feigned departure, a love note, a rendezvous in the park.
Van Buck regrets his wager and reports his nephew's scheme to
the Baroness. The latter counts on Cecile's forthright disclosure
of the love note; when it does not come, she finds the letter in
her daughter's apron and reads it. Irate more at Valentine's reference to her as a scatterbrain than at his amorous enterprise, the
Baroness dismisses Van Buck and his nephew angrily.

Valentine swears revenge, now with the approval of his uncle
(whom he softens up with dinner and wine at a local inn). He
sends off another message for a rendezvous in the woods. The
Baroness, who is in the throes of preparing a ball, locks Cecile
for safekeeping in the study, but the young girl tricks the curate

into releasing her by a pretended fainting spell and runs off to meet Valentine. While the repentant Van Buck, the Baroness, and her household are searching the woods in the dark, Valentine and Cecile meet in a moonlit clearing. The young man tries at first to exploit his advantage, but he is gradually chastened and abashed by Cecile's innocence. Why shouldn't she come out to meet him, since they are supposed to be engaged? Cecile recognized Valentine from the start: she first saw him and fell in love with him the year before at a masked ball. Didn't he remember? (He didn't, although his love notes referred to such a meeting as pretext for his sudden passion.) Why did Valentine pretend not to know her in the park; and why did his uncle keep jumping into the bushes every time she approached? Valentine abandons his seducer's pose, declaring his love for Cecile and his desire to marry her. The Baroness and Van Buck arrive in time to give the couple their blessing, as Valentine admits that "you should never swear to anything, and still less, dare anyone."

Once again, a happy ending—this time one which leaves nobody as its victim. For in reality the play has no antagonist except Valentine's own mistrust and resistance to marriage. All the characters participate fully and willingly in the triumph of love: a love which is consecrated and unobjectionable. The ostensible puppet figures, Van Buck, the Baroness, and the curate, unlike the *fantoches* of *Marianne, Fantasio, On ne badine pas avec l'amour*, and *Le Chandelier*, are neither dismayed nor defeated by love's conquest, since neither decency nor their self-interest is sacrificed by the couple's union. Quite the contrary! The Baroness' immediate and for a Musset puppet surprisingly flexible reaction to the sight of the happy pair kissing under the moonlight is: "Good evening, son-in-law. Where the deuce have you been hiding?" (III, 4).

Although the *fantoches* of *Il ne faut jurer de rien* are more clearly puppets in their comical mechanicalness than their analogues in *Le Chandelier*, the shift in Musset's attitude toward them is nonetheless—indeed, for that very reason—even more noticeable. Because it is clear that Van Buck, the Baroness, and the curate are direct legatees of Claudio, the Duke, and Bridaine, we are conscious of their alteration. This is not so true of their form—their "puppetness"—as of their sentimental implications. For in truth Van Buck is drawn as a stock comic figure: the rich uncle, the self-made man, the bourgeois whom the elegant young Valentine has an easy time turning to ridicule. Whether citing Homer on cuckoldry, mocking the oratorical periods of Van Buck's sermons, or trapping his uncle into sharing the luxury of chocolate and pastries for breakfast, Valentine makes excellent use of his verbal and mental agility in confrontation with the old man's stolid single-mindedness (I, 1). Laughter is naturally on the side of the youth, who is willing to shock and surprise, against middle-aged "common sense." Similarly, the scene in the Baroness' park subjects Van Buck to ridicule because of his mechanical alternation of objections and disappearances into the greenery, which undermines the dignity normally attached to his age and station (II, 1). Furthermore, the ease with which Valentine enlists his uncle's support for his final campaign against Cecile's virtue—aided by Van Buck's gastronomic weaknesses—makes the older man seem truly a puppet on the strings of the youth's intelligence and wiles (III, 3). As far as all this is concerned, then, Van Buck appears to embody all the essential traits of *fantoche*-dom: passivity, mechanical action, shock at the protagonists' doing, and subjection to his own material appetites.

But there are significant differences as well, between Van Buck's nature and function and those of his predecessors. For one thing, he has a certain self-consciousness. Not as much as Clavaroche, of course, but enough to be able to say, when Valentine goes too far in his abuse of his uncle: "Can you imagine a man of my age serving as a child's plaything?" or "Do you take me for a vaudeville uncle?"—when that is precisely the role he is taking (I, 1). There is always an element of lucidity in his carrying out of the indignities forced upon him by his nephew; and that emphasizes the second, primary element of distinction from the *fantoches*: his love of Valentine. If Van Buck accepts the degrading role of "vaudeville uncle," it is because he is genuinely fond of his nephew. His sermons, too, are dictated by this loving concern which makes him want to protect Valentine from his own extravagance. Valentine may tease him about his stodgy materialism; that does not prevent the young man from letting Van Buck pay his debts. No matter how Van Buck threatens to disown him, it is perfectly clear to us (and to Valentine) that he will never actually do it. This disinterested affection is a new feature in the *fantoches'* makeup. The Duke of Mantua's "love" is merely politics and vanity; Claudio's is a sinister sense of property; the Baron's concern for Perdican and Camille is part of his family obligation and does not visibly differ from his feeling of administrative responsibility as royal tax collector. In truth, Van Buck's admission into the ranks of the characters capable of love has a curious effect on our attitude toward Valentine: it gives him a nuance of ingratitude which tempers the wholeheartedness of our laughter at his uncle's expense. He thus continues the tendency inaugurated by Fortunio, with the difference that, instead of triumphing nonetheless over the puppets, Valentine will end up in complete accord with them.

Similarly, the Baroness is at the same time one of Musset's most successful caricatures and a deceptively human, sympathetic character. Her puppet-like traits are, essentially, her flightiness and her class consciousness. The former is deliciously illustrated in I, 2, when she is the focal point (or better, the roundhouse) of several simultaneous conversations, and succeeds in confusing all her interlocutors while remaining apparently sure of what it is she is talking about:

> *The Curate:* What did you think of the latest sermon, Madame? Did you hear it?
> *The Baroness:* It's green and pink, on a black background, like the little desk upstairs.
> *The Curate:* I beg your pardon.
> *The Baroness:* Oh excuse me, I was miles away.
> *The Curate:* But I thought I saw you there.
> *The Baroness:* Where?
> *The Curate:* At Saint-Roch, last Sunday.
> *The Baroness:* Oh yes, of course. Everybody was in tears; the Baron did nothing but blow his nose all the way through. I left in the middle, because the lady next to me had the odors, and I'm in the hands of the homeopaths right now . . .

or:

> *Cecile:* Mama, why don't you want me to learn the
> Viennese waltz?
>
> *The Baroness:* Because it's indecent. Have you read
> *Jocelyn?*
>
> *The Curate:* Yes, Madame. There are some beautiful
> verses, but I must admit, the base of it . . .
>
> *The Baroness:* The base is black, like the rest of the desk;
> you'll see that on palissander.
>
> *Cecile:* But Mama, Miss Clary does the waltz, and so does
> Miss Bunbury.
>
> *The Baroness:* Miss Clary and Miss Bunbury are English,
> young lady. I'm sure, Father, that you're sitting on
> them.
>
> *The Curate:* On Miss Clary and Miss Bunbury? But
> Madam . . .
>
> *The Baroness:* It's my skeins of yarn. . . . Ah, there's what
> I'm looking for. No, it's the red; where can it have
> disappeared?

The Baroness is not the only incoherent one here; but she is the center of confusion, and she sets the tone and pace for the others. That this is her normal state of mind is amply confirmed by a subsequent card game (II, 2) and by the utter panic that the arrangements for her ball throw her into, while Cecile's threatened escapade undermines all her self-possession. The Baroness' conversation then becomes an interlacing of chairs, syrups, moral maxims, and appeals for help.

The Baroness' class-consciousness mixes delightfully with her social incoherence to complete the portrait of a distinguished marionette. Her commentary on Valentine's intercepted letter to Cecile is marked more by criticism of the young man's breaches of etiquette and epistolary style than by distress at the love note's intentions—until she reads the fatal expression "scatterbrain" (which was the cause of Cecile's reticence). She makes it clear from the beginning that Valentine's refusal to accept her invitation to dinner and cards is a sign of the bad breeding so prevalent in the modern world. When the Curate agrees that contemporary young people don't bother to be polite, she retorts: "Polite! They haven't the slightest idea! And what would it matter if they were polite? My coachman is polite. In my day, Father, people were gallant . . . I'd like to have seen my brother, who was in the Prince's retinue, fall from his coach at some castle-gate, and stay overnight. He would sooner have lost his fortune than refuse to be a fourth at bridge . . ." (II, 2). Her shock at Van Buck's suggestion that Cecile is concealing Valentine's letter from her mother is couched in terms of class: how dare a bourgeois make such an accusation against a daughter of the aristocracy? And she derides the Curate's warnings of revenge by Valentine and his uncle for her brusque dismissal of them: "What, from Van Bucks? Cloth merchants? What could that possibly matter? Even if they shouted, who would hear them?" (III, 2). Like the Duke of Mantua and like Claudio, the Baroness shares in the *fantoches'* preoccupation with rank and protocol, the concern for forms and rules rather than emotions. At least on the surface.

But once again, as with Van Buck (with whom she is quickly reconciled), there is a mitigating element of sentiment which spoils the apparent machinality. If the Baroness is a puppet, she is a formidable one. In spite of her dowager airs and her sense of class, she is obviously the focus of her household, the center about which retainers, guests, and family revolve: she has a moral power that is absent from previous *fantoches*. More than that she is, like Van Buck, capable of giving and inspiring love. Cecile insists on this in her revelations to Valentine in the final scene: if she is a dutiful daughter (apart from the momentary defiance of her escapade—and that was justified by Valentine's status as fiancé), it is because she loves and respects her mother. Behind her façade of flightiness and arrogance, the Baroness is a charitable, concerned châtelaine, ready to bring food and comfort to "her" poor at a moment's notice, and never forgetful of the obligations of good fortune. Cecile's praise, which seems in no way ironic (or underlined by any irony of Musset's), strikes us as patronizing in the connotation given to "charity" today. But it is symptomatic of the pervading air of innocence, of an almost pastoral naïveté that characterizes *Il ne faut jurer de rien*, and which seems shocking after the lucid cynicism of *Lorenzaccio* and the rueful disillusionment of *On ne badine pas avec l'amour.* Nonetheless, in the context of this play, what has seemed to be a variant on Musset's typical grotesque figures turns out to be something quite different: a "real human being" (if the cliché may be forgiven) who masquerades as a puppet, rather than a puppet masquerading as a man.

Even the Curate, who is so stereotyped as to be without family or surname and thus seems to melt into the ranks of parlor-comedy clerics, distinguishes himself quite clearly from Blazius and Bridaine, his nominal ancestors. Whereas the latter were marked above all by a self-interest, a gluttony that reaches mock-epic proportions in Bridaine's monologue, the Curate is merely a bumbling hanger-on, a conversationalist and bridge partner for the Baroness. Typically, in the transformation which the *fantoches* undergo in this comedy, his general air of ineffectualness translates itself into excessive human concern: when he fails to carry out the Baroness' wishes in guarding Cecile, it is because he is worried lest something really has happened to her. She profits by his inability to remain impassive—by his sentimental weakness—to pass right over him: and we cannot help feeling the nuance of regret that we experienced at Valentine's treatment of Van Buck.

Thus Van Buck, the Baroness, and the Curate represent, individually and collectively, a parody of middle-age and of social mores. In their internal nature, their character traits, they continue the *fantoches'* ironic representation of what is no longer (or has never been) youthful, and they call to mind Musset's predominant existential theme: the fossilization of man and of human experience by time. In their inconsequential yet comically rigid interrelationships with each other, they remind us of the social parodies of *Marianne* and *Fantasio*, the ossification of human behavior, of human relationships, which we call social codes, protocol, or politics. Yet each of them evolves into something he did not seem to be, and which previous *fantoches* never were: a character endowed with internal depth, a three-dimensional figure rather than a cartoon. In all three cases, the element that catalyzes this transformation is a sense of goodness: of "charity" in the broader sense (as the Baroness exemplifies), therefore of love. Neither the existential nor the social parody takes on the note of bitterness that pervades Musset's earlier comedies, and which there makes his puppets into willing or unconscious agents of death and despair for his protagonists. On the contrary: Van Buck and the Baroness end by being "right," and Valentine ends by wholeheartedly and happily agreeing with them.

As in *Le Chandelier*, this humanization of the puppet figures has an interesting effect on the protagonists of *Il ne faut jurer de rien*. They are relatively diminished, morally and psychologically, in respect to the *fantoches* and by extension in respect to Musset's earlier heroes. The latter were in truth the only "human" characters in their plays, and their difference in species from the other dramatic figures gave them a peculiar relief, a quasimythical stature. Whether this literary procedure was "realistic" or just makes no particular difference: it was an important part of both the spiritual and the aesthetic integrity of those earlier works. On the contrary, Valentine and Cecile seem to represent an act of contrition or recantation on Musset's part, a literary penance for the excesses of his (all-too-recent) youth, and a peace offering to the older generation.

The process is marked first of all by a sort of "token integration" between the two races of characters. Dussane, the great interpreter of Musset, suggested this when she spoke of the proposed wedding between Cecile and Valentine as the marriage of "a doll with a dummy" (her term, *mannequin*, recalls Clavaroche's expression for Fortunio).[4] Dussane was referring specifically to Cecile's obedience and to Valentine's abstract status for her as a "match" (as well, no doubt, as to his dandyism). But the expressions employed by her are peculiarly apt in their indirect allusion to the *fantoches*. The two lovers do indeed remind us at several points, in specific ways, of the mechanical qualities formerly reserved to the puppets. Maurice Allem seems to have had this in mind when he spoke of Valentine's behavior toward Cecile during the scene in the park: "Cecile delivers her mother's invitation to Valentine. He refuses them with an affectation of coldness. She takes her leave and goes off. This is, in reverse,

4. "Les Héroïnes de Musset. I. Cécile," *La Revue hebdomadaire* (March 19, 1932), p. 277.

more or less the situation of Camille and Perdican at a given point of *On ne badine pas avec l'amour.*"[5] If Valentine chooses to repeat Camille's game of pride and prejudice, he thereby is reenacting the drama of mechanical reaction which we have noted in the earlier play and imitating the stiffness, the psychological rigidity, of the *fantoches.* But this rigidity is visible not only in his rejection of Cecile's polite advances, but in a variety of traits and gestures which Musset lends to his hero.

If the Valentine of Act I is a type of Romantic hero (like other Musset protagonists), he takes the part in a rather special way. This is a second-generation Romantic, a young man-about-town who copies the Romantics' life style much as the gilded youth of postwar Paris or San Francisco copied the Existentialist or Beat life style: as a mode of dress and manners. Valentine's individualism is primarily a question of fashion: his gaudy waistcoat (inherited from the *Jeunes-France* phalanges at the premiere of *Hernani*), his beard, his long hair, his indolence and eccentric hours. In other words, Valentine is a Dandy, a banal if attractive creature of the times who benefits neither from the originality of the movement's founding generations nor from the spiritual and aesthetic dignity with which Baudelaire was later to endow the idea. For a Romantic, even an epigone, Valentine is an oddly cautious young man. All his objections to marriage seem not a paean to celibate freedom but rather a distrust of modern woman and an unwillingness to take chances (here again we are oddly reminded of Camille: her refusal to give herself to any but an "eternal" lover). In contrast to Perdican's and Octave's diatribes against convent education and its stultifying effect on the emotional life of women, Valentine's wit exercises itself against his intended's supposed ruination by modern, liberal education and moral values.

> Is she taken to balls, to the theater, to horse-races? Does she go out alone in a cab, at noon, and come back at six? Does she have a clever chambermaid, a hidden stairway? Has she seen *La Tour de Nesle*, does she read Balzac? Do they take her out after a good dinner on summer evenings,

5. *Alfred de Musset*, p. 143.

when the wind is in the South, to see ten or twelve naked,
muscle-bound brutes wrestle on the Champs-Elysées?
Does she have a grave and curly-haired dancing master, a
graceful waltzer with well-rounded calves, to press her
hand when she has drunk some punch? . . . Does she spend
summers in the country with a worldly-wise lady, trusted
by the family, who leaves her playing the piano in the
evenings to stroll whispering under the elms with a cavalry
officer?   (I, 1)

If so, then the girl is spoiled forever, and the man who is fool
enough to marry her might as well be swallowing fish-bones or
drinking from a cracked glass, for all the concern he shows for
his own safety . . .

This imitation Romantic displays his true colors in the plan he
devises for Cecile's conquest and his own preservation from wed-
lock. It is not without significance that the incognito adopted by
Valentine is, give or take a few details, the same well-worn ruse
that the Duke of Mantua used in his assault on Elsbeth. The aim
is not the same: Fantasio's pasteboard adversary sought to prove
his capacity to inspire love for himself without the accessories of
rank, whereas Valentine wants to show that *any* enterprising
and presentable young man might overcome the young lady's
scruples. But the hoariness of the stratagem and its literary origin
(in Marivaux's *Jeu de l'amour et du hasard*) undeniably link the
two lovers, puppet and dandy, across time and space, providing
an inescapable commentary on the character of Valentine.

Nor, in the final analysis, is this the only stale part which
Valentine is willing to undertake. The role of convalescent in
the Baroness' garden is an equally literary one, and Valentine
himself acknowledges the fact by citing the verse of a particularly
trite Romantic elegy, Millevoye's "Chute des Feuilles":

A sickly youth, with measured step . . . (II, 1)

He thus consciously (if ironically) joins the ranks of Romantic
invalids, the most abused stereotype of an already outmoded
hero. This role-playing, coupled with the entire imitation of passion which he acts out for the benefit of Cecile, gives Valentine

a strange, inverted connection with earlier Musset heroes. Fantasio, it is true takes a part, too—that of the jester—but it is in order to achieve greater freedom of action and speech, a higher degree of honesty. Valentine, on the contrary, uses the language of passion cynically, to deceive and ultimately to protect himself against love. That at least is his intent: it is not his fault if the plan backfires, and he ends up a victim of his own defensive machinations.

Furthermore, in the end Valentine accepts one last role, this time a permanent one: the role of husband which he had categorically refused in the first scene of the play. He ends by putting on the costume with which he had symbolized his former mistress' neglect of her spouse: the dirty greenish gloves the latter donned as he left Valentine and his lady to their own devices (I, 1). I am not sure whether I can go as far as Jules Lemaître, who saw in this final turnabout the conscious suggestion by Musset that Cecile, having succumbed once to an ardent suitor, is quite likely to do so again:

> You will say, "That was possible once, because she was in love." But, in fact, nothing guarantees that, in a few years, she won't fall in love with another man. And then, with that frankness, that perfect naturalness, that adorable spontaneity which we see in her . . . you can see where that will lead . . . Valentine no longer foresees such a consequence, since he is in love. But you may rest assured that the poet foresees it for him, and that it doesn't frighten him . . . [6]

This is extrapolation from experience, a voice from another, more worldly sphere than Valentine and Cecile's (a *fin du siècle* voice, we might specify). Not only is Cecile in love, she is from the start in *permitted* love, and that is what touches and reassures the cautious Valentine. But it is true that he crowns the series of roles he plays with the very role (hopefully minus some of its decorative headgear) that he swore not to take at the outset: that is precisely the play's moral. Thus the culminating lesson of the play, and its resolution, are linked with the traits that con-

6. *Théâtre d'Alfred de Musset*, introduction by Jules Lemaître (Paris, 1889), I, xvi.

nect Valentine with Musset's earlier puppets. The play's message cannot but be taken in some degree as a refutation of what those earlier comedies were about, the triumph of some of the very antivalues the puppets stood for. Which is why the Baroness and Van Buck so heartily approve!

Valentine's moral progression is a reversal of that followed by Musset's earlier heroes. He goes from amorous skepticism to a kind of orthodox belief, rather than from belief to tragic revelation, as do Coelio and Perdican. This is all the more striking because the former attitude is closely associated in this play with a kind of Romanticism and the latter with traditional bourgeois values: marriage, fidelity, domesticity. Secondly, he tends to go from a state of relative freedom (bachelorhood, even if his is premonitory of Baudelaire's banal "Eldorado des vieux garçons") to a state of willing subjection. It is doubtless unnecessary to insist on the anti-Romanticism of such a progression, its denial of one of the movement's fundamental spiritual values. (I am, of course, talking here, as elsewhere in this chapter, of Romanticism as a spiritual and philosophical current, and not as a literary school.) Valentine trades his shopworn and conformist individualism for the comforts of a pipe and slippers, the proverbial "ball-and-chain" of married life. Closely associated with this evolution is a third progression, the hero's paradoxical movement from Romantic literary caricature (the Dandy) to bourgeois "real life." This is underlined by Valentine's speech of surrender to Cecile's honest charms. There the young man abandons his penultimate role, and therewith all *literary* roles: that of Lovelace in Richardson's *Clarissa Harlow*, the model for many a Romantic seducer. It is paradoxical because the shift from human to puppet values (in the context of the earlier plays) is here connected with an inverse movement from caricature to characterization, in terms of the hero's personality. The paradox may be entirely explicable, even commonplace, in terms of social reality: we know to what an extent nonconformism can become stereotype or caricature from the fads and movements of recent years. The fact remains that this social realism is a denial of Musset's previous dramatic and spiritual values, and of literary creations whose revolt, whose nonconformity, escaped the stereotype through their poetic originality and power. And that Musset's plays henceforth were devoid of precisely those two qualities, which gave stature to his theater in the years 1833–34.

If Cecile is not quite so symptomatic of this particular decline as Valentine, that is primarily because Musset's theater is androcentric. His heroines play an important role, but it is subordinated to that of his heroes, in whom the essential process of realization or transformation takes place. Perhaps it is symptomatic that Cecile participates even less in this process than her elder sisters do—far less. Marianne, Camille, Jacqueline all evolve in significant ways through the action of their plays; their evolution, of course, is always a function of the couple—either its union, as in the latter's case, or its tragic disintegration, as with Marianne and Camille, whose loss is an element of the hero's larger disappointment or disillusionment. Cecile, on the contrary, remains remarkably static. This is what Dussane pointed out in her sensitive analysis of the role:

> At no time does Valentine appear to Cecile otherwise than as a fiancé. The fiancé is a bit odd? She respects his oddness ... She doesn't notice his eyes lifted to heaven, she doesn't hear his sighs, his double-meanings. Valentine is piqued, he becomes irritated. Is she stupid? Is she indifferent? Is she a flirt, more subtly than he is a rake? None of all that: she is already *conjugal*. She is sure of Valentine."[7]

Madame Dussane indicates the irony of this certainty: it is based on the supposition that Valentine honestly remembers seeing her the year before, when she was taken with him, and that his suit of her is sincere. But that does not change her psychological reality in any way: Cecile remains naïve and ignorant right to the final curtain, and her certainty ends by being completely justified. We may rightfully wonder whether she makes any sense out of Valentine's attempted explanation of his plans, or whether she even tries. In any case, the explanation breaks down in confusion, and Valentine abandons all hope of setting either Cecile or himself straight on the matter.

What Cecile may lack in imaginativeness or capacity for de-

7. "Les Héroïnes," p. 278.

velopment, she more than makes up for with her two predominant traits: common sense and determination, those two bourgeois values *par excellence*. Her common sense radiates from her as a kind of substitute passion: it reaches a degree of attractive sweetness that compensates for the lost heat of Marianne (in this she is reminiscent of Elsbeth; but Elsbeth is only marginally associated with love in *Fantasio*). Perhaps it is relevant to recall that the French expression "le bon sens" connotes a certain goodness that is not particularly suggested by its English equivalent. In the case of Cecile, it almost reaches the level of poetic vision. We see from the beginning that her little head is remarkably level, that she does not let herself be carried away by fashions or fads (unlike Valentine). Thus, amidst the chaos of the second scene, when her mother is carrying on three conversations and her dancing master is vying manfully for her attention, Cecile's wistful plea to learn the waltz does not blind her to the inanities of ballroom practice. Her exchange with the dancing master takes on an almost symbolic value:

> *Dancing master:* Mademoiselle, no matter how much I tell you to, you fail to do your oppositions. Now, turn your head away slightly, and let me see your arms bent.
>
> *Cecile:* But sir, if you don't want to stumble, you have to look where you're going.
>
> *Dancing master:* Bah! that's just terrible. See here, can anything be simpler? Watch me: am I stumbling? You go to the right, you look to the left; you go to the left, you look to the right. Nothing could be more natural! (I, 2)

It is obviously not natural to Cecile, whose instinct seems to lead her intact past the pitfalls of modern life and education. No more than the dance, the novels of Balzac (or Madame de Staël or George Sand), which Valentine warned against in his argument with Van Buck, do not seem to have spoiled her judgment or inoculated her mind with the virus of dangerous sentiments. As she confesses to her fiancé, only the descriptions and landscapes interest her: the "seductions, ruses and intrigues" all seem impossibilities or lies which have nothing to do with the "real" world in which she lives. Even her love for Valentine expresses itself in practical actions, as in the "broth" which she made to strengthen him during his convalescence from his "sprain" (and which Valentine finally admits he drank with pleasure). When, amid the lyricism of the final scene—which shifts from Valentine's false, borrowed Romanticism to praise of Cecile's "solid virtues" (as Claudio would say)—her lover suggests that the planet appearing in the sky above them is Venus, Cecile replies that she thinks it is a better, chaster planet: Ceres, the goddess of wheat and bread. Her promise for the future is to "take care" of Valentine even better than she did after his accident, no doubt to protect him from his own eccentricities, which are foreign to his definition as husband. As for Cecile, even her escapades are firmly grounded in realism: if she dared disobey the Baroness and run out of the castle to meet Valentine, it was with the idea that she might thereby compromise her reputation and force her mother to accept the match that Valentine's tactlessness had almost spoiled. This charming paragon of virtue even commits her follies in the name of common sense!

Reinforcing this trait is the strong little will lurking behind her air of obedience. It is obviously Cecile who engineered the campaign initially, from the first sight of Valentine to Van Buck's proposition of a suitable match. Valentine's fantastic plan of seduction has been only a momentary diversion of this campaign —an absurdly irrelevant one we can see, when we look at it from Cecile's perspective in the final scene. Van Buck's plunges into the brush end by seeming even more comical, once we know that Cecile had observed them—just as she watched Valentine drink her broth and thereby confirm her assurance of success. If Valentine seems a bit ridiculous, and realizes it himself in retrospect, that does not appear to affect Cecile's determined conjugality. She will know how to keep him in line, to protect him from his own follies and make him like it. If ever middle-class values had a symbolic representative, a myth figure to personify the stabilizing force of will-to-reason (it seems a contradiction in terms), it would be Cecile, the domesticating force of bourgeois womanhood in her simple glory.

Cecile is thus, mythically, Marianne (and Eve) in reverse: instead of going from the stricture of convent education, from enforced ignorance, to guilty desire and knowledge, she has gone from freedom to innocence and virtue. I say "has gone" because any process of change has evidently taken place before the action of the play. Only her gradual self-revelation constitutes what might be called change: the change engendered in Valentine's feelings by the surprise of her honesty, the charm of her calm little will. With Cecile, and with Valentine's conquest by her innocence, we are in a world before the Fall, or a world in which the myth of the Fall has been strangely inverted. Valentine's fall from innocence, related in his anecdote to Van Buck, is somehow effaced by Cecile's example: it might never have existed, and the young man's confusion in the scene in the woods is either an emergence from amnesia or an entry into it:

> You told me that novels shock you; I've read a lot of them,
> some of the worst. There's one called *Clarissa Harlow*;
> I'll let you read it when we're married! The hero loves a
> beautiful girl like you, my darling, and he wants to marry
> her; but first he wants to test her. He kidnaps her and
> takes her to London; then, when she resists, Bedford arrives
> —that is to say, Tomlinson, a captain—I mean Morden—
> no, I'm mixing it up—Anyway, to cut it short—Lovelace
> is a fool, and I am too, to have tried to follow his example.
> God be praised, you didn't understand me—I love you,
> I'm marrying you, there's no truth in the world other than
> raving about love!   (III, 4)

The memory is erased, the new light eclipses the old, but it does not matter. Valentine is integrated now into Cecile's world, a world where evil deeds and bad intentions do not exist. This is an odd reversal of the resolution in Musset's earlier plays, and its dreamlike atmosphere contributes to our suspicion that it has a symbolic value in relation to them: the passage from the pathetic oneirism of Musset's youthful theater to the positivistic optimism of his premature decline.

The play thus ends in a triumph of connubial harmony which is all the more striking for its contrast with Musset's deepest personal instinct. Unlike Valentine, the author remained to the end of his life the invincible bachelor. This was not merely fortuitous circumstance, an irrelevant detail in his biography unrelated to Musset's work. It is as intimately linked to his best works as his parallel fear and hatred of old age. As Gastinel says, "For Alfred, a man who marries renounces his youth. Between the young and this deserter, a chasm immediately opens up."[8] For this inveterately skeptical young man, who two years later was to turn down the marriage offer of a woman who nonetheless devoted her entire life to him—Aimée d'Alton—to sing the praises of marital bliss is a strange and finally touching phenomenon. Amid the chaos of Musset's personal life, in transit from the exhausting fireworks of his affair with George Sand to the depressing, self-inflicted solitude of his last years, *Il ne faut jurer de rien* stands as a wonderfully deceptive monument to the possibility of love and understanding within the context of the social structure, and within the framework of human morality. The possibility of love as a final ordering principle, a basis for stability in action (and no longer merely in memory). In this affirmation all the play's characters are joined, puppets as well as protagonists, in a final reconciliation.

The familiar material is treated from a new perspective. Lovers, *fantoches*, actions, sentiments, and themes from Musset's former works are reinterpreted, revisualized. Even a large piece of material from Musset's unfinished *Roman par lettres* (which told of the sweet pain of unrequited love, in Hoffmannesque style) passes into the mill, to be transformed into wholesome flour under the beneficent influence of Ceres. The painful uncertainties to which Musset's protagonists were subjected in a hostile world, the isolation and miscomprehension to which his unhappy young people subjected themselves and each other in the desperate search for love, are reconciled in a new moral: nothing is certain—but anything is possible. *Il ne faut jurer de rien.*

8. *Le Romantisme d'Alfred de Musset*, p. 126.

Chapter 9 *Carmosine:*

The Myth Turned Fairy Tale

 The period of Alfred de Musset's life extending from 1836, the date of *Il ne faut jurer de rien,* to 1857, the year of his death, is a rich source of insight into the psychology of the artist—rich particularly in sentimental adventures of striking intensity and number. This is the side of Musset which attracted innumerable biographers for a half-century or more following Musset's death. Even the physical decline of the author has been chronicled by the literary doctors (or men of medical letters) who flourish in France as nowhere else. It is a period of immense interest to those who study the psychopathology of the creative mind. Musset's sentimental adventures, with their invariably unhappy conclusion, are complexly interwoven with his physical ills—the alcoholism and "aortic insufficiency" which led to his premature death at age forty-seven—and the remarkable alteration of his literary talent which, after the initial decline in quality from 1835 to 1838, permitted him to continue producing works of a lesser order until shortly before his death. The pathetic quality of this misspent life remains a source of fascination and conjecture. What might Musset's talents have become had he not squandered the moral resources of his youth?

Yet Musset's life seems unusually "true" in a mythic sense to the themes of his greatest literary works. Coelio, Octave, Perdican, and Lorenzo confront us with the idea of decline as a necessary function of life and human time. Andrea del Sarto, the artist as failure, gave evidence of Musset's precocious fascination with the question asked by Robert Frost's "Oven-Bird": "What to make of a diminished thing?" Musset's short story, "The Son of Titian," took up the theme once again in 1838, and turned it into a symbolic introduction to the poet's declining years. Having produced a perfect portrait of his mistress, Tizianello, second son of the great painter, bids farewell to art for the rest of his life. Musset seems to have found in this legend an idealization of his own obsessions: the praise of laziness, the renunciation of art for love, the premature fruition of a promise never fulfilled thereafter. Details of the plot (for example, an embroidered purse given the artist by his mistress, which also appeared in *Un Caprice*) indicate that this story was intended to some degree as an *apologia* to Aimée d'Alton, the life-long caretaker of his literary estate who, having been Musset's mistress and later his friend, even went so far as to wed the poet's brother Paul in order to continue the task of editing Alfred's works and bringing his plays to production after his death. A suitable conclusion, it might be said, for one of Musset's short stories.

What seemed in the dramatic works of 1833–34 to represent the ultimate pathos of life—the survival of the body following the spirit's death—became daily reality for Musset after 1840. Gustave Flaubert's succinct formula is perhaps the best summation of his life: "Musset will have been a charming youth, and then an old man."[1] The cruel terseness of this remark is deepened by our knowledge of Musset's own feelings. As Pierre Gastinel said, "I know of no adolescent who carried farther than he did the hatred of grey hair and wrinkled faces."[2] Although Musset did not live long enough to grow truly old (he seems to have done everything within his power short of suicide to prevent it), what could the fading of his youthful talent, vigor, and beauty have been for him but premature senility, painfully accentuated by the limp and stiffness, the series of debilitating illnesses, which beset his latter years? From 1840 on, Musset could no longer delude himself about the direction his health was taking. The carefree prodigality with which he had always flung himself into

1. Letter to Louise Colet of June 26, 1852. Gustave Flaubert, *Correspondance*, nouvelle édition augmentée, series 2, 1847–52 (Paris, 1926), p. 447.
2. *Le Romantisme d'Alfred de Musset*, p. 35.

excess began to take a toll on his body and spirit, leaving him exhausted where once he had sprung back. "These failings lead him to ask a painful question: is his youth disappearing? For after all, isn't it one of the signs by which a man recognizes the approach of old age, no longer to be able to commit the follies one used to allow oneself, to feel ceaselessly one's body protesting, through some ache or pain? The idea haunts Musset's spirit . . . In his eyes, didn't life end with youth?"[3] All his biographers agree that Musset's thirtieth birthday seems to have affected the poet's spirits in the way the fortieth or fiftieth does most men. The poetic texts of the period testify to it—most of all the celebrated sonnet "Tristesse," of 1840. "I have lost my force and my life / And my friends and my joy; / I have even lost the pride / That made men believe in my genius." Even the prose fiction which Musset ground out reluctantly to earn a living contains frequent hints of the author's distress, a bitterness which his dislike of this work unconsciously enhanced. The conclusion Musset gives in his short story "Frédéric et Bernerette" to an affair he had recently passed through is evidence of a frame of mind that rarely left him for long in his latter years: "I have been told that after reading [Bernerette's] letter, Frederick came close to committing a desperate act. I will not speak of it here; the indifferent all too often find reason for ridicule after such acts, when a man survives. The world's judgments are sad on this point; he who attempts to die is laughed at, and he who dies is forgotten." The cruel irony of survival, associated with the indignities of age, was to remain a source of pain to the end of his days.

Yet this period of the author's life was far from sterile in the ordinary sense of the word. He added a considerable number of works to the list of his publications, in practically every genre that he had previously explored: poetry, prose fiction, essay, drama. Musset's legendary *paresse*, which those who loved and respected him kept exhorting him to end, seems to reflect disappointed expectation on their part more than the statistical evidence of his creation. Those who awaited another masterpiece were treated only to rare satisfactions of a lesser order: the poems "Souvenir" (1841) and "Sur trois marches de marbre rose"

3. Ibid., pp. 568–69.

(1849); two or three of the short stories collected in 1854 under the title *Contes*; the plays *Il faut qu'une porte soit ouverte ou fermée* (1845) and *Carmosine* (1850). The rest is characterized by a deceptive facility—deceptive when we realize how much effort Musset exerted merely to continue producing literary works, for the maintenance of his self-esteem and financial solvency.

These considerations explain to some extent the preoccupation Musset showed for consolidating his literary reputation. The period 1840–57 saw the collection and re-edition of a good part of his works: *Poésies complètes* and *Comédies et Proverbes* in 1840; *Premières poésies* and *Poésies nouvelles* in 1852; the revised *Comédies et Proverbes* in 1854. In 1852, his election to the French Academy presupposes serious campaigning for admission to that august body. If these years did not witness a significant addition to the list of Musset's dramatic works, they were marked by several periods of active theatrical ambition that belied his vow never to return to the scene of his initial fiasco. As early as 1838 he confessed to Aimée d'Alton, then his mistress, a revival of interest in the stage: it may be that the possibility of establishing an enduring bond with her sparked concern for achieving some material success. In 1839 his liaison with the young tragedienne Rachel spurred Musset to begin a regular tragedy in verse, *La Servante du Roi*, which he never terminated, Rachel's initial interest cooling at the same rate as their love affair. It is from this period that his essay "On Tragedy" dates. In it he attempted to define a new basis for the tragic genre, a compromise between the Romantics' rejection of traditional forms and style and the neoclassical tragedy that had stagnated and repeated itself since Racine's time. For his renewal of the genre, he took as epigraph André Chenier's "Sur des pensers nouveaux faisons des vers antiques."[4] Musset's long-standing rebellion against Romantic dogma is evident in these writings. But more than that, his rejection of the original dramatic system which he himself had evolved in his armchair theater is consecrated in them—paradoxically enough because of the theatrical ambition that led to his hope

4. *Oeuvres complètes en prose*, p. 900. "Let us write ancient verses on new ideas."

of sharing in the success Rachel momentarily lent to a moribund genre. This hope was rekindled in 1850, when the actress turned briefly back to Musset for a comedy; but nothing concrete emerged from their erratic association.

Musset's absorption by the theater is evident from the series of actresses with whom he was linked during this time by either amorous or professional associations, or both. Madame Allan-Despréaux was the most influential and enduring of these: her correspondence furnishes us with some of the most lucid, sympathetic documentation we have on the poet's mind and actions. This exceptional woman was responsible in great part for Musset's belated success on the stage, since it was she who brought about the production of *Un Caprice* in 1847, at the Comédie-Française, which led to an entire series of successful Musset premieres in the following years. After Madame de Léry, she created the roles of the Marquise in *Il faut qu'une porte soit ouverte ou fermée* (1848), of Jacqueline in the Comédie-Française premiere of *Le Chandelier* (1850), and of the Countess in *On ne saurait penser à tout* (1849). Similarly, the actress Madeleine Brohan was intimately associated with the first production of *Marianne*, in 1851; the role of Lisette in *Louison* (1849), a disappointing verse comedy, was written for her sister, Augustine. An equally ill-advised work, *Bettine*, was written for the young star Rose Chéri; its lack of success seems to have had the side effect of discouraging Rachel from commissioning another comedy from Musset's flagging talent. The concentration of stage works either written or revised for performance between 1848 and 1851, as we can see from the above catalogue, is proof of Musset's surge of hope for his dramatic career. The death of his ambition can doubtless be traced to the general failure of all his new stage works, as compared with the earlier plays which he had not written for performance.

It is not surprising, given this failure, that the most interesting of Musset's plays from the last period is one he wrote for publication and not for the stage. *Carmosine* was commissioned in 1850 by Louis Véron, publisher of the newspaper *Le Constitutionnel*; it was one of Musset's few important plays not to see the light of day in the *Revue des Deux Mondes*. The circumstances of the writing of *Carmosine* are part of the poet's legend.[5] Véron offered Musset a thousand francs per act for a three- or five-act comedy. The author had already prepared the outline of a play based on Boccaccio's tenth story from the seventh day of the *Decameron*.[6] Since Musset had injured his right hand, he dictated the entire work to his governess, Madame Martellet. Véron was so pleased with it that he insisted on paying for five acts instead of the three Musset wrote; after a contest of generosity, the two men compromised on the figure of four thousand francs. Despite the generous sentiments displayed on both sides, there is something rather depressing about these circumstances which seems in keeping with the qualities of the play itself. No doubt is left in the reader's mind that compared with the great comedies, *Carmosine* is a *pièce de circonstance* that little reflects Musset's deeper emotional or artistic concerns. Despite its sentimentality it has that quality of "objectivity," of dissociation from his life, which Gastinel finds in all Musset's later production:[7] the act of dictation, which gives us one of the poet's only works lacking an autograph manuscript, provides a fittingly symbolic representation of this. Furthermore, Véron's offer, which was far more generous to begin with than any the *Revue des Deux Mondes* had ever been able to make, and his financial surcharge on delivery of the work smack suspiciously of charity, a "benefit performance" for the declining poet. Not a totally disinterested one, of course, since Musset's name still meant something despite the failure of *Louison* and *On ne saurait penser à tout* (an "imitation" of Carmontelle) the previous year, but at least a conscious gesture of solidarity going beyond the normal economic limits of such transactions. Véron is said by Paul de Musset to have been "charmed" by the play Musset handed him. The word is apt for

5. See Paul de Musset, *Biographie*, in *Oeuvres complètes*, "l'Intégrale," pp. 43–44; and Madame Martellet, *Dix Ans chez Alfred de Musset* (Paris, 1899), p. 64.

6. Jean Richer, in Alfred de Musset, *Textes dramatiques inédits*, p. 175, maintains that manuscript fragments of *Carmosine* in the poet's own hand date from as early as 1833–34.

7. *Le Romantisme d'Alfred de Musset*, p. 636.

the effect of *Carmosine* on the reader. Certainly no stronger reaction can be generated by the somewhat elaborated adaptation
for the stage of Boccaccio's slender original.

The action of the play takes place in Palermo in the thirteenth
century. Carmosine, the daughter of Master Bernard, a doctor,
and his foolish wife Dame Paque, has fallen in love with Pedro
of Aragon, the king of Sicily, whom she saw one day in a tourna-
ment. Her father despairs of curing the wasting illness that has
since claimed her, and Carmosine is resigned to dying for her
impossible love, which she has kept a secret from all around her.
Dame Paque is convinced that the girl is pining for Ser Vespasiano, a boastful courtier. Perillo, the young man to whom
Carmosine was promised before he left to earn a law degree at
Padua, returns from six years' absence to learn of his misfortune.
Overhearing the girl's plea to her father not to see him, Perillo
sends a letter to Master Bernard freeing him of his obligation: he
is going to join the King's armies. Carmosine, feeling death approach, reveals her secret to the troubadour Minuccio and asks
him to inform the King of it before she dies. Minuccio meets his
old friend Perillo at the palace and decides to help the young
couple despite themselves. He tells the King of Carmosine's fatal
love, and recites as hers a ballad he has asked the poet Cipolla
to compose. Both the King and the Queen are deeply moved. The
latter goes to visit Carmosine and speaks in behalf of Perillo,
saying that the King desires their marriage. When Pedro himself
appears in full regalia, promising to be her knight and wear her
colors in exchange for a single kiss, Carmosine accepts Perillo as
her husband from his hand.

The plot, it must be admitted, is a bit tenuous—the fault, no
doubt, of the even more slender tale from which it is taken. Of
course, even Musset's best plays are not particularly distinguished
by the richness or originality of their action; that was a quality he
willingly left to the journeyman carpenters of the popular theater.
But even in its context *Carmosine* is remarkably static and predictable. Once its givens are enunciated, we have a feeling of
ceremonial reenactment which goes beyond the fairy-tale atmosphere of its events or the stylization inherent in dramatization
of familiar material. Predictability seems to be what the play is

about, and the sense of wish fulfillment which dominates its resolution is symptomatic of the moral world in which its characters evolve. Given this atmosphere, the participants in its action have nothing to do but carry out their appointed roles, pending the happy reversal that awaits them. This is particularly true of the two protagonists, whose action in the play is limited to regretting their misfortune and accepting the pain of renunciation until the benevolent forces around them have brought about their union.

It is of course traditional of the fairy-tale genre, to which this play in many ways adheres, that the happy resolution comes from above: not so much from divine or cosmic forces as from the upper strata of the human hierarchy. Here it is the King and the Queen, in their tranquil, elevated harmony, who descend among their subjects to bring health and happiness through union. Musset makes this more than a mere *deus ex machina*: it is part of the moral structure of the entire play. Carmosine has wasted away because of an impossible love, a love aimed far too high even for a girl of her beauty and character. Her father has tried to cure her with all the art at his command; but he is only a plain-spoken, common man, and medical knowledge is not enough to bring harmony to Carmosine's body and soul. Carmosine's "sin," her departure from the normal aims of a person of her station, has been committed with a good deal of modesty and remorse— indeed, the very source of her ill health is the knowledge of her love's audacity and unreason. But she can be returned to normality only by an intervention from above, which reestablishes her balance by reconciling her with the order of things: a possible love with the King's benediction, and even his promise of token fidelity.

Musset enhances this atmosphere of submissiveness to order imposed from above by attributing the virtues of modesty and resignation to all his sympathetic characters. Master Bernard takes pride in his status as a wealthy physician only to the extent that it permits him to use his riches and science in behalf of his daughter. His failure to accomplish anything for her is a source of mortification, a reminder which he takes very much to heart that he is but an ordinary man. In his eyes, Dame Paque's supreme folly is the social ambition which makes her see Ser Vespasiano, the nobleman who divides his pretentious compliments between mother and daughter, as a possible match for Carmosine. Minuccio, the troubadour, is an interesting example of this process of leveling which affects Musset's characters. It is symptomatic that this "man of art" is nothing so elevated as a poet (even a musician, in the Romantic sense of the term), but rather a minstrel, an amuser. He does not himself set Carmosine's message to the King in verse, but has it done by a professional rimester, Cipolla (who does not appear on stage and is qualified as a pedant). Everything about Minuccio's talent is modest: he finds it impossible to learn the poem by heart in time and renounces his attempt to set it to music, ending by reading the text to the King and Queen (II, 7). His greatest quality, in the judgment of Master Bernard, is not his talent. Replying to Ser Vespasiano's praise of the troubadour's reputation at court (which gives the courtier a pretext for boasting of his own connections), the worthy doctor says:

> Is that so! Well, in my eyes, that is the least of his merits; not that I look down on a good song: nothing goes better at table with a glass of good wine. But more than a clever musician, a troubadour as they say, Minuccio is for me an honest man, a good, old and loyal friend, however young and frivolous he may seem; a devoted friend to our family, the best we have perhaps since the death of Anthony [Perillo's father]. (I, 7)

It appears almost a gesture of self-abasement on Musset's part to treat the artist with such condescension. Implicit in Master Bernard's praise of Minuccio is another surprising rejection of the author's former values: his extolling of the troubadour's "maturity." Minuccio is as worthy as an older man, despite his apparent youth. He has the virtues which the mature prize above all: loyalty, devotion, steadfastness—Master Bernard even goes so far as to say that Minuccio has succeeded to the rank vacated by the death of Perillo's father. This succession is contrary to the deepest tendencies of Musset's youthful theater: virtue there was not something one acceded to in time, it was something time dissolved.

It is this modesty which above all characterizes the two young lovers as well. Carmosine is full of compunction from beginning to end of the play because of her involuntary lack of measure in falling in love with the King. This makes her character sweet and gently appealing, but remarkably monotonous compared with Musset's earlier heroines. Her sending of Minuccio to tell the King of her love is not an attempt at self-satisfaction: Minuccio is supposed merely to inform the monarch, not to accomplish anything more concrete for her. Carmosine goes this far only when convinced of her imminent death, which obviates any vain hope for personal fulfillment. She does not have even that pride, formerly so natural to Musset's heroines, which would make her ridicule Vespasiano's absurd claim to her hand. Instead, she limits herself to paying him no particular attention, emerging from her gentle apathy only enough for an occasional word of cool politeness.

Perillo carries modesty to the point of never actually speaking of his love directly to Carmosine. Despite his appearance as early as the second scene, he refrains from presenting himself to his beloved until the third act; prior to that time he deals entirely through Master Bernard, for fear that his importunity may imperil the girl's health. When the father informs Perillo of Carmosine's illness, he offers to conceal his arrival in the city, to extend the six years' absence which has already seemed so long. When he overhears Carmosine's expression of dismay at the news of his return, he departs with admirable discretion. It is by chance that Carmosine, intercepting Perillo's farewell letter to her father, learns of his despair and his intention to go off to war. Perillo has only one moment, in the second act of the play, in which his self-respect makes him formulate a reproach against his unhappy fate —a fleeting outburst of pride. That comes when he learns from Ser Vespasiano's boasting that he has a rival for Carmosine. But even then his despair is stronger than his anger, and he resigns himself to the absurdity of the courtier's claims:

Why should I hold it against this stranger, this ridiculous automaton whom God brings across my path? Him or any other, what does it matter? I see in him nothing but Destiny,

whose blind instrument he is; I even believe it ought to
be so. Yes, it's a most commonplace thing. When a sincere
and loyal man is stricken in what he holds most dear, when
an irreparable misfortune crushes his force and kills his
hopes, when he is mistreated, betrayed, rejected by all
around him, almost always, you should note, almost always
it is a common lout who deals the final blow, and who, by
chance, unwittingly, happening upon the man fallen to
the ground, steps on the dagger buried in his heart. (II, 3)

The rhetoric of these phrases is almost that of Musset's earlier
heroes; but in the context it seems ridiculously exaggerated, compared with the moderation displayed by all except the play's one
example of overweening pride, Vespasiano. And it must be added
that Perillo returns so fully to the paths of modesty that he does
not utter a single word in the final scene, when the King and
Queen change Carmosine's mind and unite the couple in the
bonds of reasonable matrimony.

Perillo's reference to Ser Vespasiano as an automaton, in the
speech cited above, immediately raises the question of the *fantoches* in *Carmosine*, as in Musset's earlier comedies. What Perillo has to say about the courtier as a blind instrument of destiny,
carrying out the mechanical, unheroic task of destroying the sensitive protagonist, sounds like an abbreviated formulation of what
the marionettes stood for: the victory of inhuman fate over human individuals, of the mechanical over the emotional, of time
over youth. But there are several elements of this speech and of
Vespasiano's function in the play which conflict with what we
know of Musset's *fantoches.*

The tone in which Perillo speaks of Ser Vespasiano is something new in the plays we have examined. Although Octave describes Claudio as a "village pedant" (*Marianne*, I, 1) and "an
old man who has no more sense, and never had a heart" (II, 3),
it is only in passing that he deigns to mention him, as part of
his argument in favor of Coelio. Nowhere are the automatons
granted such fatal importance by the protagonists as Vespasiano
is given by Perillo. This is all the more striking in the light of
the courtier's trivial influence in the plot of *Carmosine* compared

with *Marianne* or *Fantasio*. Vespasiano, who was invented by
Musset to fill out the action of Boccaccio's brief tale, bears a
name whose very ludicrousness indicates clearly the sort of character he is. Its echo of the word *vespasienne*, that incongruously
pompous title a Roman emperor passed on to the public comfort
facilities of Paris, makes it difficult to take him serious as a rival
to Perillo.[8] Indeed Perillo's reference to his dire significance has
an inverse effect to the one intended: it strikes us as so outland-
ish, so disproportionate to the simpleton in question, that it makes
Perillo himself look rather foolish. We thus have confirmation
of our sense that this one hyperemotional speech which Musset
puts in the mouth of his moderate, self-effacing hero is meant
ironically; it underlines the theme of the beneficial effects of
resignation by showing the incongruousness of Perillo's spasmodic revolt.

More than any of Musset's previous grotesques, Vespasiano is
evidently intended merely as a comic foil, invented for that
purpose. His heavy-handed compliments to Carmosine's addled
mother and her ludicrously demure reply are exemplary:

> *Vespasiano:*   Would that I might only cleave my heart
> in two with this dagger, and offer half of it to
> a person whom I respect . . . I dare not make
> myself clearer.
>
> *Dame Paque:* And I *must* not understand you.   (I, 7)

The obviousness of Vespasiano's tactics later gives even Carmosine the opportunity to avoid his gallantry with an ironic word:
"You are courting my mother, otherwise I was about to ask you
to lend me your arm" (III, 2). But all through the play, Vespasiano is the convenient butt of everyone's jokes and insults. When
Dame Paque claims that it is he who inspired Carmosine with
love at the King's tourney, Master Bernard has an easy time
mocking her:

8. As Lafoscade points out, Perillo himself is mainly invented by
Musset; but his role is at least suggested by the anonymous husband
given to Carmosine by the King at the end of Boccaccio's story: *Le
Théâtre d'Alfred de Musset*, p. 159.

Dame Paque: Whom would she look for, in the throng,
 but the people she knows? And what other,
 amongst our friends, what other than the handsome, the gallant, the invincible Ser Vespasiano?
Master Bernard: So much so, that he toppled with his four
 hooves in the air at the first blow of a lance.
Dame Paque: It is possible that his horse may have tripped,
 and his lance was turned aside, I don't deny that;
 it is possible he may have fallen.
Master Bernard: It is most certainly possible; he spun
 through the air like a top, and he fell, I swear it,
 just as hard as it is possible.
Dame Paque: But with what an air he stood up again!
Master Bernard: Yes, with the air of a man whose dinner
 lies heavy on his stomach, and who would much
 rather remain on the ground. If such a sight is
 what made my daughter ill, rest assured it wasn't
 with love.   (I, 1)

Even the gentle Minuccio turns to ridicule Vespasiano's conde-
scendingly protective attitude toward him by referring to the
courtiers as marionettes moved by strings attached to the King's
fingers, and including in his enumeration of the puppet figures
"the soldiers of fortune, or of chance if you will, whose lance
shakes in their hands and whose feet quaver in the stirrups"
(I, 8).

Of the *fantoches'* materialism, Vespasiano retains only his
interested motives in seeking Carmosine's hand, namely the
hope of receiving her considerable dowry and the King's alleged
pledge to give him two plots of land on "his wedding-day" (the
formula is an obvious way of getting rid of importuners, but
Vespasiano has not understood that). Counterbalancing this materialism is the pseudopoetic style that Vespasiano alone culti-
vates, among all the characters of the play. The courtier's florid
eloquence is opposed to Master Bernard's praise of plain language
and the simple virtues: it is part of Musset's "de-poetization" of
his art, his rejection of the subjective lyricism which characterized

his earlier protagonists. In *Carmosine*, poetry is not the matter of vision which the Romantics and their successors believed in. It is strictly a function of that mannerism and cult of form which we associate with a certain stereotype of the medieval court of love: the Sicilian school for example. One of Vespasiano's most exasperating public defeats comes at the hands of the giggling young things who draw him into a typical amorous dispute: "Which is better: the lover who dies of grief at no longer seeing his mistress, or the lover who dies of pleasure on seeing her again?" (II, 6). In the face of their obstinately reiterated shriek —"The one who dies!"—Vespasiano can only sputter his impotent bewilderment and stalk off. Yet it is his pretension to poetic expression that leads him into such humiliations: if he were satisfied to be a simple clod, Musset suggests, there would be nothing seriously wrong with him. *Si tacuisses.* But this is not at all the radical opposition between kinds of life that integrates Musset's earlier puppet figures into their dramatic context. Vespasiano is merely ludicrous, not sinister, alien or menacing. At no time does his suit threaten Perillo's love or the outcome of the play—except perhaps in the young man's mind, and that only for a moment. Vespasiano's function is decorative rather than integral to the action of the play; the mere suggestion that the opposite might be the case is enough to make Perillo ridiculous.

For the real message of *Carmosine* is that everything will turn out for the best, if only we trust to Providence and authority. Vespasiano's mistake, if we were to take him that seriously, would be trying to force that authority by his dogged importunateness, instead of waiting patiently for it to act according to its own superior lights. The mature characters in the play point this out to their impatient or overreaching juniors. Minuccio, who (as we have indicated) is remarkable for his precocious "maturity," illustrates it in his advice to Perillo. Although his words seem at first to reiterate the hymn to passion and suffering in the name of love which Musset sang in his "Nuits," his conclusion is more prudent:

Your heart has somehow been wounded. Whose has not?
I won't tell you to struggle against your grief now, but

rather not to attach and chain yourself to it with no hope
of return, for a time will come when it will be over. You
can't believe that, can you? All right, but remember what
I'm going to tell you:—Suffer now if you must, weep if
you will, and don't be ashamed of your tears . . . Far from
stifling the torment which oppresses you, rend your breast to
clear a path for its escape, let it burst forth in sobs, in sighs,
in prayers, in threats; but I repeat, do not engage the future!
Respect that time which you no longer count on, but which
is far wiser than we are, and for a sorrow which must be
fleeting, do not prepare the most durable one of all,
regret, which renews exhausted suffering and poisons
memory!   (II, 2)

In other words, do not do anything rash, which might jeopardize
your happiness to come. Play the game of passion for its thera-
peutic value, but with a calm, appraising eye on your investment
in the future. A most reasonable artist this, one who fully justifies Master Bernard's respect! Perillo, who at any rate is a man
of law—thus a fairly conservative type at heart—does not go
beyond his tirade and his demand of service in the King's armies:
a highly indirect form of suicide, which passes through official
channels and therefore risks being cut short by official wisdom.

Minuccio's advice is influenced by what he already knows concerning Carmosine's impossible love. He does not underestimate
the gravity of her illness, and the serious difficulty which it and
its strange cause represent for Perillo's and her happiness. But his
"wisdom"—the sagacity born of experience—makes him con-
fident in the outcome of the two lovers' separate appeals to the
highest authority, the King. It is true that neither Perillo nor
Carmosine approaches him with the intention of resolving their
problem by royal fiat, or of receiving direct gratification of their
profound desires (which moreover do not coincide): their in-
nate modesty forbids it. But Minuccio, promoting their causes as
ambassador to the King, seems to suppose that some such resolution will come, whether or not it takes the form that each of the
lovers expects. For as "entrepreneur général" of serenades and
"shopkeeper" of love songs (II, 2), Minuccio is a loyal, produc-

tive subject who believes completely in his monarch's good offices. Gone are the days when poet and revolutionary were synonymous: this purveyor of lyrics is as solid a bourgeois as any silk merchant or notary.

We are thus immeasurably far from the world of *Lorenzaccio*, both politically and aesthetically. Just as the latter play represents in terms of Florentine history the political situation of France following the *révolution ratée* of 1830, Carmosine seems to echo in a more dilute and sweetened form the situation of France in 1850 through the Sicily of 1280. Here we have a Pedro of Aragon called to the throne of the Two Sicilies after the Vespers have put an end to the old Angevine monarchy: a dim reflection of the events of 1848 which had deposed the house of Orleans and placed at the head of a short-lived Second Republic that very Louis-Napoleon who was soon to become Emperor Napoleon III. Musset's Pedro seems to be a preshadowing of the latter event—or at least an expression of the poet's desire for it. For Pedro, the recent bloody events (Vespers or Revolution) were intended to restore liberty and internal harmony, not to promote social upheaval. His tirades in the fifth scene of Act II are those of an irate father returning from an absence, to find that his family has been bickering instead of building prosperity:

> Is this unhappy kingdom so accursed of heaven, so inimical
> to its repose, that it can not keep the peace at home while
> I carry on war abroad! ... This one is stirred by pride, that
> one by greed. They squabble over a privilege, over a
> jealousy, over a grudge; while all of Sicily calls for our
> swords, they draw knives over a wheat-field. Is it for this
> that French blood has been flowing since the Vespers?
> What was your battle-cry then? Wasn't it liberty and the
> fatherland? ... Why did you overthrow a king, if you do
> not know how to be a people? ... When a nation has arisen
> in hatred and in anger, it must lie down again like a lion,
> in calm and dignity ... We are all involved, we are all
> responsible for the bloodbaths of Easter day. We must all
> be friends, or else risk having committed a crime. I have
> not come to pluck up Conradin's crown from beneath the

scaffold, but to leave my own to a new Sicily . . . If, instead
of helping one another, as divine law commands, you
disrespect your own laws, by the cross of God I'll remind
you of them, and the first one of you who crosses his
neighbor's hedge to rob him of a penny, I'll have his head
chopped off on the boundary-stone of his field . . .   (II, 5)

Good Queen Constance takes pains to reassure his fearful subjects of Pedro's deep kindness and concern, and to intercede for
mercy on their behalf. The King is nonetheless that idol of all
bourgeoisies in troubled times, the benevolent despot who will
restore order after internal strife, who will consolidate the new
liberties for those who can afford to profit by them, by protecting
the *status quo* of property and privilege. It is difficult not to see
Carmosine with the jaundiced eyes of Marxist criticism, so far
has Musset departed from that "critical realism" which may be
imputed to his earlier works. Here the voice is overwhelmingly
juste-milieu, middle class and authoritarian-liberal, and justifies
one East German critic's despairing commentary on all of Musset's later theater: "It is revealing of the ruling class of the Second
French Empire that it quashed the young Musset's 'rebellious-
ness,' interesting itself in his socially 'uncommitted' plays and
giving them its applause."[9] What is true of Musset's successful
post-1834 comedies is doubly true of *Carmosine*, which not only
turns its back on the poet's earlier revolt, but substitutes a contrary political viewpoint for the one that he abandoned. It would
be excessive to say that Pedro of Aragon is a rehabilitation of
Cosimo de Medici: the two characters are too different in stature
and dramatic significance to justify so facile a comparison. But
the political virtues for which Pedro stands in *Carmosine*, and
in whose name he exercises a benign and sympathetic influence,
are reminiscent of Cosimo's form of "law and order," the praise
of harmony as the final aim and the necessary end of revolution.

This political quietism is also reflected on the plane of *Carmosine's* sentimental action. The young heroine's unreasonable love
for her monarch is a sickness that must be cured. If her father's
potions are incapable of reestablishing her spiritual and physical

9. Werner Bahner, *Alfred de Mussets Werk*, p. 85.

order, help must come from above: first from the royal inter-
cessor, the Queen, and then from the ultimate authority, the spirit
of sovereignty descended among his common subjects to dispense
justice and charity. The religious overtones of this intervention
are probably incidental: there is little conscious theological symbolism in Musset's works, and the play is too fragile to support
any such interpretation. But the myth of passion in Musset's
earlier works is subjected to a curiously inverse dogmatism here:
instead of the irresistible power of love which transcends moral
and social limits, we find an encroachment of society's norms on
the sentimental aspirations of the young hero and, particularly,
heroine. Nowhere do we find more than in *Carmosine* the justification of Pierre Gastinel's characterization of the lovers in Musset's later drama: "The sentiment which stirs them is accom-
panied by such respect that, even when requited, physical desire
never speaks loudest; even rejected, they manage to forget themselves . . . They have in common qualities which make us forget
their faults: a goodness which would shun playing with another's
happiness as a crime, a sincerity which does not hesitate to admit
its wrongs; no aggressive pride, no stupid vanity, no selfish-
ness."[10] Gastinel, it is true, considered *Carmosine* to be an exception to the poet's general decline, a return to his earlier manner and vision.[11] Insofar as that vision was intimately related to
Musset's emotional viewpoint as formulated by Perdican, however, it does not seem possible to consider the play in this light.
Even more than Musset's parlor comedies, *Carmosine* evokes the
author's decline, his rejection of the world his youthful ardor had
created, *because* it apparently returns to the fantasy and imaginativeness of the earlier works.

In *Carmosine*, the dream of love is resolved by a return to
reality. It is the kind and gentle Queen who carries Musset's new
message to the lovesick heroine. She cures Carmosine's wasting
illness by exposing it to the light of day, taking it out of the
realm of mystery (and shame) and transferring it to the plane
of the tangible, the everyday:

10. *Le Romantisme*, p. 627.
11. Ibid., p. 625.

Imagine that this prince's sister, or his wife if you will, has been informed of this love, which is the secret of my young friend, and that, far from feeling aversion or jealousy toward her, she has undertaken to console her . . . to take her out of her solitude, to give her a place beside her in the very palace of her husband . . . Suppose that she wants this child who dared to love so great a prince to dare to confess it, so that this love, hidden in unhappy solitude, may be purified in the light of day and ennobled by its very cause.

(III, 8)

The Queen does not intend to yield her royal husband up to her bourgeoise rival. She means, rather, that Carmosine's love will be transformed by a fatherly kiss into a less fatal form, public adoration, and that Carmosine's position relative to the King will be "regularized"—she will join the royal household as maid of honor to the Queen. Once she is absorbed (one is tempted to say "coopted") into the order of things, her love thus normalized into a permissible state, the reasons for Carmosine's illness disappear as if by magic into the reigning harmony of the court of Palermo. She has, it is true, a moment of revolt upon learning that her cherished secret has become common knowledge. But her shame gives way before the onslaught of goodness and assimilation which terminates the play. Her personal will to happiness, out of phase with the general well-being, gives way to an acceptable form of love, a permissible channel to the sentiment which motivated it. And she does this because it is willed from above. As the Queen says, in her final, convincing plea: "Yes, it is the King who wishes first of all that you get well, and that you come back to life; it is he who thinks that it would be a great shame for so beautiful a creature to die of so noble a love—those are his own words . . . It is I who wish that, far from forgetting Pedro, you see him every day; that rather than combatting a penchant for which you ought not to reproach yourself, you should yield to this sincere impulse of your soul toward what is fine, noble and generous . . ." (III, 8).

How well this parallels the political implications of *Carmo-*

sine! Carmosine's love of Pedro is simply the movement of all good subjects toward their monarch's inherent superiority, translated into hyperbolic terms. As all good subjects accept the beneficent will of their ruler, so Carmosine will subordinate her excessive desires to his jurisdiction, accepting a suitable husband from his hand, and thus restoring the sentimental balance of the kingdom! As orthodox religion teaches us that earthly love is the just reflection of divine *caritas*, so Perillo's and Carmosine's marriage will be sanctified by its submission to royal will, its inspiration by the ideal example provided in Carmosine's pure passion for the King.

This is a sad fairy tale. Sad, in its representation of the distance traveled by the Romantic spirit since the 1820's and 1830's, when imagination and revolt were synonymous: here we find the French equivalent of "God's in his heaven, all's right with the world," the Gallic Victorianism that Napoleon the Little was to bring. Sadder still in its testimony to the decline of that fresh, impertinent, and passionate irony that gave Musset's love comedies their peculiarly mordant vigor. Never again would the French theater rediscover this rare combination of sincerity and pose, of poetry and rhetoric, of sentiment and skepticism, which Musset invented and then lost. His imitators and emulators, from Rostand to Anouilh and Giraudoux, have never succeeded in equaling this composition, this equilibrium. A trace too much pose, a slight excess of irony, and the delicate structure loses its stature, slides into the trivial or the mean. The miracle of the young Musset was the degree of dignity, of nobility, which his genius lent to those "imperfect and base creatures" which his wit and his sentiment elevated to the rank of true heroes.

Chapter 10 The Originality

of Musset's Theater

The distance separating *Carmosine* from the great plays of 1833–34, sixteen years in time, but light-years in terms of force and vision, is thus paradigmatic of Musset's artistic decline. It is, of course, no consolation to find in this descending curve the mythic fulfillment of the author's familiar themes. Musset's biography is a pathetic tale, devoid of redeeming heroism or tragic catharsis. All of his contemporaries —friends, lovers, and enemies alike—testify volubly to the disintegration of his public and private personality which accompanied an artistic decline no less poignant for the former dandy's vain attempts to keep up appearances.

But his contemporaries, with rare exceptions like Gautier and Paul de Musset, were unaware of the significance to the theater of what Alfred had created in his brief period of greatness. No one could foresee that six or seven of his plays would become staples of the Comédie-Française; more significantly, no one could have imagined that a work like *Lorenzaccio*, judged simply unplayable in its original form, would be an important part of that theatrical renascence known as the Théâtre National Populaire, or the hit of the 1970 Prague theater season; or that the fluid, shifting perspectives of *Les Caprices de Marianne* would provide a dramatic base for the film technique of Jean Renoir's *La Règle du jeu*. The "cinematic" quality of Musset's drama, which was noted as early as the 1920's, makes it apparent that the motion picture was not so much a device which revolutionized the concept of dramatic structure as the necessary realization of an evolving theatrical vision in search of its technological means. The works of a Musset or a Büchner are part of a historical becoming whose results are now being felt fully in the contemporary flowering of the cinema.

Musset's biography as a creator thus transcends the disappointments of his life and his self-fulfilling myth of failure. The importance of his dramatic work has gradually been appreciated and analyzed by critics over the past fifty years. Its originality, which makes it one of the first examples of what can be termed "avant-garde" theater, can finally be assessed in the context of a stage and screen that have come of age. But that originality is not so easy to define. Our continually increasing body of information concerning the environment and the traditions in which the artistic figures of the past evolved their peculiar style or vision makes it a far less simple matter today to isolate that original "genius" which Musset's own, more innocent Romantic generation found in predecessors like Sophocles, Dante, or Shakespeare. It is all the more difficult in dealing with so young an author: the precocious, although they tend to proclaim their individuality louder than their elders, inevitably bear deeper marks of their spiritual and artistic nurturing than do the Goethes, Beethovens, and Matisses. Even the boy genius Rimbaud spent a relatively long apprenticeship with Baudelaire and Banville. Musset's theatrical personality is further complicated by his desire to adapt Shakespearean dramatic practice to the ways of the French stage, and by his expressed admiration for Schiller, for Molière, for Racine. The direct lineage between Musset's comedies and Marivaux's, also, with perhaps a collateral link via Beaumarchais, has been frequently cited, although the bonds between specific plays, themes, and techniques have not been clearly delineated. The influence of Richardson and, particularly, of Byron on the character of Musset's heroes has received thorough study. The sources and spirit of a peculiarly German fantasy which Musset (with Gérard de Nerval) translated more authentically than any of his compatriots, especially in *Fantasio*, before he passed it back to Büchner, have interested French Germanists like Jean Giraud and Albert Béguin. Italian and Spanish sources and alternative influences for everything have been exhaustively documented

over the past century or more. Little remains to be stu
in this domain, beyond the inevitable "further notes" which strew
every great artist's path.[1]

   And yet the artistic originality of Musset's plays shines through
all this impressively cluttered scaffolding. It can first be felt as
a vague "distinctiveness," as a divergence from the particular
models he admitted to following. If, for René Clair, who mounted
On ne badine pas avec l'amour at the TNP in 1958, "Musset is a
Shakespeare who might have known Marivaux,"[2] the philosopher Alain found in his theater a radical "un-Shakespeareanism":
"If I ever went so far as to compare Musset and Shakespeare (as
many are tempted to do), I would on the contrary oppose them
to each other."[3] For his turn-of-the-century appreciator Jules
Lemaître, the spirit of Musset's dramas was foreign to both
Shakespeare and Marivaux: "Neither Shakespeare's nor Marivaux's theater could give us an idea of Musset's theater, if it did
not exist: for there is really something more there, something
absolutely original and irreducible, an intellectual consistency,
a certain *quality* of vision, sentiment and expression which is
only his, and which is all of him."[4] This seems subjective or im-
pressionistic. But it evidences a conviction among readers of dis-
cernment which bears further analysis.

   Certainly a factor which radically distinguishes Musset from
Shakespeare (or from Marivaux or Molière) is the remarkable
youthfulness which radiates from his best dramas. This is not
true in the same way that Musset's lyrics are now considered
poetry for adolescents, whose pathos and grandiloquence fade
once the age of indulgent self-interest is outgrown: that is the
Musset of Heinrich Heine's untranslateable quip: "un jeune homme de beaucoup de passé," or Lamartine's cruel portrait: "Blond-

   1. For all these "influences" cf. Léon Lafoscade, *Le Théâtre d'Alfred
de Musset.* See also, in particular, Pierre Nordon, "Alfred de Musset et
l'Angleterre," *Les Lettres Romanes* (1966–67); and Jean Giraud, "Alfred de Musset et trois romantiques allemands," *Revue d'Histoire Littéraire* (1911–12).
   2. Cited by Guy Leclerc, *Les Grandes Aventures du théâtre* (Paris,
1965), p. 248.
   3. "Marivaux-Musset," *Mercure de France*, 50 (1950), 582.
   4. *Théâtre d'Alfred de Musset*, I, v.

haired child, waxen-hearted young man, / Poetic plaything of soft poesy . . . / You who take your vague whim for passion . . ."[5] Unlike his lyrics, Musset's plays succeed in objectifying the "youthful condition," the eternally repeated drama of the young—their anguished fear of adulthood and its inevitable betrayal of youth's instinctive, generous passions; the sense of impotence and rage at the contradiction between ideal, or dream, and reality. This anxiety is one that seems to be captured by those who flower prematurely—a Musset or a Jarry, a Rimbaud or a Radiguet. Few have produced so complete a body of work as Musset, however, during their brief period of vision. That is what constitutes his drama's enduring dialogue with the young, at the same time that the aesthetic perfection of these works renders them continuingly accessible to those beyond the generation gap. In Leclerc's words, "It is he who most luminously reflected the state of mind of the younger generation in the first half of the nineteenth century, and who retains to our day the most amazingly modern appeal."[6] Despite the outmoded sound of some of Musset's Romantic rhetoric and of his terminology (Lorenzo's lost "virtue," for example, or the convent-bred compunctions of his heroines), the delicate balance of sentiment and irony, idealism and cynicism, which imbues his heroes, their thirst for experience and their fear of failure, their exaltation of love at the expense of morality and wisdom—all remain a unique representation in traditional literature of the permanent drama of youth. The slogan of Coelio and Octave, those marvelous alter-egos whose unselfish friendship is

5. Cited by Gastinel, *Le Romantisme*, p. 590. Cf. Jacques Copeau's penetrating remark about this other Musset, whose deceptive "sincerity" dominates many of the lyrics, but especially the *Confession*: "He lavishes at once all that is noblest and all that is basest in his nature: 'I have never put my knee to the ground without putting my heart in it.' It is this perversion of 'sincerity,' this collusion of the flesh with the soul, which is the fatal poison of his debauchery. This suffering libertine could never worship anything but purity . . . Musset was never able to recover from his youth. Despite his forced marches, he could never cross and leave behind him that region of life where 'knowing nothing in the world, desiring everything, the young man feels the seed of all the passions at once.'" "Le Théâtre d'Alfred de Musset," p. 21.

6. *Les Grandes Aventures du Théâtre*, p. 247.

as modern as their opposing forms of inebriation, might well be "Make love, not law," in the face of their antagonist, the middle-aged judge Claudio, just as Fantasio's disdain for the Establishment leads him to flight into the irrational, the unorganized, and Lorenzo's profound sense of betrayal goes beyond political violence into cosmic despair and self-destruction.

The intense air of "relevance" is perhaps unexpected in an author who was one of his generation's principal antirealists, whose *Fantasio* has typically been qualified as the "dreamiest of dreams." But in an age when social and political commentary has been inextricably mingled with psychedelic fantasy, this may not seem so paradoxical as it once did. The uneasy marriage of drugs and commitment, of dropping out and protest, has accustomed our generation to forms which the nineteenth century suspected only in certain privileged moments (often, as in the case of Musset and Rimbaud, associated with abuse of alcohol, sex, and drugs). But this is precisely what constitutes another facet of Musset's original theatrical personality, the coupling of relevance with fantasy which has permitted his works, in that acid test (if the expression may be permitted) of artistic universality, to be interpreted as "critical realism" (as it is by the Marxists,)[7] or as philosophical and psychological documentation of the profoundest sort,[8] or pure "theater," divorced from the realm of reality by the sheer poetry of its language and dramatic technique.[9] *Lorenzaccio* is both a well-documented recreation of Florence in 1536, with its political factions and social struggles, and a highly personal expression of the hero's—and Musset's—internal spiritual conflict. *Fantasio* is both a satirical commentary on marriages and the reason of state—Princess Louise's wedding to Leopold of Belgium—and a lyrical, inebriated paean to freedom and chaos. *On ne badine pas avec l'amour* begins as a stylized comedy, with grotesques and chorus, and ends as something like

7. See, for example, Henri Lefebvre, *Alfred de Musset dramaturge*; and Werner Bahner, *Alfred de Mussets Werk*.

8. Bernard Masson, *Lorenzaccio ou la difficulté d'être*; Joachim-Claude Merlant, *Le Moment de "Lorenzaccio" dans le destin de Musset*.

9. Louis Jouvet, *Tragédie classique et théâtre du XIXᵉ siècle*; Jacques Copeau, "Le Théâtre d'Alfred de Musset."

Romantic melodrama. *Les Caprices de Marianne* blends elements of Renaissance Italian comedy with observations on the captivity of woman in nineteenth-century society and a hymn to the "new" morality. Whether we call this eclecticism or elusiveness, one of the chief traits of Musset's originality is the indefinability of his theater according to traditional genres, definitions, or viewpoints. No better example of Musset's complexity in these respects can be cited than the production of *Lorenzaccio* by the Za Branou Theater of Prague, in which the poignant relevance of the author's political ideas to the reality of post-1968 Czechoslovakia was intensified by a highly stylized, intensely modern staging employing masks, semiabstract sets, disciplined mass movement, and electronic audiovisual devices.[10]

This suggests a further aspect of Musset's theatrical personality: this literary drama, written in defiance of the contemporary theater and freed from the practical requirements of the stage as his time and tradition conceived it, is eminently, essentially playable, as succeeding generations in the theater have come to realize. In this respect it differs significantly from enterprises like Ludovic Vitet's *Scènes historiques* and Renan's *Drames philosophiques*, or even the later Hugo's *Théâtre en liberté*. Theatrically, Musset's armchair shows are far freer than Hugo's, whose *liberté* is mainly verbal and political. Yet Hugo's dramatic scenes were imagined as "unplayable theater," which "could not be presented on our stage such as it exists."[11] But Musset's works have demonstrated their practicability in a wide range of theatrical contexts. For his freedom somehow remained subject to theatrical principles, even if they were not those observed by the contemporary stage. Aside from his normal playgoing, Musset had seen Shakespeare done by Kemble's troupe; he had taken part in family and society theatricals. These limited experiences seem to have confirmed a stage instinct which he possessed beyond any of his contemporaries in the theater. Dumas' and Scribe's involvement in the day-to-day problems of producing their plays

10. Under the direction of Otomar Krejca, in a Czech translation by Karel Kraus, at the Odéon-Théâtre des Nations, Paris, May 11–16, 1970.

11. Quotation from Hugo's preface cited by Georges Ascoli, *Le Théâtre romantique*, p. 172.

—Scribe's clever engineering of his comedies to the observed reactions of his audiences, Dumas' protean activities as writer, director, publicist, actor, costumer, set-designer and machinist, even Hugo's need to provide sketches of costumes and sets for *Marion de Lorme* and *Hernani*, contrast sharply with Musset's *pudeur*, his hesitation even in later years to take an active part in production of his works.[12] Yet he was the most professional of them all, because his instinct transcended the narrow limits which the nineteenth-century French stage set to its ambitions and its definition of theater. No one is more qualified to speak of this than Jacques Copeau:

> Musset said verses marvelously, a supreme art among
> poets when they master it . . . His gift for imitation goes
> so far as to reproduce with his body the expression, the walk,
> the age and the physical habits of the people he observes.
> It is this actor's instinct which proclaims any born dramatist.
> Musset has a sense of acting. See his reflections on a
> certain "exit" of Mlle Pressy in the *Barber of Seville*; they
> denote a man who sees what goes on on the stage, an un-
> common gift. He is interested in production. See his review
> of *Gustave III*, March 14, 1833 . . . But he does not under-
> estimate the importance of their art . . . And he understands
> their problems . [. He admires Rachel, for the right reasons,
> which he expresses well . . . Finally, he takes an interest
> in the material conditions of performance, in the dimensions
> of the stage, its "layout" as we say today, and he lingers
> with Voltaire to determine what influence the theatrical
> customs of his time might have had on Racine's tragedies.[13]

Musset's instinctive sympathy for Shakespeare (which did not turn him automatically and arbitrarily against Racine, as Romantic dogma willed) let him see that there was a deeper theatrical logic to be found than that of the unities. Shakespeare's stage, more flexible than the contemporary French proscenium stage, had greater potential for the dramatic imagination: it of-

12. Cf. Allevy, *La Mise en scène*, pp. 117–18.
13. Alfred de Musset, *Comédies et Proverbes*, introduction by Jacques Copeau (Paris, 1931) I, v.

fered Musset possibilities beyond the linear structure and the Cartesian rationalism that governed even the Romantics' attempts at liberation. He saw that stage reality might and should be other than a reasonable transposition from "real life" and evolved a principle of elliptical development and allusive dialogue, the music and rhythm of scenic organization, which the Symbolists were much later and only gradually to bring (or restore, after the "realist heresy") to the theater. In the words of Copeau, "He possesses the secret of light composition. I do not mean something mawkish or weak by that. But an agility, a joyousness. True power in art is delicate and explosive. It abolishes real duration at one stroke. At one stroke the poet has entered his own world. There he is in command of everything. An image, an allusion, a passage, a break, a balancing of scenes or speeches, and perhaps even less, is enough for him to stir up the powers of illusion, to awaken a desire in the imagination and to satisfy it at the same moment."[14] No doubt Musset's sense of dramatic composition resulted from the theatricality which his family and friends all remarked in his character, and which made him don a great yellow overcoat and lie chanting on the floor of his room during spells of remorse for his misspent youth, or illuminate his room with candles and torches when he was expecting the "visit of the Muse," as when he wrote the "Nuit de mai."[15] He felt that theater is not the illusion of reality but illusion itself, as a function and need of the human spirit. His dramatic structures, his dialogue, his rapidly shifting settings all speak to that need rather than to the need to be reassured about probabilities and logic. Without overstepping the boundary of whimsy, wish fulfillment, or fairy tale in his major works, he had the instinctive *métier* to create a world firmly governed by its own invincible logic, peopled by characters who, on a variety of levels, are theatrical beings, difficult to imagine in real life (as are their settings) yet inevitable and true on the stage.

Part of the reason for this resides in their language, which succeeds in being natural in its context, and unreal at the same time.

14. Ibid., p. xviii.

15. Paul de Musset, *Biographie*, in *Oeuvres complètes*, "l'Intégrale," pp. 23, 31.

Nobody we know speaks Musset's poetic prose.[16] Yet its balance and rhythm, its music, make it remarkably speakable; it "lies well in the voice." Musset's ear for dialogue (which incidentally makes his verse also so deceptively casual when he wishes it) has nothing to do with the imitative realism, the ear for the vernacular, of a Courteline. But an actor with a sensitive ear and a sense of style—that which actor-poet Jules Truffin termed a "lilac voice"—can make it sound as true and unforced as any theater language written.[17] For Musset had the good sense to root his *enfants du siècle* in the solid linguistic tradition of the Enlightenment to which his taste naturally drew him. Auguste Brun says: "The language we hear in the *Comédies* . . . is easy to identify: it is that which characterizes the 18th century in France. But at times romanticism slips in with its rhetoric, its phraseology, its poetical images . . ."[18] This mixture is typical of Musset's personality. His images, however, are not merely decorative, as they would have been in eighteenth-century usage and as they remained even in much of the Romantics' theatrical dialogue (the current which leads to the poetry of *Cyrano*). They are the very basis of his logic. All of Musset's characters, even his minor figures and his grotesques—who have been characterized as "clods of genius"—utter their ideas metaphorically or allusively. This gives the sequence of his dialogue a peculiar elliptical quality all its own, analogous to the elliptical progress of his scenes. Boissy referred to this as Musset's "indirect language," and asserted that he was alone among French dramatists in using it. Thus Marianne talks of precious and cheap wine to Octave when she is really opening the dialogue of seduction (*Marianne*, II, 1); Fantasio speaks of blue tulips, and of mechanical dolls, to Princess Elsbeth, in opposition to her impending marriage (*Fantasio*, II, 1 and 5); Camille asks Perdican about a picture in a gallery when she wants to be persuaded not to join a religious order (*On*

16. For an examination of Musset's dramatic language, see Auguste Brun, *Deux Proses de théâtre: Drame romantique, Comédies et Proverbes.*

17. Barbey d'Aurevilly referred to Musset's theater as "a lilac struck by lightning." Both quoted by Gabriel Boissy, *Le Figaro* (April 9, 1920).

18. Brun, *Deux Proses*, p. 59.

ne badine pas avec l'amour, II, 5). The examples could be multiplied at will. Even the sense of prosaic boredom to which Musset's heroes are subject tends to find a symbolic expression: a cotton nightcap covering the city of Munich; counting from one to infinity; deploring a botched sunset; sitting in the sun staring at one's new suit or watching one's wig grow . . . But a witty eighteenth-century critical spirit is never far behind the Romantic *Weltschmerz.*

Here again we find the unmistakable echo of Musset's voice: this "mixture of wit and sentiment, of pathos and comedy, of fantasy and truth, of passion and irony, of sadness and buffoonery, an inimitable and unique blend which constitutes the charm, the originality, the secret and the miracle of Musset comedy."[19] Musset alone among French Romantic dramatists possessed the mastery that enabled him to avoid the temptations of sentimentality, facile virtuosity, bombast, exoticism, diabolism, Byronism —all the *isms* to which the Romantic flesh was heir. The tendencies are all latently present: Musset was not a shy recluse from his times. But every tendency has its corrective, with the result that we are constantly being surprised yet at the same time feel a reassuring sense that he is not going to betray us by lapses into the maudlin, sensational, or excessive.

Beyond the unique voice, the elliptical structure; the balance of emotion, intelligence, and taste; the sense of true theater; the rare expression of youthful passions and anxieties—beyond all these the theater of Alfred de Musset possesses for us today a virtue we may seek in vain in French drama of his century: its expression of deep and insistent ethical preoccupations of our day. Behind its lightness, its wit, its amorous sentiment, his theater is uncommonly serious. In the words of one of his most perceptive commentators, Bernard Masson, "An entire dialectic of personal existence is sketched out in this singular theater, which formerly passed for one of fantasy and laughter."[20] But it took almost a century, and painstaking examination of the texts and of Musset's life, to discover this. We take it for granted, in an

19. Maurice Donnay, "Les Comédies de Musset," *Revue française* (June 22, 1924), 682.
20. *Lorenzaccio ou la difficulté d'être*, p. 51.

era when metaphysical anguish can be represented by clowns and tramps, that seriousness has its derisive or destructive laughter. But the literary climate of Musset's century did not favor such an appreciation of his part-time buffoon, Fantasio; his pasty-faced, effeminate jester-assassin, Lorenzo; or his grotesque caricatures of the aging and conformist, the *fantoches*.

It took the efforts of Léon Lafoscade, Jean Giraud, and above all Pierre Gastinel to reveal the truth about this "waxen-hearted young man."[21] More than any of his literary contemporaries who paid extensive lip service to German thought and letters, Musset had read and understood the German artists and philosophers. He knew Shakespeare, he translated DeQuincy, he read widely in modern English literature. He spoke less Italian, perhaps, than George Sand, as she discovered in their celebrated escapade to Venice, but he read Dante, Boccaccio, Bandello, and Leopardi (whom he admired intensely, a revealing taste at a time when Leopardi was almost unknown in France). By a duality worthy of his best comedies, which reveals the roots of his literary creation in the depths of his personality, Musset took pains to hide under the mask of the handsome playboy this other Musset, intellectually solid, preoccupied with the pervasive human problems of his and our day: the complex nature of love, the painful difficulty of communication, the temptation of conformity, the conflict between the individual and society, the idealist's simultaneous aspiration toward fulfillment and toward death, the struggle and incomprehension between generations, the inexorable conquest of man by time.

The quotation from *Fantasio* which opens this study is a fitting epigraph to Musset's theater: the theater of solitude. No body of dramatic work of his time or nation—indeed few *oeuvres* of any time—better express the dilemma of modern man, caught between the defense of his own dignity and the collective needs of mankind. No one foresaw or felt more clearly, more intimately, than he the incomprehension between generations and peoples which has come to be a predominant concern today. Nor has anyone better expressed the comical incongruity, the tragic

21. *Le Théâtre d'Alfred de Musset*; "Alfred de Musset et trois romantiques allemands"; *Le Romantisme d'Alfred de Musset*.

absurdity of the struggle pitting man against himself, across the barricade of time and space, in a battle of incomprehension and dogmatism which prevents its participants from seeing that the face glimpsed through the smoke and blood is their own, distorted by the enemy within us all who will one day claim each of us as his victim. The thirst for love to break down the barrier of the body's isolation, and love's paradoxical obligation to use that body, the locus of our solitude, for its expression is what gives their terrible poignancy to Musset's lovers and heroes: to Coelio, Octave, and Marianne; to Perdican and Camille; to Lorenzo, Philip Strozzi, and Ricciarda Cibo; even to Fantasio, the cosmic jester in the Princess' garden, who utters the magic formula amid the quips and paradoxes inspired by his ennui: "Quelles solitudes que tous ces corps humains!"

Bibliography

Editions

Un Spectacle dans un fauteuil, Part One, Paris, 1832. (Contains *La Coupe et les Lèvres, A Quoi rêvent les jeunes filles*, and *Namouna*.)

Un Spectacle dans un fauteuil, Part Two, 2 volumes, Paris, 1834. (The first volume contains *Les Caprices de Marianne* and *Lorenzaccio*; the second, *André del Sarto, Fantasio, On ne badine pas avec l'amour*, and *La Nuit Vénitienne*.)

Comédies et Proverbes, Paris, 1840. (Contains all the works of Part Two, and in addition *La Quenouille de Barberine, Le Chandelier, Il ne faut jurer de rien*, and *Un Caprice*. The text used for the Gastinel and Van Tieghem editions.)

Comédies et Proverbes, "seule édition complète, revue et corrigée par l'auteur," 2 volumes, Paris, 1853. (Contains the poet's revised versions of most of the foregoing, plus *Il faut qu'une porte soit ouverte ou fermée, Louison, On ne saurait penser à tout, Carmosine*, and *Bettine*. The text used for the Allem edition.)

Théâtre d'Alfred de Musset, with an introduction by Jules Lemaître, 4 volumes, Paris, 1889–91.

Correspondance (1827–1857), collected and annotated by Léon Séché, Paris, 1907.

Comédies et Proverbes, with an introduction by Jacques Copeau, 2 volumes, Paris, 1931.

Oeuvres complètes de A. de Musset, Comédies et Proverbes, text established and presented by Pierre and Françoise Gastinel, 4 volumes, Paris, 1952. (The prose texts of *Spectacle dans un fauteuil* are based on the 1840 edition of the *Comédies et Proverbes*, the rest on the 1856 reedition of the revised *Comédies et Proverbes*.)

Les Caprices de Marianne, mise en scène and commentary by Gaston Baty, Collection "Mises en scène," Paris, 1952.

Textes dramatiques inédits, presented by Jean Richer, Paris, 1952.

Théâtre complet, text established and annotated by Maurice Allem, "Bibliothèque de la Pléiade," Paris, 1958.

Oeuvres complètes en prose, text established and annotated by Maurice Allem and Paul-Courant, "Bibliothèque de la Pléiade," Paris, 1960.

Oeuvres complètes, text established and presented by Philippe Van Tieghem, "l'Intégrale," Paris, 1963.

Il ne faut jurer de rien, text established and presented by Bernard Masson, Paris, 1966.

Books

Affron, Charles, *A Stage for Poets: Studies in the Theater of Hugo and Musset*, Princeton, 1971.

Allem, Maurice, *Alfred de Musset*, edition reviewed and corrected, Paris, 1947.

Allevy, Marie-Antoinette, *La Mise en scène en France dans la première moitié du dix-neuvième siècle*, Paris, 1938.

Ascoli, Georges, *Le Théâtre romantique*, 5 fascicles, "Les Cours de Sorbonne," Paris, 1936.

Bahner, Werner, *Alfred de Mussets Werk. Ein Verneinung der bürgerlichen Lebensform seiner Zeit*, Halle, 1960.

Bailey, Helen Phelps, *Hamlet in France: From Voltaire to Laforgue*, Geneva, 1964.

Barine, Arvède, *Alfred de Musset*, Paris, 1893.

Baty, Gaston, and Chavance, René, *La Vie de l'art théâtral des origines à nos jours*, Paris, 1932.

Bock, Margarete, (née. Sachs), *Symbolistisches in den Dramen von Alfred de Musset*, Berlin-Charlottenburg, 1936.

Brun, Auguste, *Deux Proses de théâtre: Drame romantique, Comédies et Proverbes*, Gap, 1954.

Carmontelle (Louis Carrogis), *Proverbes dramatiques*, Paris, 1822.

Centre National de la Recherche Scientifique, *Le Théâtre tragique*, studies assembled and presented by Jean Jacquot, Paris, 1962.

Decugis, Nicole, and Reymond, Suzanne, *Le Décor de théâtre en France du Moyen Age à 1925*, Paris, 1953.

Descotes, Maurice, *Le Drame romantique et ses grands créateurs (1827–1839)*, Paris, 1955.

Des Essarts, Emmanuel, *Le Théâtre d'Alfred de Musset*, Clermont-Ferrand, 1889.

Dimoff, Paul, *La Genèse de Lorenzaccio*, Paris, 1936; revised edition, Paris, 1964.

Dumas, Alexandre, (père), *Lorenzino*, Paris, 1842.

Evans, David Owen, *Le Drame moderne à l'époque romantique (1827–1850)*, Paris, 1937.

Flaubert, Gustave, *Correspondance*, new edition, augmented, second series (1847–52), Paris, 1926.

Gastinel, Pierre, *Le Romantisme d'Alfred de Musset*, Rouen, 1933.

Gauthiez, Pierre, *Lorenzaccio*, Paris, 1904.

Gautier, Théophile, *Histoire de l'art dramatique en France depuis vingt ans*, series 1–6, Paris, 1858–59.

Gochberg, Herbert S., *Stage of Dreams*, Geneva, 1967.

Houssaye, Arsène, *Les Confessions, souvenirs d'un demi-siècle 1830–1880*, Paris, 1885.

Hugo, Victor, *Théâtre en liberté*, in *Oeuvres de Victor Hugo*, volume 18, Lausanne, 1962.

Jouvet, Louis, *Tragédie classique et théâtre du XIXe siècle*, Paris, 1968.

Lafoscade, Léon, *Le Théâtre d'Alfred de Musset*, Paris, 1901; reprinted without reference to the original edition by Nizet, Paris, 1966.

Lebois, André, *Vues sur le théâtre de Musset*, Avignon, 1966.

Leclerc, Guy, *Les Grandes Aventures du théâtre*, Paris, 1965.

Lefebvre, Henri, *Alfred de Musset dramaturge*, Paris, 1955.

Lemaître, Jules, *Impressions de théâtre*, volume 10, Paris, 1898.

Lyonnet, Henry, *Les "Premières" d'Alfred de Musset*, Paris, 1927.

Martellet, Madame, *Dix Ans chez Alfred de Musset*, Paris, 1899.

Masson, Bernard, *Lorenzaccio ou la difficulté d'être*, Paris, 1963.

Mérimée, Prosper, *Le Théâtre de Clara Gazul*, Paris, 1922.

Merlant, Joachim-Claude, *Le Moment de "Lorenzaccio" dans le destin de Musset*, Athens, 1955.

Musset, Paul de, *Alfred de Musset, sa vie, son oeuvre*, Paris, 1877.

Nguyen Manh Tuong, "Essai sur la valeur dramatique du théâtre d'Alfred de Musset," unpublished thesis, Montpellier, 1932.

Nicoll, Allardyce, *The Theater and Dramatic Theory*, London, 1962.

Pommier, Jean, *Autour du drame de Venise*, Paris, 1958.

———, *Variétés sur Alfred de Musset et son théâtre*, Paris [1944].

Renan, Ernest, *Oeuvres complètes*, 35 volumes, Paris, 1863–1926.

Richter, Jean-Paul, *Choix de rêves*, translated by Albert Béguin, Paris, 1964.

Rothschild, Suzanne A., *A Critical and Historical Study of Alfred de Musset's "Barberine"*, Paris, no date.

Sainte-Beuve, Charles-Augustin, *Causeries du lundi*, volume 13, Paris, 1858.

Sand, George and Musset, Alfred de, *Correspondance. Journal intime de George Sand (1834)*, Monaco, 1956.

Sarcey, Francisque, *Quarante Ans de théâtre*, 8 volumes, Paris, 1900–02.

Shroder, Maurice Z., *Icarus: The Image of the Artist in French Romanticism*, Cambridge, Mass., 1961.

Stendhal, *Racine et Shakespeare*, Paris, 1965.
Tonge, Frederick, *L'Art du dialogue dans les Comédies en prose d'Alfred de Musset. Etude de stylistique dramatique*, Paris, 1967.
Van Tieghem, Philippe, *Musset, l'homme et l'oeuvre*, Paris, 1945.
Vilar, Jean, *De la Tradition théâtrale*, Paris, 1955.

Articles

Alain, "Marivaux-Musset," in *Mercure de France*, 50 (1950), 577–583.

Bachem, Rose M., "Musset's and Browning's Andrea del Sarto," *Revue de Littérature Comparée*, 38 (1964), 248–254.

Bidou, Henry, "Le Théâtre d'Alfred de Musset," *Conferencia* (October 15, November 1 and 15, December 1, 1920).

Bowman, Frank Paul, "Notes Toward the Definition of the Romantic Theater," *Esprit Créateur*, 5 (1965), 121–130.

Clavel, Maurice, "La Grande Société anonyme," *Le Nouvel Observateur*, 265 (December 8–14, 1969), 47–51.

Copeau, Jacques, "Le Théâtre d'Alfred de Musset," *Revue universitaire* (October 1, 1931).

Denommé, Robert T., "The Motif of the Poète maudit in Musset's *Lorenzaccio*," *Esprit Créateur*, 5 (1965), 138–146.

Dimoff, Paul, "*Une Conspiration en 1537* de George Sand," *Revue de Paris* (December 15, 1921), 673–708.

Donnay, Maurice, "Les Comédies de Musset," *Revue française* (June 22 and 29, 1924).

Dussane, Béatrix, "Les Héroïnes de Musset. I. Cécile," *La Revue hebdomadaire* (March 19, 1932); "II. La Capricieuse: Marianne," ibid. (March 26, 1932), 421–440.

El Nouty, Hassan, "L'Esthétique de *Lorenzaccio*," *Revue des Sciences Humaines*, fascicle 108 (October–December 1962), 589–611.

———, "Théâtre et anti-théâtre au 19ᵉ siècle," *PMLA*, 79 (1964), 604–612.

Falk, Eugene H., "Musset's 'Lorenzaccio'," *Tulane Drama Review*, 2 (February 1958), 32–37.

Frenzel, Elizabeth, "Mussets Lorenzaccio—ein mögliches Vorbild für Dantons Tod," *Euphorion*, 58 (1964), 59–68.

Giraud, Jean, "Alfred de Musset et trois romantiques allemands," *Revue d'Histoire Littéraire*, 18 (1911), 297–334; 19 (1912), 341–375.

Gravier, Maurice, "Georg Büchner et Alfred de Musset," *Orbis Litterarum*, 9 (1954), 29–44.

Grimsley, Ronald, "The Character of Lorenzaccio," *French Studies*, 11 (January 1957), 16–27.

Jansen, Steen, "Alfred de Musset dramaturge. *A Quoi rêvent les jeunes filles* et la technique dramatique d'*Un Spectacle dans un fauteuil*," *Orbis Litterarum*, 21 (1966), 222–254.

Jeune, Simon, "Une Etude inconnue de Musset sur Hoffmann," *Revue de Littérature Comparée*, 39 (1965), 422–427.

————, "Musset caché," *Revue d'Histoire Littéraire*, 66 (1966), 419–438.

————, "Souffles étrangers et inspiration personnelle dans *Les Caprices de Marianne*," *Revue des Sciences Humaines*, new series, fascicle 121 (1966), 81–96.

Lafoscade, Léon, "La Genèse de 'Lorenzaccio'," *Revue des Deux Mondes* (November 15, 1927), 433–437.

Lanson, Gustave, "Mariage de Princesse. Vérité et fantaisie dans une comédie de Musset," *Revue de Paris* (March 1, 1913), 32–46.

Lombard, Charles M., "French Romanticism on the American Stage," *Revue de Littérature Comparée*, 43 (April–June 1969), 161–172.

Masson, Bernard, "Le Masque, le double et la personne dans quelques Comédies et Proverbes," *Revue des Sciences Humaines*, fascicle 108 (October–December 1962), 551–571.

Maurois, André, "Alfred de Musset: Les Comédies," *Revue des Sciences Humaines*, fascicle 101 (January–March 1958), 17–29.

Mauzi, Robert, "Les Fantoches d'Alfred de Musset," *Revue d'Histoire Littéraire*, 66 (1966), 257–283.

Moreau, Pierre, "L'Ironie de Musset," *Revue des Sciences Humaines*, fascicle 108 (October–December 1962), 501–514.

————, "A Propos d'*On ne badine pas avec l'amour*," *Information Littéraire*, 8 (January–February, 1956), 1–5.

Nordon, Pierre, "Alfred de Musset et l'Angleterre," *Les Lettres Romanes*, 20 (1966), 319–333; 21 (1967), 28–46, 123–140, 238–256, 354–368.

Plard, Henri, "A Propos de 'Leonce et Lena,' Musset et Büchner," *Etudes Germaniques*, 9 (1954), 26–36.

Schnerb, Claude, "Fantasio ou la destruction d'un mythe," *L'Illustre Théâtre* (Spring 1955), 24–25.

Shaw, Marjorie, "A Propos du 'Fantasio' d'Alfred de Musset," *Revue d'Histoire Littéraire*, 55 (1955), 319–328.

————, "Deux Essais sur les comédies d'Alfred de Musset," *Revue des Sciences Humaines*, fascicle 93 (1959), 47–76.

Sices, David, "Multiciplicity and Integrity in *On ne badine pas avec l'amour*," *The French Review*, 43 (February 1970), 443–451.

————, "Musset's *Fantasio*: The Paradise of Chance," *The Romanic Review*, 58 (February 1967), 23–37.

Simon, John K., "The Presence of Musset in Modern French Drama," *The French Review*, 40 (1966), 27–38.

Starobinski, Jean, "Note sur un bouffon romantique," *Cahiers du Sud*, 61 (1966), 270–275.

Van Tieghem, Philippe, "L'Evolution du théâtre de Musset des débuts à *Lorenzaccio*," *Revue d'Histoire du Théâtre*, 4 (1952), 261–275.

Vial, André, "A Propos d'*On ne badine pas avec l'amour*," *Revue des Sciences Humaines*, fascicle 101 (January–March 1958), 55–67.

Index